C000104168

ST ANTONY'S/MACMILLAN SERIES

General Editors: Archie Brown (1978–85), Rosemary Thorp (1985–92) and Alex Pravda (1993–), all Fellows of St Antony's College, Oxford

Recent titles include:

Christopher Abel and Colin M. Lewis (*editors*) WELFARE, POVERTY AND DEVELOPMENT IN LATIN AMERICA
Jeremy Adelman (*editor*) ESSAYS IN ARGENTINE LABOUR HISTORY, 1870–1930
Orlando Albornoz EDUCATION AND SOCIETY IN LATIN AMERICA
Amatzia Baram CULTURE, HISTORY AND IDEOLOGY IN THE FORMATION OF BA'THIST IRAQ, 1968–89
Gail Lee Bernstein and Haruhiro Fukui (*editors*) JAPAN AND THE WORLD
Archie Brown (*editor*) NEW THINKING IN SOVIET POLITICS
Archie Brown (*editor*) POLITICAL LEADERSHIP IN THE SOVIET UNION
Deborah Fahy Bryceson FOOD INSECURITY AND THE SOCIAL DIVISION OF LABOUR IN TANZANIA, 1919–85
Victor Bulmer-Thomas STUDIES IN THE ECONOMICS OF CENTRAL AMERICA
Sir Alec Cairncross PLANNING IN WARTIME
Helen Callaway GENDER, CULTURE AND EMPIRE
Rodolfo Cerdas-Cruz THE COMMUNIST INTERNATIONAL IN CENTRAL AMERICA, 1920–36
Anuson Chinvanno THAILAND'S POLICIES TOWARDS CHINA, 1949–54
Colin Clarke (*editor*) SOCIETY AND POLITICS IN THE CARIBBEAN
David Cleary ANATOMY OF THE AMAZON GOLD RUSH
John Crabtree PERU UNDER GARCÍA
Alex Danchev (*editor*) INTERNATIONAL PERSPECTIVES ON THE FALKLANDS CONFLICT
João de Pina-Cabral and John Campbell (*editors*) EUROPE OBSERVED
Robert Desjardins THE SOVIET UNION THROUGH FRENCH EYES
Guido di Tella and Carlos Rodríguez Braun (*editors*) ARGENTINA, 1946–83: THE ECONOMIC MINISTERS SPEAK
Guido di Tella and D. Cameron Watt (*editors*) ARGENTINA BETWEEN THE GREAT POWERS, 1939–46
Guido di Tella and Rudiger Dornbusch (*editors*) THE POLITICAL ECONOMY OF ARGENTINA, 1946–83
D. R. Dorondo BAVARIA AND GERMAN FEDERALISM
Saul Dubow RACIAL SEGREGATION AND THE ORIGINS OF APARTHEID IN SOUTH AFRICA, 1919–36
Anne Lincoln Fitzpatrick THE GREAT RUSSIAN FAIR
Michael B. Froman THE DEVELOPMENT OF THE IDEA OF DÉTENTE
Haruhiro Fukui, Peter H. Merkl, Hubertus Müller-Groeling and Akio Watanabe (*editors*) THE POLITICS OF ECONOMIC CHANGE IN POSTWAR JAPAN AND WEST GERMANY
Heather D. Gibson THE EUROCURRENCY MARKETS, DOMESTIC FINANCIAL POLICY AND INTERNATIONAL INSTABILITY
Heather D. Gibson and Euclid Tsakalotos (*editors*) ECONOMIC INTEGRATION AND FINANCIAL LIBERALIZATION
Avner Gil'adi CHILDREN OF ISLAM
David Hall-Cathala THE PEACE MOVEMENT IN ISRAEL, 1967–87
John B. Hattendorf and Robert S. Jordan (*editors*) MARITIME STRATEGY AND THE BALANCE OF POWER

The Communist International in Central America, 1920–36

Rodolfo Cerdas-Cruz

Translated by Nick Rider

in association with
ST ANTONY'S COLLEGE
OXFORD

© Rodolfo Cerdas-Cruz 1993
This translation © Nick Rider 1993

All rights reserved. No reproduction, copy or transmission of
this publication may be made without written permission.

No paragraph of this publication may be reproduced, copied or
transmitted save with written permission or in accordance with
the provisions of the Copyright, Designs and Patents Act 1988,
or under the terms of any licence permitting limited copying
issued by the Copyright Licensing Agency, 90 Tottenham Court
Road, London W1P 9HE.

Any person who does any unauthorized act in relation to
this publication may be liable to criminal prosecution and
civil claims for damages.

First published 1993 by
THE MACMILLAN PRESS LTD
Houndmills, Basingstoke, Hampshire RG21 2XS
and London
Companies and representatives
throughout the world

ISBN 0–333–53822–6

A catalogue record for this book is available
from the British Library.

Copy-edited and typeset by Povey–Edmondson
Okehampton and Rochdale, England

Printed in Great Britain
by Antony Rowe Ltd
Chippenham, Wiltshire, England

Series Standing Order (St Antony's/Macmillan Series)

If you would like to receive future titles in this series as they are published,
you can make use of our standing order facility. To place a standing order
please contact your bookseller or, in case of difficulty, write to us at the
address below with your name and address and the name of the series. Please
state with which title you wish to begin your standing order. (If you live
outside the UK we may not have the rights for your area, in
which case we will forward your order to the publisher concerned.)

Standing Order Service, Macmillan Distribution Ltd, Houndmills,
Basingstoke, Hampshire, RG21 2XS, England

Contents

v

Preface

The revolutions witnessed in Latin America, and above all those in Central America, have all exhibited a dynamic interrelationship between those factors that are specifically internal and external forces and circumstances. The latter have in some cases incontrovertibly become of decisive and primary importance. Central America and the Caribbean have for centuries been a theatre for confrontations and conflicts, first between European powers seeking influence over and control of the area and then, since the nineteenth century, between these same powers and the United States.

Ideologically, a medieval scholasticism was followed in Latin America by a liberalism that did not succeed in ever fully taking shape in a system that was viable and rooted in social realities, for which it would have required a bourgeoisie capable of being its instrument in society, a class that did not exist. Later, moreover, even while the traditional post-colonial confrontation between liberals and conservatives continued unresolved, the influences in the ideology of socialism and anarchism began to reach American shores, without there being to any great degree a proletariat, so to speak, capable of fulfilling the historic mission assigned to it in theory.

It was almost as if the continent was an immense social laboratory in which theories and concepts could be tested and discarded, or a battlefield on which one doctrine or another was never entirely defeated, but survived alongside all others in an everlasting dispute that was as sterile as it was directionless, from conservatism and nineteenth-century liberalism to positivism, anarchism, socialism and communism, passing through the social doctrine of the Catholic Church, all putting forward their conceptions and in one way or another revealing their aspirations, possibilities and limitations.

The social tragedy of the Latin American peoples, however, remained complete and undiminished, and their search for economic progress and desire for positive social change and political liberty, expressed through a whole series of attempts at national and social emancipation, commonly concluded in bursts of violence and repression that caused the deaths of thousands of victims. In Central America in the 1920s and 1930s three situations developed that were dissimilar in social and political terms but were all of great significance for the future of the region, where their influence is still strong in the present-day turmoil:

(a) In Nicaragua, with the figure of Augusto César Sandino, where a movement of national liberation appeared that sought the emancipation of the country from the interventionism of the United States that had made it into a *de facto* protectorate, attempting to achieve this by means of an impressive and hard-fought guerrilla campaign.

(b) In El Salvador, where an insurrection of a social rather than a national character occurred, associated with the figure of Agustín Farabundo Martí, which sought to change the oppressive social structures that had proletarianized the peasantry following the expropriation of their ancestral lands, by means of a soviet-type revolution that culminated in the horrific massacres of 1932.

(c) In Costa Rica, the only democratic state in the region, with a legal Communist Party, where the path chosen was that of meaningful social and political reforms, in an effort to broaden democracy and modernize the country. Only in this case were positive results of a permanent nature achieved.

The Communist International, which at its Second Congress had approved some contradictory theses by Lenin and M. N. Roy on the national and colonial question, attempted to put them into practice in this small neck across the American continent. After holding all its discussions on the revolution and its character, the Party and its nature, the importance of Latin America for the imperialist powers, the formation of soviets in backward peasant areas, and so on, it had the opportunity to test the veracity of its theses and concepts in practice. It first tried to do so in Nicaragua, where it eventually withdrew after declaring General Sandino a traitor who had sold himself out to American imperialism. It then went on to El Salvador, where under its influence the Salvadorean uprising of 1932 took place that resulted in the massacre of tens of thousands of peasants. In this case too the International withdrew, forgetting the dead and defaming their leaders. Finally, in the case of Costa Rica, where some successes and advances actually were obtained, the Comintern limited itself to a politics by correspondence, without any real influence, and in the present book we consider why this in fact saved the small local Party from suffering a catastrophe similar to that inflicted on the movement in the other two countries.

This book seeks to follow the evolution of these three case histories step by step, within the context of the ideological and political framework laid out by the International itself. For this purpose we have studied its Congresses, Plenums and resolutions, its minutes, discussion papers and correspondence. In all of this research the overall objective has been to gain a clear grasp of the movement's conception of the revolution in the colonial, semi-colonial and dependent world, to observe its application in the three situations chosen for analysis, and to draw up a balance of the results. This in essence makes up the following study. The possibility that has recently arisen of the opening up of the archives of the Communist International in Moscow, following *glasnost* and *perestroika*, will no doubt reinforce the growing interest of historians, political analysts and social scientists in what actually happened within the Comintern, both in its internal workings and in relation to its actions in Latin America as a whole and Central America in particular. However, we believe that with regard to the latter, and to the specific application of the concepts and theses of the Communist International to the realities of its society, we have clearly established and documented with this study the fundamental elements of what took place at that time.

RODOLFO CERDAS-CRUZ

Introduction

The elaboration of the strategy and tactics of the Third International was undertaken on the basis of the theoretical formulations of Marx, Engels and Lenin, and the practical experience of the European revolutions of the last century, and the Russian revolutions of the twentieth, that is, those of 1905 and February and October 1917.

For Marx, social evolution is a historical-natural process governed by laws that are not only independent of the will, consciousness and intentions of human beings, but which also determine the latter's same will, consciousness and intentions. The passage of society through certain determined stages thus becomes necessary and inevitable; these stages may sometimes be accelerated and their negative aspects reduced, but it will never be possible to leapfrog over them.

For this reason, the fact that the colonial and underdeveloped peoples exhibited a level of backwardness that placed them a century or more behind the most advanced countries of the West made it imperative for these countries to make great efforts to bring about conditions that would permit capitalist development within their borders. This stage, painful but necessary, was therefore seen as an obligatory point of transit, apart from in a few exceptional situations, such as would be the case with the traditional Russian communes or *mir*, which Marx and Engels conceived could in certain circumstances, above all in terms of the international situation, serve as a point of departure for a direct transition to communism. Another way of looking at it would be to say that the role of the colonial and underdeveloped countries, like that of the minority nationalities, was regarded as practically worthless, unless it was inserted in the perspective of world capitalist development.

Nevertheless, in spite of these theoretical concepts in his ideas, Marx's own understanding of the colonial problem was more complex, though it never systematically developed to permit the full integration of the colonial question into his theory of the socio-economic structure of capitalism. In the case of Ireland, specifically, Marx perceived the structural connections, the mutually determinant bonds between the metropolis and its colonies, but without drawing from this any conclusions of a general nature. It was however because of this perception that he came to state that his years of study of the Irish

1

question had led him to the conclusion that 'the decisive blow against the English ruling classes (and it will be decisive for the workers' movement all over the world) *cannot* be delivered in England but *only in Ireland*.'[1]

Despite this observation, Marx never saw the Ireland–Great Britain relationship as a general phenomenon, nor as an example of the structural relationship between the colonial and capitalist worlds, evidenced by his statements on Mexico, South America and the Slav peoples. In his final analysis, the specificity of the colonial world and its development faded before the overwhelming impact of an all-powerful capitalism that was expanding on a worldwide level. The universal ambitions of capitalism made capitalist relations of production germinate wherever it established itself. These new relationships tended to break down the old social relations of production, and integrated the backward nations into the worldwide expansion of capitalism at a vertiginous pace. The advanced countries, Marx said, did no more than put before the more backward nations their own future, which was none other than one of capitalist development. Whatever or whoever opposed this development would not only be swept aside by the onward flow of history but would also be reactionary, retrograde and ultimately futile in nature.

The fact of being aware of the laws governing capitalist society did not make it any more possible to 'leap over stages'. Subjectivity could not go beyond the objective conditions that the social world and the corresponding mode of production imposed upon it. It was possible to accelerate the process, but impossible to avoid it. As Marx wrote, 'Even when a society has begun to track down the natural laws of its movement . . . it can neither leap over the natural phases of its development nor remove them by decree. But it can shorten and lessen the birth-pangs.'[2]

According to Marx, the objective material basis of a society is not determined by the will or knowledge of a person or a class but by the level of development of its productive forces. One period is distinguished from another not so much by what it produces as by how it produces it. It is from this factor that the social relations of production are derived, and so too the classes and their conflicts, and their superstructural manifestations, particularly the apparatus of the State.

These conditions constitute a precise underlying framework that will mark out, objectively, the limits of social and political action. Out of this background, and not from any arbitrary subjectivity, must arise the economic, political and social tasks that will necessarily have to be undertaken in each country at any particular time. What these tasks are, whether they are of one type or another, will in turn determine for the workers' movement the alliances to be made, the objectives to be pursued, and above all the revolutionary prospects of the proletariat in its progress towards the future socialist revolution.

The English and French revolutions in this sense together represented a classic model of bourgeois revolution. However, Marx and Engels distinguished between one and the other, considering the English revolution as classical from the point of view of economics and the French from that of politics. This absence of agreement between the economic and the political spheres already gave warning of the later over-simplifications and mechanistic interpretations that would be put forward on revolutions not just in Germany and Russia, but also in the colonial world, and which would characterize the theoretical approach of the international communist movement.

In the specific examples of Germany, firstly, and later of Russia, the sluggishness and delay in the bourgeois revolution with regard to the classic model created particular conditions of development that made it necessary to introduce still more qualifications into the original Marxian conception of social evolution. In both countries revolutions took place at a point when a relatively developed proletariat with class consciousness and organization already existed, and was itself in confrontation with a timid and hesitant bourgeoisie that was very different from the class that had played a decisive role during the French revolution. This placed these examples at some remove from the classical models, and gave them certain similarities with the colonial and dependent world.

The proximity of two revolutions, the bourgeois and the proletarian; the need simultaneously to undertake general democratic tasks alongside those of agrarian reform and transformation; the urgent need to consolidate an independent State power and regain the natural resources of a country from foreign hands, and so on, would all tend to amalgamate the historic tasks of the bourgeois revolution into the national liberation revolutions of the colonial and semi-colonial world, though in conditions that gave notice, to say the least, of the imminence of a socialist revolution.

In the case of the German revolution, Marx had no doubts with regard to its character, which he considered to be bourgeois–democratic and not socialist. The fact that the country was undergoing great economic growth and possessed a well-developed working class did in his judgement take away from its revolution its bourgeois-democratic nature. However, neither was it a case of a simple bourgeois revolution of the classic type, since questions relating to the socialist stage of the revolution were already being put forward. In effect, two distinct revolutions could be seen to be appearing within it, in a manner which simultaneously brought together and separated different forces that were all opposed to a common enemy. There was unity between bourgeois and proletarians in their struggle against feudal domination, great landholders and the privileges, legal hierarchies, servitude and so on, typical of pre-capitalist Europe. There was confrontation and conflict, however, in that it attempted to replace the domination of the feudalists with a new system of overlordship, that of capital over labour, of the bourgeoisie over the proletariat.

In this situation the primary need of the proletariat, according to Marx, was to preserve their independence as a class in the revolution, by creating their own party organization, their own armed workers' committees and their own class policies. This would make it possible to develop the bourgeois-democratic revolution without pause or interruption, and transform it into a proletarian socialist revolution. Consequently the slogan put forward by Marx for the German communists at that time was that of the Permanent Revolution.[3]

Lenin, faced with a much more complicated situation, sought to respond to a similar dilemma in the case of the Russian revolution. In his 1905 pamphlet 'Two Tactics of Social Democracy in the Democratic Revolution'[4] he set out to define what he saw as the basic questions posed by the imminent revolution in Russia, as follows:

(a) The nature of the revolution.
(b) The role of the bourgeoisie, of the proletariat and of the peasantry in the revolution.
(c) The problem of alliances.
(d) The route and means of transition by which the bourgeois revolution could be transformed into a socialist revolution.

This theoretical formulation elaborated by Lenin with reference to the Russia of the turn of the century, together with his evaluation of the revolutionary experience of 1905,[5] was to be of decisive importance in the conceptions regarding the colonial and semi-colonial world that later predominated in the Communist International: first, because it was of course the theses of Lenin that were eventually triumphant in the Russian Revolution itself; second, because it was Lenin who, together with M. N. Roy, drew up the theses on the national and colonial question that were approved at the Second Congress of the Comintern, in 1920; and finally, because Lenin's ideas were between 1920 and 1928 raised to the status of an obligatory movement in the colonies and semi–colonies – and later, moreover, in the Stalinist interpretation, they became an unchallengeable dogma for the whole of the international Communist movement.

The Russian Revolution gave a powerful stimulus to the development of colonial and semi-colonial independence struggles, above all in India and China, though its influence was also felt to varying degrees throughout the entire world, including Latin America. The fact that in India and China an imposing mass of seven hundred million human beings had been set in motion, led the leaders of the Russian Revolution to give particular attention to the events taking place there. However, their approach was entirely based on the Marxist categories that had been developed up to that time, and on the supposition, at times openly stated, that these revolutions would repeat the historic cycle already experienced by Soviet Russia. 'Inexorably and with mounting momentum they are approaching their 1905', wrote Lenin on the colonial countries in May 1922, in an article marking the tenth anniversary of *Pravda*.[6]

What was expected was a bourgeois-democratic revolution in which proletarian methods of struggle would be used, or at least their use would be attempted, under the hegemony of the working class, with its own vanguard Party. The objective, however, was the realization of social and economic tasks specific to the bourgeois revolution, which was the stage still pending resolution in these countries.

The interpretation of the colonial system according to classical Marxist formulae came up against increasing difficulties in its attempts to give an account of a reality that was extraordinarily complex, and escaped Marxist dogmatic of categories. The following were the most significant of the central theses of Marx, Engels and Lenin that served as theoretical and political orientation for the international Communist movement in the colonial and dependent world:

(1) The nature of the revolution in those countries where precapitalist modes of production have not been eliminated is bourgeois-democratic.

(2) This revolution, contrary to the classical experiences of England and France, cannot and should not be carried to its conclusion by the bourgeoisie. It is the proletariat that should and can bring about its full implementation.

(3) The proletariat should constitute themselves into a separate party, independent of the bourgeoisie and the petit-bourgeoisie, and form alliances with the agricultural proletariat and the peasantry, pulling the latter away from the sphere of influence of the liberal petit-bourgeoisie. On this basis the proletariat should then subsequently conquer political hegemony and establish themselves as the vanguard of the revolution.

(4) The proletariat should not limit their task as a class to the constitution of an independent workers' party. It will be necessary for them to translate this independence into social and State organization by means of the formation of workers' councils that will, from the first stages of the revolution, be the seeds of a duality of power that will be resolved, by dialectical development, in the establishment of the dictatorship of the proletariat.

In these theses a basis was laid out for the transformation of the bourgeois-democratic revolution, the bypassing of which was impossible since it corresponded to an objective stage of development of the productive forces, into a proletarian socialist revolution. The political instrument with which this would be achieved was via a revolutionary dictatorship of the workers and peasants, under a system of soviets, and through a process of permanent revolution, in the Marxist–Leninist sense.

In terms of methodology, the political and ideological practice seen in the discussions held within the Communist International would follow – particularly after the death of Lenin – a common pattern, that was to have frankly pernicious consequences. This was the drawing of an analogy between the process under examination, in whichever of the colonial, semi-colonial and dependent countries it happened to be at the time, and one of the stages of the Russian Revolution, according to the level of development found in the country in question. Accompanying this would be an obligatory reference to the interpretations of Lenin on the national and colonial question, and his theory of imperialism. Under Stalin, Lenin's theses were converted into dogmas, most particularly in the Russocentric interpretation put forward by Stalin himself.

Evidently such theoretical instruments were wholly insufficient for the correct formulation of the problems of the colonial, semi-colonial and dependent world. Generalization of this kind lost all contact with the historical, cultural, social and political realities of the countries on the periphery of the main centres of imperial power. The calls that were repeatedly heard for problems to be examined in concrete terms were never able to overcome the theoretical and political trammels that such a system of categories superimposed on reality represented, and which ordered and prejudged all information coming from this reality. Those noteworthy efforts that were made to go beyond this distorted vision of a world that remained unknown were disregarded, with consequences that were truly tragic.

As hopes for immediate revolution in Europe receded following the failure of the revolution in Germany, and the main focus of revolutionary turbulence shifted to Asia, the discussions between the principal leaders of the International on the revolution in the colonial, semi-colonial and dependent world were regarded with ever greater importance in the course of the 1920s. Subsequently, however, with the failure of the Chinese revolutionary movement of 1927, the rise of fascism in Europe and the threat of a war against the USSR the national and colonial problem would once again be relegated to a clearly secondary position.

Nevertheless, in spite of this ebb and flow of interest the same particular complex of problems, deeply rooted in reality, could be seen to be struggling time and again throughout this period to demand attention in the deliberations of the Comintern. In effect, in the colonial, semi-colonial and dependent world, was the revolution simply a bourgeois-democratic one, or rather something that went beyond the latter, though without becoming a socialist revolution? What kind of revolution was it, what were its driving forces, its tasks, its prospects and its international significance? What value did the social categories of class party, bourgeoisie, petit-bourgeoisie, working class, peasantry, soviets and so on have in the specific context of the economic, social and cultural realities of the multifarious variety of countries taken in under the labels of colonial, semi-colonial and dependent? And lastly, in this respect, what, in concrete terms, should be the strategy and tactics to be followed by the national sections of the Communist International?

In spite of later developments in the International, the basic theoretical formulation of the movement's position on this subject, other than simple analogies with the Russian Revolution based on formal rather than structural analysis, consisted essentially of the so-called theses on the national and colonial question by Lenin, approved, with the additional contributions of M.N. Roy, at the Second Congress. Up to then the view that had predominated was that expressed in the 'Manifesto of the Communist International to the

Proletariat of the Entire World', written by Trotsky and unanimously approved at the first Comintern Congress in 1919. In this text it was stated that only the proletarian revolution could guarantee the free existence of the minor nations, through the liberation of productive forces that this revolution would bring about. It went on:

> The emancipation of the colonies is possible only in conjunction with the emancipation of the metropolitan working class. The workers and peasants not only of Annam, Algiers and Bengal, but also of Persia and Armenia, will gain their opportunity of independent existence *only when* the workers of England and France have overthrown Lloyd George and Clemenceau and taken State power into their own hands. Even now the struggle in the more developed colonies is more than the struggle for national liberation; it is assuming an explicitly Socialist character. If capitalist Europe forcibly dragged the backward nations of the world into the capitalist whirlpool, then Socialist Europe will come to the aid of the liberated colonies with its technology, its organization, its spiritual forces, in order to facilitate their transition to a planned and organized socialist economy.
>
> Colonial slaves of Africa and Asia! *The hour of proletarian dictatorship will also be the hour of your own liberation!*[7]

It was not until the Second Congress of the Comintern that the colonial question was actually approached in a direct and specific manner. Shortly beforehand Lenin had published his famous 'Thesis on the National and Colonial Question' which represented a hazardous attempt to offer an acceptable interpretation of the situation in a world that was unknown and only recently awakening, and to propose, with an even greater degree of risk, strategic orientations and tactics for use in its national and social emancipation.

Manabendra Nath Roy, a young Indian who after many travels had taken up residence in Mexico, attended the Congress as a delegate for the latter country. He had behind him only his intelligence, experience and revolutionary spirit. He did not represent any real organization, and the true focus of his political concerns was not Mexico or Latin America, but his own homeland in India.

According to the account given by Roy in his memoirs, he had already prepared his own theses, which ran contrary to those of Lenin. When the Soviet leader became aware of this, he openly invited Roy to present them to the Congress and set them against his own. Roy refused, because this would have been to confront a legendary revolutionary in circumstances that could only have led to his actions being misinterpreted. Lenin then suggested the possibility of bringing together both theoretical positions and presenting them to the Congress as one, leaving it to the future, according to what might be revealed by subsequent events and the systematization of actual experience, to see which of them most corresponded to reality.[8]

This compromise solution was simply no solution at all. It placed together alongside each other entirely different strategic orientations and tactics, and gave the status of a fundamental element of theory to a body of ideas that were essentially contradictory within themselves. The attitude of the international Communist movement to these theses has been in the best tradition of dogmatism and rigidity. Many years later, for example, in 1969, Carlos Rafael Rodríguez, First Deputy Prime Minister of Cuba and a veteran Communist militant in the Popular Socialist Party,[9] a member organization of the Comintern, would write that with the theses for the Second Congress, 'The Leninist theoretical corpus on colonial problems was complete. One can be sure that with the Theses and their defence in the Second Congress of the Communist International, Lenin considered that (the movement's) ideas on the subject had been definitively laid out.'[10]

As a result, the provisional nature of the text and the idea that it should be regarded as conditional on subsequent practical experience disappeared, a fact that would impede any systematic re-examination of the document in the light of any errors or successes in the little-known colonial world. The observation made at the time by Lenin and recalled by Roy, that 'we were exploring new ground and should suspend final judgement pending practical experience',[11] thus lost all its meaning. Instead, the end result was the simultaneous application of contradictory theses that would only serve to justify criticisms thrown against the local leaders of the movement for the failures of the International, and to save the political face of those who were truly responsible, situated in the upper levels of the organization.

A very brief examination of these theses can reveal their obvious contradictions and the falsity of the idea that Roy's could simply be supplementary to those of Lenin: first, for example, in the theory of the party. For Roy, the real source of strength in the underdeveloped countries would be found not in the small nationalist groups but in great mass revolutionary parties. This meant, in his judgement, that the International should promote revolution in the colonies by means of the agitation of such parties. Communist Parties should be created in all these countries and undertake active political work and agitation as a basic requirement for the successful establishment and expansion of the great mass revolutionary party.

Closely associated with this concept were his ideas on the role of the educated intermediate sectors and the negative role of bourgeois nationalism, and an immediate concern for the social question within the colonies.

The overall import of such ideas could not ultimately be other than a combination of the classic Marxist–Leninist party of a new type, first conceived by Lenin in the conditions of Czarist Russia, with a large-scale, primarily agrarian social movement that also included among its bases of support sectors of the petit-bourgeoisie. This raised the question of precisely how the Communist International would be able simultaneously to build up and promote a broadly-based national liberation movement, forge the alliances necessary to do so, bring forward the social objectives to be undertaken by a future socialist revolution, and equally combine this national liberation process with the overall needs of the world proletarian revolution.

Roy's discussions with Lenin left him with the impression that the Soviet leader was ignorant of the relation of social forces in the colonial countries. Lenin frankly admitted to him his lack of knowledge of colonial realities, and said that in his arguments on this subject what he was doing was to situate these countries within the broader context of his general theoretical understanding of the problem. As Lenin saw it, the effect of imperialism was to maintain the backward and colonial countries in social conditions of a feudal nature, which impeded the development of capitalism and the satisfaction of the demands of the native bourgeoisies. The character and meaning of the colonial movement was that of a bourgeois-democratic revolution, and for this reason he argued against Roy that, 'Every stage of social evolution being historically determined, the colonial countries must have their bourgeois-democratic revolution before they could enter the stage of the proletarian revolution.'[12] The Communists should, however, avoid a situation in which the nationalist bourgeoisie would have full control over the leadership of the national liberation movement, a movement that would nevertheless in whatever circumstances be a factor objectively favourable to the international socialist movement.

Roy maintained that the colonial bourgeoisie was different from those of the imperial homelands, while conversely it could not be differentiated either economically or culturally from the feudal social order. For him the nationalist movement was ideologically reactionary, and its victory would not necessarily signify that of a bourgeois-democratic revolution. The example of Gandhi brought out still more clearly the differences between Lenin and Roy in this regard. For the former, Gandhi was a revolutionary, in that he was an inspirational figure and leader of the masses who sought independence. For Roy, on the other hand, basing himself on Plekhanov and his critique of populism, Gandhi was politically revolutionary but socially a reactionary.

Lenin's position was simply that the International should support the colonial national liberation movements. However, Roy argued that this idea could only be given real substance through the organization of Communist Parties in the colonies, with the objective of revolutionizing the social orientation of the movement under the pressure of organized workers and peasants. This, in his judgement, was the only means of genuinely aiding the colonial peoples in their struggle for national liberation, as the bourgeoisie, for fear of revolution, would always ultimately come to a compromise with imperialism in exchange for a few concessions. In such circumstances, Roy maintained, the working class should be prepared to take over the leadership of the struggle for national liberation and transform it into a mass revolutionary movement. Thus, in the same way that for Lenin the revolution in Russia had brought together two revolutions, the bourgeois-democratic and the socialist, so too for Roy, in the colonial world, the revolution of national emancipation was interlinked with a social revolution that only the Communist movement, organized in independent parties, could carry forward.

It was also at the Second Congress that attention was first given to the question of Latin America, which was described as a colonial base for United States imperialism. One of the US delegates, Fraina, argued that it was the Communist Party of the United States that should 'take the initiative in the organization of Communist Parties in Latin America. American imperialism cannot be defeated except by a revolutionary movement embracing the whole of the Americas'.[13] Arguments like this, taken together with the contradictory positions of the leaders of the International on the colonial world, within which Latin America was indiscriminately included, made a powerful contribution to creating a state of political and ideological confusion that would take on tragic proportions when its effects were seen in practice in Central America.

Succeeding Congresses of the International remained bogged down in discussions on the general principles of the revolution in the colonial countries. The primary centre of attention was naturally the Chinese revolution, but the participants in the debate included delegates from every part of the world, and Latin Americans among them.

The Fifth Congress in 1924 was attended as an observer by Víctor Raúl Haya de la Torre, founder and leader of the APRA (American Popular Revolutionary Alliance).[14] This Congress saw the launch of the slogan of the 'United Anti-Imperialist Front' for the colonial countries, a slogan that had also been adopted by Haya de la Torre, though with a meaning substantially different from that given to it in the International. This was above all due to the influence of Zinoviev, for whom the United Front could not be understood outside of the process of bolshevikization of Communist Parties that the Congress had agreed to push forward. The Front in this view should have as its fundamental base of support a worker–peasant alliance. The clear objective would be the formation of a worker–peasant government, which for Zinoviev was simply a slogan to be used for propaganda and agitational purposes in substitution of the real aim: the establishment of the dictatorship of the proletariat. Consequently, this worker–peasant alliance and its corresponding government would be directed equally against imperialism, the bourgeoisie and even, too, the petit-bourgeoisie.

The United Front was not, then, understood in any broad and flexible sense but in a highly restrictive manner, both in terms of the classes participating and in the objective laid down. If to this was added the movement's glaring ignorance of the realities of Latin America, it was evident that such a strategy and such tactics would become insuperable obstacles for the unification of the various political movements that existed in the continent at that time. This conception of the United Front, the sectarian exposition of which was heard by Haya de la Torre at the Fifth Congress, laid the basis for the Comintern's subsequent breach with the APRA. Equally, it also constituted the immediate source for the development of contradictory policies that would acquire particular significance in the case of the national liberation struggle led by Augusto César Sandino in Nicaragua, and in the attempt at social revolution under Agustín Farabundo Martí in El Salvador.

In the period that went from the Fifth to the Sixth Congress, in 1928, the attention of the Comintern was centred on two main topics; firstly, the so-called partial stabilization of capitalism, and secondly, the transfer of the main focus of revolutionary tensions to the peripheral countries, and Asia and Latin America in particular.

As a result of these discussions a concern to develop a better understanding of Latin America became more visible in the International. This shift in attitude was also encouraged above all by the great deal of speculation that there was at that time on the possibility of an inter-imperialist clash between the United States and Britain in competition for the dominant position in the region. According to Bukharin, this opened up the possibility of developing movements in Latin America that would be capable of destabilizing world capitalism, and most particularly US imperialism, the strongest, youngest and most vigorous of all the world imperialisms. Hence periodic studies were undertaken on the evolution of the region and the expansion of the United States and the other powers, and it was concluded that 'the South American continent is, with China, the land of the future for the great imperialist powers'.[15]

Nevertheless, there was still no integrated understanding of the developments that took place in the continent or their significance for the world socialist revolution, nor even a real comprehension of what immediate events actually were happening there. A typical example of this was when Vitorio Codovila, of the Argentinian Communist Party, attempted at the Seventh extended Plenum of the Executive of the International in 1926 to give a detailed analysis of the situation and went so far as to claim, against all the available evidence, that in Central America there already existed 'a revolutionary movement of the petit-bourgeoisie and of the workers and peasants that is seeking to establish a government like that of Mexico'.[16]

A variety of events in the region caught the attention of the leaders of the Comintern, such as the situation in Mexico, or the holding of the Pan-American Conference in Havana in 1928. However, in terms of real knowledge of the area there was no improvement. All efforts were centred on resolving the question of how to adjust reality to pre-established theoretical formulae, and the International did not manage either to undertake a clear diagnosis of the different countries of the region, or to put forward definite strategies with which to confront their problems. Nor were any advances made in the theoretical categorization of the different types of countries that made up the area.

At the Seventh Plenum it was agreed to strengthen two organizations that would be of the first importance in events in Central America. These were International Red Aid, which would play a major role in the crisis in El Salvador in 1932, and the League against Imperialism, which would do so in the case of Sandino's movement in Nicaragua.

Central America would nevertheless still have to wait for quite some time before it was really 'discovered' by the Comintern. One only has to recall that all the Latin American countries were included in the undifferentiated bloc of 'colonial, semi-colonial and dependent countries', and commonly, though not always, also thrown in under the designation of 'the Orient', which arbitrarily lumped together social and political realities as dissimilar as those that could be found in Asia, Africa, Latin America and even Japan.[17] And, at the same time, one could also say that in reality the Communist International never genuinely discovered Latin America.

The Programme Commission of the Executive Committee of the International adopted the 'Draft Programme of the Communist International' on 25 May 1928. In its fundamentals this text acquired the position of a basic theoretical guide for the Latin American Communist movement, with the final modifications that were introduced in the course of the debate upon it at the Sixth Comintern Congress, which followed immediately afterwards.[18]

A report on the colonial question was presented to the Sixth Congress, prepared by Otto Kuusinen. It was a work of complete improvisation that suffered, as was wholly unavoidable, from the gravest of defects. The fact that its author, in no way familiar with colonial problems, had been given the task scarcely a few weeks before the Congress can account perfectly for the deficiencies in his report. It also, however, indicates to us the reality of the manner in which such questions were dealt with in the organization.

In addition a supplementary Co-Report was also prepared, written by Jules Humbert-Droz, that was specifically dedicated to Latin America, and which was presented at the thirty-second session of the Congress on 16 August 1928.[19] The principal points discussed in it were the nature of the revolution, the nature of the Party, the tasks to be undertaken and the problem of alliances. Attention was drawn to the importance of Latin America, which, the report said, was growing ever greater due to its position as one of the most acute focuses of conflict in the entire international situation, as a consequence of the rivalry between the old imperialism of Britain and the young and vigorous imperialism of the USA. The revolutionary movement against the process of colonization undertaken by the Americans throughout the region had, in the opinion of the author, become one of the most important revolutionary elements in the international socialist revolution, and, most of all, in the struggle against potentially the most powerful of all the existing imperialisms.

Recognition was given in the report to the differences between the North, predominantly consisting of countries that were essentially agrarian and lacking in an industrial proletariat, and the Southern Cone. In the latter a working class did exist, and there were processes of social differentiation much deeper than in the rest of the continent.

On the characterization of the nature of the revolution in Latin America, Humbert-Droz recalled that this problem had previously led to differences between the Latin Secretariat of the Comintern and the Executive Committee. He criticized the Russian delegate Trevine for his claim that in Latin America the revolution was neither bourgeois-democratic (as Humbert-Droz himself maintained) nor directly socialist.[20] For Humbert-Droz the Latin American revolution, in addition to being bourgeois-democratic, was directed against imperialism and the great landowning magnates, and represented a base of support for the international proletariat and the world socialist revolution. The possibility of developing an autonomous capitalism in the region did not exist; instead, there was a basis for a rapid and direct transition from a bourgeois-democratic to a proletarian revolution. It was therefore necessary for the proletariat to acquire hegemony within the Latin American revolutionary movement, as it was this class that must give it its orientation, provide it with leadership and determine its organizational structure. Hence, the central task of the Communist Parties was to secure this hegemony in the revolutionary struggle, establishing a bloc of revolutionary forces made up of the working class, both industrial and agricultural, the landless peasantry, and the revolutionary petit-bourgeoisie. The latter would have to be opposed whenever it sought to take over hegemony from the proletariat, as any success on its part would cause the movement to deviate into the launching of military coups, with mass support, that would culminate in the Generals taking control of the process for themselves and compromising the historic scope of the revolutionary movement.[21]

According to Humbert-Droz, the central slogan and overall general position of the Communist movement for Latin America should be the struggle for the establishment of the democratic dictatorship of the workers and peasants. Consequently, the International should assist the Latin American Communists to convert their Parties into authentically bolshevik organizations, with an inflexible application of the 21 conditions for entry into the Comintern, and to combat both anarcho-syndicalism and the efforts of the reformists of Amsterdam, above all in the field of labour organization. 'Only if these conditions are fulfilled,' the report declared, 'will the Latin American revolutionary movement attain its historical objectives and make possible the development of the bourgeois revolution into a socialist revolution, into a true dictatorship of the working class.'[22]

However, in spite of all this apparent clarity, the arguments of Humbert-Droz left unanswered the very questions that were formulated in the Co-Report itself. While the Latin American revolution was declared to be bourgeois-democratic, it was also said that an independent bourgeoisie with a national outlook capable of carrying such a process forward did not exist. The working class, little developed, organizationally weak, found itself swamped by an ocean of democratic petit-bourgeoisie that exhibited significant anti-imperialist tendencies. It was, however, this same working class that had to neutralize the latter, larger class, pass from the democratic to a socialist revolution and establish the dictatorship of the proletariat in the region. Clearly, in the face of such adverse realities this was simply a case of a declaration of good intentions, which did not lead to any real conclusion.

Bukharin, for his part, persisted in stressing the world historical significance of the conflict between the United States and Britain, which as he saw it took on a decisive character in their confrontation over the control of Latin America. 'I repeat and underline,' he said, 'that the conflict between the United States and England is the axis of all the existing antagonisms in the capitalist sector of the world economy.'[23]

A contribution of great importance was made to these debates by the Ecuadorean delegate Ricardo Paredes Romero,[24] who argued for the use and development of the category of dependent countries, as the most applicable to the situation of the Latin American states. In doing so he put forward, in a detailed manner, a series of classificatory categories, objectives, forms of organization and types of prospective alliances. Unfortunately, however, his solidly based intervention did not meet with sufficient response for it to be translated into either resolutions or specific policies for the region.

The main debate, meanwhile, was still unable to overcome the insurmountable obstacles set by a methodology that only proposed analogies with the Russian Revolution and the adjustment of reality to pre-established and schematic ideological formulae. Rebellions by some of the delegates against this manner of proceeding were recorded in the minutes, but did not alter the outcome. Trevine, in arguing against Humbert-Droz, said:

Well then: it is not my fault if the situation . . . is such that neither
the bourgeois-democratic revolution nor the socialist revolution are
in progress . . . Humbert-Droz has himself recognized that the
countries of Latin America did not contain the necessary conditions
for the development of an independent national capitalism. This
means that in these countries it will be impossible to install a
bourgeois regime. Foreign capitalism is developing there, but the
country remains feudal. Since there is not the least possibility of
developing a national capitalism, one should not expect that the
revolutionary movement that is emerging in the countries of Latin
America should have a bourgeois-democratic character. Instead of
seeking to apply to these revolutionary movements already existing
formulas such as 'bourgeois-democratic revolution', 'socialist revolution', it would be more worthwhile to consider these movements as
they really are.[25]

Clearly there was an immediate need for the development of a new
historical and political category for Latin America that would have the
capacity to reflect the particularities of the colonial and semi-colonial
world, and above all the dependent Latin American states. It should
also have made it possible to go beyond the sterile schematic system of
bourgeois-democratic revolution on the one hand, and socialist
revolution on the other, linked together by a bridge that would have
to be crossed over rapidly, thanks to the hegemony of a proletariat that
was non-existent or scarcely beginning to form. It is equally clear,
however, that this was not done, and so the movement's resolutions
and directives remained lodged within the old dogmas and preconcep-
tions. Questions such as the nature of the Party, the hegemony of the
working class, alliances with other classes, the nature of the revolution,
the stages through which it has to pass, the struggle against
imperialism, the tasks to be undertaken in the agrarian field, the
problem of armed insurrection, the creation of soviets and so on, were
integrated into a programme in formal terms, but without the
fundamental theoretical problems with which such questions were
indissolubly interlinked, even after having been correctly formulated,
let alone resolved.

A short time later it would become necessary to formulate a new set
of theses referring specifically to Latin America, in order to take into
account the political, economic and social developments that were seen
to be taking place in the region. However, the Sixth Congress would
nevertheless still be one of the main sources of inspiration for the

Communist Parties of Latin America, with all the necessary consequences in terms of political policies and lines of action based in erroneous conceptions divorced from reality.

The Sixth Congress of the Comintern had also approved the admission into the organization of Cuba, Ecuador and Colombia, whose delegates enriched the debates with contributions based on actual experiences, though without this being reflected in any great progress being made. On 25 February 1929 a conference of Latin American labour organizations was held in Montevideo, followed by a conference of the Communist Parties of the region in Buenos Aires, in June of the same year.[26] The most important delegate at both meetings was Humbert-Droz, who took part under the *nom de guerre* of Luis.[27]

Humbert-Droz, like Bukharin, had begun to be aware of Stalin's negative influence, which was an important factor among the motives for his apparent exile to the remoteness of Latin America. His contact with the reality of the region revealed to him a continent that was infinitely rich and varied, and of which there was a profound ignorance within the International. However, this was not sufficient for him to modify his own pre-established systems of thought. It can be noted that the theses in his Co-Report were written before his journey, and yet the ideas in them were to be reproduced more or less unaltered in the final resolutions of the Communist conference in Buenos Aires.

In these resolutions the Latin American revolution was defined as bourgeois-democratic, agrarian and anti-imperialist. Its axis consisted of the proletariat, though the petit-bourgeoisie and even the national bourgeoisies also had a certain anti-imperialist role to play. A situation should be avoided, it was urged, in which either of these classes could become predominant in the process, as this would inevitably lead to a compromise with imperialism. It was for this reason that the APRA was attacked as the mouthpiece of the radicalized democratic petit-bourgeoisie, and its social and political ideas denounced as reactionary.

It was intended to undertake a more exact study of Latin America, and a 'Draft thesis on the revolutionary movement in Latin America' was nominally prepared by the Secretariat for Latin America of the Executive Committee of the International, though in reality it had been drawn up, in Spanish, by the Latin American Commission at the Sixth Congress. This document was distributed in the various Latin American countries and Spain, and described as the primary text 'on the prospects of the revolution in Latin America and the tasks of our Parties and the revolutionary proletariat'.[28]

In it great insistence was made on three points: that the revolutionary classes should be under the hegemony of the working class and its Party; that the democratic petit-bourgeoisie had to be neutralized in order to guarantee the transition from a democratic to a socialist revolution; and that the final objective was the establishment of a Federation of Soviet Republics of Latin America.[29] It was following this that the constitution of soviets of workers, soldiers and peasants became part of the agenda for the whole of the Communist movement, and was actually attempted in Cuba and El Salvador.[30]

In Europe, meanwhile, the rise of fascism coincided with the consolidation of Stalin in power. Given that the International had on more than one occasion and in different ways become one of the strongholds of opposition to the Soviet leader, as had happened in the cases of Zinoviev and to some degree of Trotsky, Roy, Bukharin and others, the interest shown by the Soviet Party in the Comintern was subsequently reduced to a minimum. This was reflected in the despatch to its leadership of intellectuals and politicians of secondary status, which accentuated a tendency towards its effective elimination as a functioning entity.[31]

A few years later the Communist movement began once again to talk of the benefits of a united front, and the national sections were recommended to form Popular Fronts. A meeting of South American Parties in 1934 gave support to this new line, the Cubans being the first to put it into practice. In turn the Peruvian Communist Party for its part proposed, in the same spirit, a political union with the APRA, after having previously fought against the latter as a typical representative of the democratic petit-bourgeoisie that had to be neutralized, and rejected the APRA's own concept of the United Front.[32]

It was not until the Seventh Congress, in 1935, that the Communist Parties of Peru, Colombia, Costa Rica, Indochina and Venezuela were formally admitted into the International, which had previously classified them only as sympathizers. By that time the Presidium of the Comintern already included Blas Roca of Cuba, Prestes of Brazil and Díaz, of Mexico. This Congress opened the period of the Anti-Fascist Popular Front.

It is of interest to note that among the materials provided for the delegates was a description of the member Parties. This document bears witness to the depth of the prevailing disinformation regarding Central America. On El Salvador, it said that the Communist Party had first been organized in 1930 (which meant that it had not existed when it was represented in the Communist conference in Buenos Aires in 1929), and an account was given of the Party's attitude during the insurrection of 1932, which the document mistakenly also placed in 1930. It was claimed that following this episode the reconstruction of the Party had been initiated in 1933, when persecution had supposedly ceased. With regard to Honduras, the report said that the local Party had existed since 1927, had since been decimated by repression and was then in the midst of a process of reconstruction, with some 300 to 500 members who were still being organized. Turning to Guatemala, it was stated that a previous attempt at organization in 1925 had been rapidly crushed, but a process of Party reorganization had been begun in 1930, which, however, had also suffered brutal repression at the hands of the tyrannical regime in power in the country. It was estimated that the group who were still attempting to organize as a party of the Guatemalan working class consisted of some 80 militants. Costa Rica had organized its Party in 1931, which operated legally, was active among the labour unions of the country, published the newspaper *Trabajo* and in 1933–4 had led a major strike in the banana plantations and won seats in the national parliament and municipal councils. Regarding Nicaragua, the document gave a brief account of the *Sandinista* campaign and recognized that it had not been possible to form a Communist Party there, repeating the criticisms already made by the Communist movement against the supposedly petit-bourgeois position and identity of Sandino.

In spite of what efforts were made to modify the International's clearly mistaken policy on the colonial and dependent world, it would not be possible to change the organization into anything other than an organizer of defeats. As Fernando Claudín wrote in his book *The Crisis of the Communist Movement*, referring to the Comintern, 'The sudden volte-face at the Seventh Congress will not cause it to be reborn. It will be its swan-song.'[33]

The differences between the Congresses before and those after the Sixth Congress in 1928 are important to underline. In the first six Comintern Congresses there was debate, intellectual inquiry, audacity and creativity, albeit upon a basis of objective knowledge of the social, economic and political realities of the colonial, semi-colonial and dependent world that was frankly feeble. Following the Sixth Congress, however, these were only apologetics. These Congresses were gatherings of well-marshalled delegates providing adulatory standing ovations for the Leader and the movement's supposed revolutionary successes; ritualized conclaves from which the real problems of colonial emancipation and the transformation of semi-colonial and dependent societies became ever more remote, to the point of being virtually lost from sight. It is because of this collapse of real debate that it would be possible, many years later, for Carlos Rafael Rodríguez, present Deputy Prime Minister of Cuba and formerly a militant of the old Popular Socialist Party led by Blas Roca, in his time a member of the Executive Committee of the International and of its Caribbean Bureau, to make the following admission: 'Only in May 1969, fifty years after the Second Congress of the Communist International, did the differences in the economic and semi-colonial development of Asia and Africa come to be recognized in a text dealing collectively with the problems of the Communist movement.'[34]

The near-absolute predominance of a methodology based on comparison and analogy facilitated quick analysis, but places the movement on a course that was wholly mistaken. It was this incomprehension of the realities of colonial, semi-colonial and dependent countries, combined with the movement's subordination to the increasingly State-oriented objectives of the Soviet Union, themselves conceived within a vision that though employing internationalist rhetoric remained essentially Russo-centric, that ultimately determined the strategy and tactics of the Communist International in Central America; that is, in Nicaragua, with the campaign by Augusto César Sandino against American intervention, in El Salvador, with Agustín Farabundo Martí and the peasant insurrection of 1932, and in Costa Rica, with the only legal Communist Party in the region, which was saved from disaster precisely due to its weak links with the Comintern.

This is what we intend to examine in the following chapters.

1 A Revolution in Incubation: Nicaragua in the 1920s

CENTRAL AMERICA IN THE COMINTERN BEFORE SANDINO

Although Central America is frequently mentioned from the first in the documents of the International, in practical terms the development of the Communist movement in the area went through a prolonged process of gestation that did not produce any real effects until the end of the 1920s and the beginning of the next decade. The first mention of the region appeared in the Call issued on the foundation of the International Communist Women's Movement, which contained a declaration of support for the Communist group in Cuba and the Communist group of Central America.[1]

Naturally, the existence of these Communist groups, as they were called, was only of very remote political significance, in as much as they could be the points of departure for the building up of genuine political organizations in the future. Occasional articles about different countries of Central America appeared in publications of the International. Thus, in 1922 a short article was published on Guatemala, in which an analysis was given of the dependency of the Central American states and of the imperialism of the United States.[2]

Sporadic pieces of news were given about some of the most significant events in the isthmus, though on the basis of information originating in external sources, from the United States, Cuba or Mexico. Reports of this kind appeared, for example, on the presence of US customs inspectors in Latin America, on El Salvador and Nicaragua, and on the development of the banana workers' strike at La Ceiba in Honduras,[3] and denunciations were published of the imperialist policies of the United States in the region.[4]

Demetrio Boersner has pointed out that in the summer of 1932 a group of Guatemalans calling themselves the 'Workers' Socialist Unification' took a decision to unite with other Central American

22

revolutionaries and form a Communist Party of Central America. They informed the Executive Committee of the International, which in return sent them a few somewhat irrelevant tactical instructions. They were simply exhorted to struggle against the oppressive domination of American imperialism and in favour of the revolutionary union of the worker's and peasants' movement of the Central American countries.[5]

Previously, in 1929, some further information had also been published about Guatemala, with a description of the living conditions of its workers, and a few general statements about the economic situation of the country. The existence of the following workers' organizations was reported: the Regional Federation of Labour (FRT),[6] with 13 unions and 2200 members and under the influence of the Communist Party, which formed part of the Central American Workers' Confederation (COCA)[7] and, from 1928, of the Red International of Labour Unions (the *Profintern)* the 'Workers' Federation for the Legal Defence of Labour',[8] reformist in nature, very strong numerically, and affiliated to the Pan-American Federation of Labour; and the Union Action Committee,[9] with around a thousand supporters, and under the influence of the anarchists.

There was also, according to this same article, another series of autonomous organizations in the country, the largest of which was the Society for Workers' Life Insurance,[10] with 2950 members, some of whom were under Communist influence. It was claimed in this article that the Communist Party of Guatemala had been founded in 1922, had undertaken a great deal of activity and had contributed to the formation of the Communist Party of Honduras. It was made up, it said, above all of unionized workers, with only an insignificant membership among peasants. It had published several newspapers, such as *El Comunista* (1922), *Nuestra Palabra* (1923) and *Vanguardia Proletaria* (1925) which had all been banned by the government. A great many strikes had supposedly been carried on under the direction of the Party, from its foundation up to the strike of April 1929 in Puerto Barrios.[11]

A similar article was published about Honduras, which laid emphasis on the struggle against the fruit companies and the penetration of American capitalism. It denounced the intervention of the foreign companies in political life and the control exercised by US imperialism over every aspect of the life of the country.[12]

All these reports should be regarded critically, particularly whenever they refer to the existence of Communist groupings. It is symptomatic that today it is admitted, officially, by the international Communist movement that the Communist Party of Guatemala was created after

1940; while with regard to Honduras, if one did see a certain development of a labour and strike movement, from a political point of view the existence of an organized and functioning Communist Party is virtually imperceptible.

Quite different was the case of Nicaragua, where in the absence of a Communist Party the presence of leading figures of the Communist International nevertheless did make itself felt, when they were sent to join the *Sandinista* movement, in an underdeveloped and dependent country, virtually under occupation, in the 1920s, by the United States Marines.

SOCIO-POLITICAL BACKGROUND OF THE SANDINISTA CONFLICT

The history of Nicaragua, a small country in Central America, with an area of 145 000 square kilometres, has been determined by its privileged geographical position, which makes it one of the most suitable sites for the building of an inter-oceanic canal across the American continent.

In 1920, Nicaragua had a population of scarcely 638 000 inhabitants.[13] Its principal export products were coffee, bananas, timber, gold and sugar. In the subsequent decade, the percentage composition of its exports by product was as shown in Table 1.1.

Table 1.1   Nicaragua: percentage composition of exports by product, 1919–30[14]

	1919	1920	1921	1922	1923	1924	1925	1926	1927	1928	1929	1930
Coffee	50	27	29	30	35	56	45	62	45	58	54	45
Bananas	4	7	17	25	19	13	14	9	16	16	18	27
Timber	13	18	11	9	16	10	15	10	19	11	12	6
Gold	12	12	12	13	7	6	5	5	7	3	4	5
Sugar	5	22	16	8	12	8	12	7	5	4	2	4
Maize	1	–	–	1	–	–	–	–	1	1	2	1
Hides	3	3	1	2	1	2	2	1	1	2	1	1
Sawn	–	–	–	–	–	–	–	–	1	–	–	–
Silver	2	3	3	3	2	1	1	–	–	–	–	–
Cocoa	–	–	–	–	–	–	–	–	–	–	–	–
Rubber	1	–	–	–	–	–	1	1	–	–	–	–
Cotton	–	–	1	–	–	1	–	–	–	–	–	–
Lard (pig fat)	–	–	1	2	–	–	–	–	–	–	–	–

The percentage of exports sent to the United States fluctuated during those ten years between 86 per cent, in 1920, and 50 per cent, in 1930, without ever going below 50 per cent[15]. As for the percentage of imports that originated in the USA, this went from 81 per cent to 61 per cent in 1930, never being less than 60 per cent.[16]

As one can see from Table 1.1, by this time coffee and bananas had already taken over from the earlier supremacy of mining, which up until 1917, always under the control of foreign capital, had been the principal economic activity. The dominant élite linked to the production of coffee had consolidated its position politically on an internal level, although, as we shall see, its role was limited to that of an intermediary for the United States. This group of coffee growers held in its hands the ownership of the land, and exercised a type of domination over the mass of rural labourers that resembled the personal overlordship exercised by the *encomenderos*,the *conquistadores* granted sweeping rights over the land and its inhabitants by the Spanish Crown in colonial times.[17]

The banana companies, for their part, were in full-scale production. The banana-growing enclave was combined with a mining area of a certain importance, which, added to the strategic and military interests of the United States in the Caribbean region, made Nicaragua one of the key points, together with Cuba, Puerto Rico, Haiti and Panama, in the domination of the area by the USA.

The standard of living of the great mass of peasants was extraordinarily low. Figures for 1920 indicate that only 19 per cent of the school-age population between 6 and 19 years old, inclusive, received any kind of formal education.[18] The state of health of the ordinary people was equally deplorable. A report from the period states that 'the relevant authorities are of the opinion that of every five children that are born only three reach maturity'. Of those who survived approximately 90 per cent were chronically infested with parasites. On reaching adulthood, syphilis and malaria were added to their problems. The government dedicated approximately 12 US cents per capita per year to the area of health.[19] An American author, in summarizing the situation, pointed out that many of these barefoot labourers earned no more than $5 or $6 a month. In the cities, he wrote, they lived in earth-floored shacks on the outskirts, with their children playing naked in the mud. Their diet consisted of beans, rice and plantains.[20]

Since the activities previously mentioned, the production of coffee and bananas, were the most important sectors of the Nicaraguan economy, the internal domination of the coffee growers was practically total. In consequence, the disputes between the Liberal and Conservative Parties – in reality, the expression of the rivalry between the municipal authorities of two cities, León, agricultural and Liberal, and Granada, trade-based and Conservative[21] – were in effect no more than a quarrel between a trading bourgeoisie and an agro-exporting one, neither having the necessary imagination to see any other way of attaining power than by vying with each other for the favours of American imperialism.

The non-existence of industry and the predominance of an agrarian economy based on semi-monoculture meant the absence of a genuine working class, as, apart from the mass of peasants tied to the coffee estates, the only groups in the country that resembled a working class were the agricultural proletariat of the banana-growing areas, which – due to the particular system of work organization in the banana enclave, did not have the characteristics necessary to be able to play an independent role – and a certain number of workers in the mines.

Still further from being able to play such a role, and with even worse conditions, was the *peón* of the great estates, linked to his master by means of a personal bond that has been compared to one of slavery, since it encouraged forced labour and established a social relationship of a hereditary nature[22] between the labourer and the *hacendado*.

This being the situation, everything would seem to suggest that it should therefore have been up to the sectors represented by small craftsmen, rural smallholders, groups of intellectuals and so on to take on a significant role, both socially and politically, in the Nicaragua of that time. However, the structure of the social relations of production did not permit the real rise of these sectors, except until after the Second World War, when the political and military dominance of the regime of Anastasio Somoza was virtually absolute, and again prevented them from occupying such a position.

The American military intervention of 1927 and the subsequent resistance by Sandino brought the possibility of an irruption of sections of the population from outside the great bourgeoisie into the Nicaraguan political process, and into the corresponding struggle for power. The nationalist mentality of Sandino's movement, and the nature of its social base, meant that it constituted a double threat for the dominant forces in Nicaragua: the agrarian and commercial bourgeoisies on an internal level, and the imperialist policies of the USA on an external level. It is within this iron triangle that one should situate the struggle of the *Sandinista* movement, to whose internal weaknesses, socially and organizationally, would be added the contradictions produced by the tendencies that would seek to have influence over it: those of the Communist International, and the *Aprista* movement.[23]

It is necessary, therefore, to look at the actions of Augusto César Sandino within the complex process of the economic and military expansion undertaken by the United States in Nicaragua, in order to fully understand both the significance of Sandino's revolt and the real nature of his struggle.

NICARAGUA, BETWEEN A REPUBLIC AND A PROTECTORATE

The United States, whose political and strategic interest in Nicaragua dates from the first half of the last century,[24] had by the beginning of the 1920s achieved an absolute financial, political and military control over that Central American country. Previously, they had secured the partial withdrawal of Britain from the area, by means of the Hay-Pauncefote Treaty, which allotted the United States exclusive rights to the construction of a canal through Nicaragua.[25]

Banking and the railways were entirely under their control. The Nicaraguan government owned all the shares in the National Bank and the Pacific Railway, but the Board of Directors of each of these institutions included an experienced group of American members familiar with their respective fields. These Boards of Directors held their meetings in New York. The National Bank also kept its reserves in New York, and the Nicaraguan government first consulted the International Acceptance Bank before adopting any kind of financial measure.[26]

This control was not limited solely to railways, but covered every significant means of communication. Telegraphic communications were in the hands of All American Cables, while radio was for the most part under the control of the Tropical Radio Company, a subsidiary of the United Fruit Company.[27]

The principal American investors in the country included the Cuyamel Fruit Company, the Standard Fruit Company and the United Fruit Company itself. The Central American Exploration Company was the owner of a gold mine and a concession of four million acres for mining purposes. Also present were Salvador Mines Ltd, The Continental Mines Ltd, the Constanza Consolidated Mining

Company and a number of smaller mining interests. Several timber interests and the Public Utilities Consolidated Corporation also had substantial holdings in the country.[28] In addition, from 1923 the Bragman's Bluff Lumber Company held a concession for the exploitation of close to 50 000 acres of forests.

We can therefore state that the Nicaragua of the 1920s was a country with a limited-product economy that was completely dependent on the economy of the United States. This dependency was, naturally, indissolubly linked to the political and military domination exercised by the United States over the little republic.

The direct political and military intervention by the American government in Nicaragua first became evident, in this century, in 1909.[29]

After provoking the fall of the Nicaraguan President, José Santos Zelaya, the State Department sent a special agent to Nicaragua and made the principal leaders of the revolt sign an agreement known as the Dawson Pact, one of the clauses of which committed the Nicaraguan government to request a loan from American bankers and revoke certain concessions granted by Zelaya to non-American companies and institutions. The American government, for its part, would provide its 'good offices' in dealings between 'The Republic of Nicaragua and certain American financiers of high standing' in order to secure the loan.[30] The debts owed by Nicaragua to Britain would be transferred to American bankers, who would thus become its sole creditors.

This was explained as follows by the then US President, William Howard Taft:

it is obvious that the Monroe Doctrine is more vital in the areas surrounding the Panama Canal and the Caribbean region, than in any other area. It is, therefore, essential that the countries within this sphere should be freed from the embarrassments caused by heavy foreign debts and chaotic national finances, and by the danger, always present, of international complications arising out of internal disorders. Hence, the United States has gladly encouraged those American bankers who were eager to lend their assistance in the financial rehabilitation of these countries ... The Republics of Central America and the Caribbean possess great natural riches. They need only some stability and the means of financial regeneration in order to be able to enter into an era of peace and prosperity that will provide them with wealth and happiness, and, at the same time, engender secure conditions that will lead to a flourishing commercial intercourse with this country.[31]

From 1911 onwards, the Nicaraguan government was so indebted towards American bankers that the whole of its income was dedicated to the servicing of foreign debt.

From December 1911 a Controller of Customs was appointed, who under the agreements signed with the bankers had to be a US national, and was named by the bankers themselves in consultation with the State Department. It is interesting to note the opinion on the subject of Dana Munro, an expert in international relations at the State Department, who believed that the establishment of US customs inspectors, like those already operating in Santo Domingo, was an additional objective that was inherent within, and perhaps of greater importance than, the projects to supply loans to Nicaragua and Honduras. The apparent success of the experiment in the Dominican Republic, Munro wrote, had led 'Taft and his advisers to see in American control of customs almost a panacea for the ills of the disorderly Caribbean countries, a practice that would discourage revolutions and also make possible the repayment of foreign claims and the construction of much-needed public works.'[32] With regard to such 'much-needed public works', we can say that of the fifteen million dollars lent to the Nicaraguan government by the New York firm of Brown Brothers & J.W. Seligman in 1911, only $500 000 went towards public projects, the rest being consumed by the servicing of debts and interests owned to the bankers, and by payments made to American companies.[33]

The American government had succeeded in installing as President Adolfo Díaz, an employee of the Luz and Los Angeles Mining Company, of which the then US Secretary of State, Philander Knox, was a major shareholder. Díaz was, in the words of Raymond Leslie Buell, 'the most pro-yankee figure in the country'.[34] Díaz would go so far as to demonstrate the unconditional nature of his support by asking for the first time, on 2 December 1911, for a treaty to be signed that would permit the United States to intervene openly in the affairs of Nicaragua, a request he would repeat in 1912, and which would lead ultimately to the permanent military occupation of the country.[35]

The conclusion of the Chamorro–Weitzel Treaty between the governments of the United States and Nicaragua on 8 February 1913 is one of the most demonstrative instances of the total domination of the former over the Central American republic. This treaty granted the

United States an option, in perpetuity, to build a canal in any part of Nicaraguan territory, a naval base in the Gulf of Fonseca, freedom of navigation for the US Navy in Nicaraguan territorial waters, and a lease of ninety-nine years, to be extended at the wish of the United States, over the Great and Little Corn Islands, all in exchange for three million dollars. The US Secretary of State presented the treaty to the Senate in Washington, which, however, rejected it as it considered it inadmissible.

Nevertheless, on 5 August 1914 General Emiliano Chamorro, Minister-Plenipotentiary and special envoy of Nicaragua to the United States, signed, together with William Jennings Bryan, the current Secretary of State, a new agreement to be known as the Bryan–Chamorro Treaty. The outbreak of the world war would give a new stimulus to US interest in the canal route through Nicaragua, and its economic and political control over the latter was reinforced by the signing of further agreements with the bankers.

The Bryan–Chamorro Treaty reproduced almost exactly the conditions of the Chamorro–Weitzel agreement, and laid down, among other things, that:

Article 1: The government of Nicaragua grants in perpetuity to the government of the United States, free from all taxation or public duties, the exclusive proprietary rights necessary and convenient for the construction, operation and maintenance of an interoceanic canal by way of the San Juan River and the Great Lake of Nicaragua, or by any other route through the territory of Nicaragua.

In Article 3 a modification was made in the destination of the three million dollars that were to be received by the Nicaraguan government. In the Chamorro–Weitzel Treaty these three million were assigned to general expenses, but under the new agreement they had to be dedicated exclusively to reducing the current debt of Nicaragua, that is, to reimbursing the American bankers.[36]

The Central American Court of Justice, founded in 1907 with the direct involvement of the United States, declared the treaty null and void, as it considered it to be in violation of the sovereignty and territorial integrity of Nicaragua, Honduras and Costa Rica (Judgements of 10 November 1916 and 9 March 1917).[37]

The government of Nicaragua, indignant over this decision, withdrew its judges from the Court, which thus received a blow from which it would not be able to recover.[38] A wave of protest built up throughout the Americas against the treaty, which was denounced as shameful. Voices were also heard repudiating the treaty in the US Senate itself.

Senator Elihu Root wrote, in a letter to his colleague Paul Fuller:

I am beset by doubts and fears when I think of the question whether the government of Nicaragua, which concluded the Treaty, is really the genuine representation of that people and whether it can be regarded, in Nicaragua and in Central America, as a legitimate and free agent to grant it; for I have read the report of our Marines in Nicaragua and I find in it these words: 'The present Government is not in power due to the will of the people; the elections were for the most part fraudulent.' And further on in the same report I have read the statement that the opponents of that Government constitute three quarters of the country . . . Can we conclude a Treaty that is so serious for Nicaragua, in which it concedes to us perpetual rights in that territory, with a President of whom we have good reason to believe that he does not represent more than one-fourth of the subjects of the country, and who is sustained in his position by our military forces, and to whom, as a consequence of the Treaty, we would pay a considerable sum of money for this same President to have at his disposal?[39]

For his part, Senator William Borah declared:

I have never considered the Treaty with Nicaragua to be a treaty concluded with the Nicaraguan people. We made a treaty with ourselves. We made a treaty with a government that represented us from the other side of the negotiating table . . . We made a treaty with a government that was our instrument. This is one of the most indefensible transactions of which I have knowledge in international life.[40]

A student of Latin American affairs, John Kennet Turner, has summarized the conclusions of a confidential report that was drawn up by the Foreign Relations Committee of the Senate in 1914:

(1) That the permanent occupation of Nicaragua was carried out by the Taft administration with the object of maintaining in power a President who was opposed by an overwhelming majority of the citizens of his country. (2) That this President, Adolfo Díaz, was

brought to power not by the votes of the Nicaraguans, but by the armed forces of the United States, at the orders of the President of the latter. (3) That as a means of installing Adolfo Díaz in the Presidency and maintaining him there we undertook a series of illegal military campaigns, killed hundreds of Nicaraguans, overthrew three successive governments, seized public and private property and prosecuted a war of conquest to the point of taking complete possession of the country. (4) That in the Presidency Adolfo Díaz found that he could do nothing of his own volition, but instead had to receive orders like a mere servant. (5) That the American domination of Nicaragua did not bring the slightest benefit to the people of Nicaragua; that the liberties of Nicaraguan citizens were permanently abolished; that the government of Nicaragua, under the American protectorate, is purely an autocracy, administered by foreigners, which finds itself obliged to maintain the threat of a regime of terror suspended over the Nicaraguan people in order to remain in power. (6) That the entire purpose of the war undertaken by the United States against the small republic was to oblige Nicaragua to submit to the plundering of its wealth by American financiers. (7) That Woodrow Wilson continued in every detail the projects for conquest initiated by Taft; that the exploitation of Nicaragua with the aid of American guns was under the Wilson administration given an air of legality, as the treaty with Nicaragua was ratified because Wilson recommended it. (8) That the principal features of this treaty, the sale of a canal concession and the leasing of some naval bases, were matters that were conceived after the satisfaction of the real objectives, with the aim of putting up a screen that would conceal the purely financial purposes of the protectorate. (9) That the current arbiter of the destinies of Nicaragua, under the American protectorate, is none other than the representative or local agent of the New York Bankers' Syndicate, for whose exclusive benefit the occupation was carried out and the Convention signed.[41]

Díaz remained in the Presidency until 1 January 1917, when the United States transferred Emiliano Chamorro from the post of Ambassador in Washington to that of President of Nicaragua.

During both the Presidency of Chamorro and those of his successors yet more agreements were signed with American bankers, and the grip of American domination was tightened still further.

In 1926 Chamorro was once again at the head of the government when a revolt broke out led by José María Moncada, a member of the Liberal Party, with the stated aim of overthrowing Chamorro and handing power to the candidate to whom it was rightfully due under the Constitution, Dr Juan Bautista Sacasa. The Americans blamed the Calles government in Mexico, which they had already accused of bolshevism because of its independent foreign policy, charging them with having encouraged the Liberal rebellion in Nicaragua in order to gain control of the Caribbean.

In Mexico, General Obregón referred to the American accusations as 'professional jealousy', and Calles was still more forthright, asking, 'What person in his right mind could conceive the idea that Mexico, a country in the midst of a process of organization, without the army for any kind of conquests, without even the shadow of a navy, could plan to endanger the defences of the Panama Canal or those of any other country?'[42]

The Communist International also made a statement on the subject, declaring:

> Everywhere, in China, in Nicaragua, in Java, the imperialists invoke, as the ultimate proof of the need for bloody repression, the struggle against bolshevism. The imperialists give the name bolshevism to any effort for the liberation of the oppressed peoples. By doing so they wish to discredit bolshevism. They do not realize that all those who are honest, just and lovers of freedom and valor then declare themselves in favour of bolshevism, and that they themselves thus develop the class consciousness of the masses and their level of organization.[43]

The United States once again placed in the Presidency their unconditional ally, Adolfo Díaz.

A short time later the Liberals established an autonomous government in Puerto Cabezas, which was recognized by the government of Mexico. Díaz received an emergency loan from the United States of $300 000, followed by another of six million dollars, and even before he had been recognized by the US as President of Nicaragua hastened to label the aid given by Mexico to the Liberals part of a worldwide bolshevik plot, and in an extensive document openly requested American military intervention. He claimed that it had been made impossible for his government to protect the lives and interests of

Americans and other foreigners resident in his country, and declared that whichever means were chosen by the State Department to offer such persons the protection he could not give them would enjoy his absolute confidence.[44]

On 23 February 1927, a wire from the Associated Press made clear the wishes of Adolfo Díaz:

> The Conservative President Adolfo Díaz, recognized by Washington, desires that the United States should formally assume the protection of Nicaragua for one hundred years, which could be extended. The project will be presented to the Nicaraguan Congress tomorrow, Thursday, Sr. Díaz having every confidence that it will be approved. When a draft of the proposal was made public last night, Díaz declared that the relevant treaty would give the US the right to intervene whenever it were necessary for the purpose of maintaining responsible government and ensuring free elections in his homeland.[45]

In this treaty, Díaz would also give over to the United States a guarantee of the canal-construction rights, as well as the right to appoint a financial consultant with supreme authority over State expenditure and an American inspector to oversee the collection of all State revenues. In addition, the United States would prepare plans for the formation of a Nicaraguan 'Constabulary' (National Guard) under the command of American officers.

The United States, however, was not prepared to take up a Protectorate over Nicaragua in such an overt manner, since the existing situation already permitted them every kind of political and economic advantage, and hence the head of the Latin American Section of the State Department, Stokely Morgan, was quick to state that they had no interest in a treaty of the kind proposed by Díaz to their legation in Managua. Nevertheless, at the same time as declarations of this sort were being made, thousands of Marines were landing in Nicaragua to maintain Díaz in power.

Inside the United States, Senator Burton K. Wheeler said on 6 March 1927, in the Forum in Boston, that:

> Kellogg's policies have led to an armed intervention in Nicaragua on behalf of a puppet President, put there by the United States and imposed on the people against their will for the sole reason that, no matter what he may cost Nicaragua in so doing, he is ever-ready to

serve the New York bankers who for seventeen years have exploited that country in a pitiless way, under the aegis of the State Department.[46]

He went on to add, brusquely:

Our State Department, throwing American honour to the dogs, recognized Adolfo Díaz as President of Nicaragua. In order to do so, it had to violate the spirit and the letter of a treaty that it had itself sponsored, it had to entangle itself in every kind of legal chicanery and political manoeuvres in the vain hope of making the worst of causes appear to be the best in the eyes of the people of Nicaragua, who rightly despise the puppet-mascot of our State Department. And when it failed in carrying off the crude deal it had tried to force upon the people of Nicaragua, it hurriedly began to send warships, Marines and bombers in order to continue its cowardly and dishonourable programme of brutal thuggery.

Who is this puppet of our State Department? He is an old favourite. He is a perfect rubber stamp. He is an ideal 'yes man'. Not only does he take orders from our State Department, he anticipates them. Don Adolfo, sitting in the Presidential Palace in Managua, could easily be confused with a phonograph dog listening to his master's voice ... In its double role of loan agent and guardian angel for a few New York bankers, our State Department has been using Díaz one day on and one day off ever since it helped to bring about the revolution in Nicaragua in 1909, which led to the fall of the government of Zelaya. He is one of the two men at its disposal. The other was Emiliano Chamorro. Of the two, Díaz is the most easily manageable instrument.[47]

The extent of American domination over Nicaragua was such that, in the opinion of Harold Norman Denny, the United States had during most of the previous two decades governed the country more completely than the US Federal government did the different States of the Union. For Denny, it was an unquestionable fact that, however vehemently the State Department might reject the term, the United States exercised a protectorate over Nicaragua, occupying the country with its armed forces. He pointed out that over the years since 1911 the United States had at different times chosen Presidents in Nicaragua, maintaining them by force of arms, dictated constitutional precepts, and said what laws had to be approved by the country's Congress. In the case that the Congress failed them, they had got the Presidents to introduce measures by decree, and imposed their will in this way. Moreover, as if this were not already enough, they had eliminated the Nicaraguan army, and were building a new force, with US Marine officers.[48]

Following Moncada's victory at the battle of Muy Muy, in March 1927, 2000 US Marines arrived in Nicaragua under the command of General Logan Feland, and in April President Coolidge named Henry L. Stimson as his personal representative in the country, with exceptional powers.[49]

On 29 April, three representatives of Sacasa held a meeting with Stimson, and on 4 May, following a second meeting in Tipitapa between Stimson and Moncada, a truce was declared and the Conservative forces evacuated the town of Boaco. On 8 May, the Council of Liberal Generals agreed their surrender, without waiting for the presence of one of their members who was absent, Augusto César Sandino.

On 12 May Moncada surrendered to Stimson, a fact that should not surprise us if there is truth in the claim made by De Nogales, that in 1912, while another revolt was in progress against Díaz, Moncada was in New York receiving a salary paid by the latter for carrying out some special tasks in the city.[50] His good relations with Díaz dated from that time.

Moncada took his submission to the extreme of decorating the US Admiral Latimer with a 'medal of peace', a crucifix from which the figure of Christ had been removed in order to be able to present it to the American officer as a decoration.[51] Only the General who had been absent from the meeting that had agreed to the surrender, Augusto César Sandino, rejected this capitulation, and made the following statement: 'Not only do I consider Moncada a traitor, but also a deserter who has gone over to the enemy. Nobody ever authorized him to leave the Constitutionalist ranks in order to enter into secret treaties, in the name of the Constitutionalist Army, with the enemy, and more specifically with the invaders of our country . . . Moncada has made himself responsible for a crime that cries out for vengeance.'[52]

2 The Indigenous Origins of the Sandinista Movement

SOCIAL ORIGINS OF THE SANDINISTA ARMY

In an effort to fulfil his desire to restore the dignity and sovereignty of the Nicaraguan people,[1] General Augusto César Sandino initiated an independent insurrectionary movement in Las Segovias. A mechanic originally from a family of relatively prosperous peasant farmers from Niquinohomo, he had taken part in the constitutionalist war with the aim of returning the government to its legitimate head under the constitution, Dr Juan Bautista Sacasa. Following the sudden capitulation of the constitutionalist Army, Sandino took a firm decision to continue fighting, only this time directly against the American Marines who remained in military occupation of the country. In order to do so he withdrew to the mountains, and with an initial nucleus of a hundred men who had already been fighting alongside him before then founded the 'Army in Defence of the Sovereignty of Nicaragua'.[2] This small first group would shortly be joined by hundreds of new combatants, who for seven years would struggle heroically against an invader who was both numerically and technically very much more powerful.[3]

The officers of the Sandinista army were of different nationalities, social origins and political ideologies, their basis of unity being a fervent determination to expel the American invader from Nicaraguan territory. Sandino told the American journalist Carleton Beals:

> I have officers from Costa Rica, from Guatemala, from El Salvador, from Honduras, and even two or three from Mexico, who came here attracted by the justice of my cause, but they are in a minority. The backbone of my army is Nicaraguan, and the officers who have stayed at my side the longest are Nicaraguans. I have received many officers from abroad, but in the majority of cases I have dismissed them. Our army is made up of workers and peasants who love their country.[4]

37

The information we have available regarding the social and cultural background of Sandino's principal lieutenants tends to indicate this same heterogeneity in their ranks. Nevertheless, although one does find some officers who were former manual workers, and illiterate, it is noticeable that there were many who had some level of education – they could read and write, which, in the conditions that, as we have described, existed in Nicaragua at that time, was indicative of a certain social and economic level. Some of these officers had formerly been owners of land: small proprietors, such as, for example, Miguel Angel Ortez;[5] medium-sized landholders, like Juan Gregorio Colindres;[6] and even some large landowners, such as Ramón Raudales[7] and the Miskito Member of Congress Adolfo Cockburn,[8] albeit they were landowners who had already been ruined, either by soldiers in the service of the government or by the American troops themselves.

It can therefore be said, with some foundation, that there was in the leadership of the Sandinista movement, in social terms, a predominance of elements of agrarian origin who formed part of a petit bourgeoisie. This phenomenon would not have been in any way unusual, but was very important in that it indicated the existence of fertile ground for the opposing development of two kinds of ideological influence within the Sandinista movement: that which came from the Peruvian APRA, which sent leading figures such as Esteban Pavletich to Nicaragua; and the influence of the Communist International, through its representatives, the Salvadorean Agustín Farabundo Martí and the Venezuelans Gustavo Machado and Carlos Aponte, and through those of its front organizations that were most involved, the 'Hands Off Nicaragua' Committees, and the League against Imperialism.

The main body of the Sandinista army was recruited from among the poor *mestizo* and Indian peasants who worked on the coffee estates. Some used to join up before a guerrilla operation, and afterwards return to their work.[9] The banana-growing areas, particularly after the world economic crisis had begun in 1929, also provided support for the Sandinista forces. The Indians of the Mosquito Coast gave massive support to the movement, and collaborated in a number of military actions.[10]

The army also recruited a good number of its members from among the workers in the mines, which were American-owned. Members of the urban lower middle classes, office workers, civil servants, professionals and shopkeepers, together with smaller and medium property-owners also gave support to the movement, many of them not through armed combat, but as propagandists for the Sandinista cause, or in the political infighting of the different parties, seeking to establish alliances outside the two traditional parties.

In 1927 Salomón de la Selva, a Nicaraguan poet whose personal career took him from the offices of the Pan-American Union in Washington to the trenches of anti-imperialism, via the Mexican Regional Workers' Confederation (CROM),[12] said:

> The Sandinista movement is the true nationalism of Nicaragua. This nationalism, under pressure of force of circumstance, has two wings: one civil, the other militant. The cowardice of the Americans has lain in labelling those of one wing bandits, and saying of the others that they are only a scarce minority . . . More and more those in the civil wing of nationalism are becoming convinced that there remains no way forward other than direct action, that is, that one must go to war, that one must take up a rifle, that one must kill Marines and traitors.[13]

This 'civil wing' mentioned by de la Selva included a good many intellectuals and professionals from the classes described above, who found themselves in opposition to the interests of imperialism.

POLITICAL AND IDEOLOGICAL LIMITATIONS IN THE ANTI-IMPERIALISM OF SANDINO: THE CONTINUED INFLUENCE OF THE LIBERAL–CONSERVATIVE CONFLICT

The movement of Augusto César Sandino was limited by a mental outlook that understood imperialism as a fundamentally external phenomenon. Such an approach lost sight of the mutually determinant dynamic between the economic and political links with the outside world, and the internal configuration of the different social classes.

However, this incomprehension of the complex relationship between the internal and the external, in a country like Nicaragua, was not a failing that was exclusive to Sandino. The Communist International was no more able to resolve the problem, as one can see from the treatment it gave to the revolutionary role of the middle and petit bourgeoisie in the colonies, the clarification of which would have to await the formulations of Mao Zhedong on the Chinese revolution. If it were possible to establish a common denominator for all the different positions put forward with regard to this question, it would be the one-sided nature of their respective approaches, either laying emphasis solely on the external element, and giving a revolutionary role to the bourgeoisie as a whole, or fundamentally stressing internal factors, with a total denial of any revolutionary role for the local bourgeoisie.

In the case of Sandino it would be precisely this problem, which he could never clarify satisfactorily, that would in the final analysis lead him to his death. It is because of this that we can say that *Sandinismo*, which had originated in the context of a struggle to secure the government for the Liberal Juan Bautista Sacasa, always carried with it the weight of its earlier links with the Liberal Party.[14] On several occasions, Sandino made an exception of the Liberals when referring to the servility that he saw in the Conservative Party with regard to the United States, and insisted on differentiating between one Party and the other, conferring on the Liberals a non-existent independence, when both were representatives of the interests of the internal dominant classes and equally tied to the coat-tails of imperialism.

In his Manifesto of 26 August 1927, issued from his headquarters in El Chipote, Sandino declared that he would remain in arms as long as the government was Conservative, and would only hand over his arms to a government of Liberals. Afterwards, he went on, he would seek to find in civilian action the 'true patriot' who could give new direction to the affairs of Nicaragua.[15]

In the Manifesto published on the occasion of the attack on El Ocotal, where some four hundred US Marines and two hundred Nicaraguan soldiers were garrisoned, Sandino said that this battle was a means of demonstrating that they were an organized force that remained in operation, as a protest and in defence of the constitutional rights of Dr Sacasa. At the end of the Manifiesto he made the President of the United States, Calvin Coolidge, responsible for everything that was taking place in Nicaragua, because he had insisted on maintaining in power Adolfo Díaz, an individual regarded with contempt by all good Nicaraguans.[16]

The persistence of his Liberal affiliations can be seen once again in the 'Manifesto of the Constitution of the Army in Defence of the Sovereignty of Nicaragua', of 2 September 1927, which defines this army as being composed of Nicaraguan Liberal volunteers, and 'Indohispanics' (*Indohispanos*).[17] Nevertheless, in this same document Sandino also swore before his fatherland and before his army not to have political commitments towards any one sector, and that his actions were guided only by the highest patriotism.[18] On 1 January 1929, in reply to letters sent to him by the US Brigadier General Logan

Feland and Rear Admiral D. F. Sellers urging him to surrender, Sandino wrote that it was patriotism that had sustained him in opposing force with force and refusing absolutely to recognize any right of interference of the United States' government in the internal affairs of Nicaragua, thus demonstrating that the sovereignty of a people was not open to discussion, but had to be defended by taking up arms. It was this same sentiment, he added, that also moved him to declare:

> that only with *General José María Moncada could I enter into an agreement for the achievement of an effective peace in our country, since he, being a member of the Liberal Party, which he betrayed, could rectify his mistakes,*[19] by means of an undertaking that he could contract with us, with the Nicaraguan people, and with the Liberal Party itself, to respect the conditions that would be proposed to him by our Liberation army. It is on the basis of the foregoing that I declare to you that in order to arrive at this effective peace agreement with Gral. José María Moncada we put forward as a first and *absolutely indispensable* condition, the withdrawal of the American forces under your command from our territory.[20]

At one point in the struggle, Sandino appeared to be clearer in his ideas regarding the equal role played by both the two traditional political parties. On the occasion of the 1932 elections, supervised by the United States, but this time with the Liberal Juan Bautista Sacasa as Presidential candidate, Sandino stated, in instructions sent to General Horacio Portocarrero on 15 December 1931, that all their efforts should be directed towards securing military control of Nicaragua by force of arms, and obstructing whatever kind of electoral farce it was intended to carry out in the country under foreign supervision.[21] Also, he declared in a Manifesto of January 1932:

> Compatriots: Proceed with dignity and remember that you have been the victims *both of the yankees and of those politicians.*[22] Anyone who runs after those individuals and goes to vote in the booths watched over by the yankees will do nothing more than offer the most lamentable homage to foreign bayonets . . . To hope for national dignity from Chamorro, Díaz, or Espinoza and Sacasa, is, compatriots, stupidity of the worst kind, above all when one can already see approaching, victorious, the Army in Defence of the National Sovereignty of Nicaragua.[23]

In a letter to José Zelaya, of 11 March 1932, Sandino said that responsibility for the events in Nicaragua lay with the foreign policy of the USA, and with those Nicaraguans who had done nothing other than flirt[24] with the invaders, contributing with their pusillanimity to providing the Americans with the pretext they required for their intervention in the country.[25]

In August 1932, he went so far as to say that the political leaders, whether Liberal or Conservative, were 'a gang of trash, cowards and traitors, incapable of leading a patriotic and courageous people', who had already abandoned these bosses and improvised their own leadership from among the workers and peasants themselves. He went on, 'Still, even today when there is so much light and exemplary conduct to be seen, these failures of politicians continue to argue among themselves for the caresses of the foreign lash, and are squabbling like so many dogs and cats in a sack to gain a Presidency based on foreign tutelage, which we will not permit.'[26] However, he then went on to say that the actions of the men of his army of workers and peasants 'would be beneficial for our politicians of the past, who *if they rectify their errors, could merit our respect,*[27] with the exception of those of the kind previously mentioned (Adolfo Díaz, Chamorro, Moncada, Cuadra Pasos and others), due to their having destroyed with their materialistic ambitions the bond of nationality that they had possessed'.[28]

Sandino appeared to believe at that time that neither Nicaragua nor himself, as the leader of the resistance, could harbour many expectations with regard to either the Conservative or the Liberal leaders. He said that Nicaragua would only be free through the bullet and at the cost of its own blood, and that the politicians 'who argued among themselves for the invader's whip' would be superseded in a not very distant future, when the people would take over the reins of State power.[29]

In a letter to General Pedrón Altamirano of 9 November 1932 Sandino commented that although the elections had already gone by (on 6 November), they were still waiting to find out whether it was against Sacasa or the Conservatives that they would have to continue fighting, as he did not believe that they would be far into the new year before the US forces would withdraw, or as he put it, 'whatever happens the pirates will leave on 2 January'.[30] In instructions to his Generals Umanzor and Morales on 18 November he ordered that under no circumstances should they refrain from harassing the enemy, whichever candidate were elected.[31]

Soon, however, there was a further re-emergence of the contradictions in Sandino's ideas, the product of a lack of understanding of the phenomenon of imperialism and of its relation to internal forces. As a result, in spite of the fact that his attitude appeared to be one of radical opposition to the new government imposed by the Americans, without any vacillations over its Liberal or Conservative composition, in reality he valued the election results in a significantly different manner according to who eventually emerged as the winner. This was due not only to understandable considerations of tactics, but also to the absence of a coherent conceptual apparatus. He said to Altamirano:

> if power remains with the Conservatives, I think neither they will seek an agreement with us nor us with them, and we will settle the matter with bullets; whereas with Sacasa we would propose that the military control of the Republic be given to our Army, for which we would require that the Minister of War was one of the members of our Army, and similarly that the Ministry of Finance and that of Foreign Relations were occupied by persons designated by our Army, for which purpose we would choose Doctor Escolástico Lara, for Finance, and Calderón Ramírez for Foreign Relations; equally, the commanders of the garrisons of La Loma in Managua and La Pólvora in Granada would have to be members of our Army, with battalions of our own troops.[32]

On 24 December 1932, Sandino called upon Salvador Calderón Ramírez, Doctor Escolástico Lara, Doctor Pedro José Zepeda and General Horacio Portocarrero to represent him in the conversations 'for unity and peace' being organized by the Patriotic Group, set up on the initiative of the Minister Sofonías Salvatierra, which were to be held between representatives of all the political parties. In his public statement Sandino said:

> we have been informed that the Nicaraguan people as a whole awoke in patriotic reaction at the sound of our weapons of liberation, and that they are unanimously interested that a patriotic understanding should be reached with our Army. *We are resolved for our part that if the government of Sacasa is free and does not carry with it either public or private commitments to the United States of North America, we will undertake discussions for peace in the town of San Rafael del Norte.*[33]

Once again we see him pass over the links between Sacasa and the US government, to which he had been the Ambassador,[34] and which had just presented him with the Presidency of Nicaragua. In such circumstances Sandino was still able to admit the possibility that the former might not have any public or private obligations towards the United States.

In the 'Basis for Peace', proposed by Sandino on 3 January 1933, he made plain yet again his lack of awareness of the unbroken and organic relationship between imperialism and the dominant classes in Nicaragua, on whom he insisted in conferring an independence that could only be utopian. The different points of the 'Basis' were:

(1) That the first citizen of Nicaragua who should find himself invested with the government of our Republic . . . and sincerely representing the interests of our nation, should request and obtain, by force if necessary, the immediate withdrawal of the American occupation forces in Nicaragua. And that he should in turn accept the support of our Army . . . for the complete maintenance of order in our Republic. (2) That the Government of Nicaragua should also accept and support the proposal to hold a conference in the capital of the Argentine Republic between representatives of the 21 governments of our America by race and that of the United States, in order to examine all matters relating to the project of transcendental importance according to which the United States seeks to build, as their exclusive property, an inter-oceanic canal and instal a naval base in the territory and territorial waters of Central America. (3) That the government of Nicaragua that accepts the first and second points of this agreement, should also accept the right of the Nicaraguan people to remove it from power, in cases where it failed in the fulfilment in whole or in part of the conditions here stipulated.[35]

In addition to these conditions, Sandino also presented to the peace discussions his Peace Protocol, in which he said that in order to reach an agreement it would first be necessary to be fully informed of the political programme that would be undertaken by Doctor Sacasa during the four years of his administration; to be convinced that he would dispense absolutely with foreign interference in the finances of Nicaragua; to be informed of the administration that would be established with regard to the so-called National Guard; and also, again, to know whether Sacasa had subscribed to pacts of any kind with the American forces. In point V of the Protocol he asked that it be put on record that his Army requested the revision of the Bryan–Chamorro Treaty, as being one that had notoriously been imposed on the Nicaraguan government by American intervention. He also demanded that the canal route through Nicaragua and the possible site for the construction of a naval base in the Gulf of Fonseca be declared of 'Indohispanic' nationality (*Indohispana*) by the Latin American Congress that it was proposed to hold in Argentina.[36]

The Marines departed, and Sandino signed a peace agreement, believing that by doing so he avoided further US intervention, that he thought might have taken place on the pretext of needing to continue to fight against him. He entirely failed to appreciate the process through which the Marines had gradually been carrying out the 'Nicaraguanization of the war', in the same way that many years later they would undertake Vietnamization in Vietnam, nor did he recognise that this withdrawal was carried out at the precise moment when the Nicaraguan armed forces were able by themselves to put down any movement that could endanger American interests.

The manner in which he perceived the role of the National Guard, a force that had been formed and trained in the clear image of colonial repressive bodies, was one more area in which Sandino suffered the consequences of his ideological limitations, as his anti-imperialism was limited to opposing the undisguised military manifestations of intervention, and did not recognize the deep roots of dependency.

Raymond Leslie Buell, an American commentator on foreign affairs and a supporter of US intervention, refers with a degree of surprise to the fact that 5000 US Marines had spent three years trying to capture Sandino and his followers, who did not amount, he wrote, to more than 500 men. However, he noted that from April 1929 responsibility for the campaign against 'banditry' had gradually been transferred by the Marines to the National Guard, made up of Nicaraguan soldiers, but commanded exclusively by American officers. This, Buell thought, had given 'new energy' to the fight against Sandino.[37]

Sandino, however, though aware of the links between the Guard and the Marines, persisted in believing that the submission of the force to a system of regulations within the constitution would be enough to put an end to the problems it originated.

Even when, after the signing of the peace agreement, the Guard was eliminating his men, by then themselves unarmed, Sandino still said that this was happening because the Guard 'being unconstitutional, was irresponsible'.[38] He also said, 'I have nothing to say about whether there should be a Guard or not, nor about the people who should lead it; I myself, as the citizen that I am, am obliged to pay the taxes necessary to maintain the Army or the Guard, or whatever it is called; what I want is only that we should be given constitutional guarantees and that the Guard should be brought within the Constitution.'[39] To President Sacasa he said that the basic need was to know 'both the constitutional status of the Guard, and the other means of guaranteeing the lives of his men'.[40]

This lack of a clear political vision that was so apparent in the Manifestos and actions of Sandino was not shared by Anastasio Somoza, the Director of the National Guard, and the most faithful and consistent guardian of the interests of American imperialism in Nicaragua.

Somoza did not look favourably on the fact that Sandino still retained 600 men, with a certain quantity of arms, in the mountains of Nueva Segovia, even though this was after the General had signed peace with the Liberal Sacasa.

Somoza, disregarding the Peace Protocol, continued to pursue and kill *Sandinistas* and to imprison anyone suspected of wishing to join Sandino's encampments in Wiwilí. In an interview given to the press in February 1934, Sandino stated:

I will not hand over our arms to the National Guard, because it is not a constitutional authority . . . It cannot be demanded of me that I should comply with what was stipulated in the agreements if the other party has not complied with them either. Please look at the agreement . . . it says that I will gradually hand over the arms to duly constituted authority. The National Guard is not a legally constituted body; therefore, I am not obliged to hand over the arms to them. It was also stipulated that we would be given guarantees, and this has not been fulfilled. Let the National Guard be brought within the Constitution, and then I will hand over my boys. Or they should guarantee to me that it shall be done as I indicate and I will bring the arms myself, by plane. The question is that there are here not two but three States: the force represented by the President of the Republic, that of the National Guard, and my own. This is truly absurd. The Guard does not obey the President. I do.[41]

While Sandino trusted in the good faith of the Liberal President, the US Embassy and the Director of the Guard, with the knowledge of Sacasa, were preparing the ambush in which Augusto César Sandino would die, together with his Generals Estrada and Umanzor, on 21 February 1934. Not much more time would pass before Sacasa was himself overthrown by a military coup, which gave absolute control over the government of Nicaragua to Anastasio Somoza.

Alongside Sandino's determined anti-imperialism and nationalism, conceived within the limitations that we have indicated, there coexisted in him a variety of beliefs of a more or less esoteric nature, based on theosophy, which influenced his thinking. However, such beliefs were by no means peculiar to Sandino. There is every indication that this was a widespread phenomenon among the petit bourgeoisie of Central America, even those who enjoyed a certain level of culture. It is necessary to mention this factor here, as the picture would not be complete if it were omitted, since it throws a good deal of light on the obstacles that must have been encountered by both *Apristas* and Communists as they tried to impose their respective lines upon the movement led by Sandino.

Sandino's 'esotericism' revealed itself for the first time in his writings on 14 October 1930, when, as we shall see, he had already broken with the Communist International, and the *Aprista* Esteban Pavletich was similarly no longer with him in Las Segovias.

In the language of General Sandino theosophical terminology acquired very specific connotations. He used it to impose his authority on his subordinates and to instil courage, determination and confidence into his troops. He told them that the mission of the chosen ones was to come down to Earth to wipe out injustice, and that every man who fought for the liberty of the peoples of the world was continuing the work of Jesus and others of the chosen.

For Sandino, the Final Judgement would be the day that would see the destruction of injustice on Earth, and the establishment of the reign of justice, which he called the Reign of Light and Truth. He declared that on that day the oppressed peoples would break the chains of humiliation with which the imperialisms of the world had kept them subjugated, and that the trumpets that would be heard on that day would be the clarions of war, sounding the hymns of the oppressed peoples against the injustice of the oppressors.

Sandino also said that Nicaragua had been chosen to initiate the judgement of justice against injustice, and light the fuse of the proletarian explosion against the imperialists of the Earth. He believed in premonitions, and admitted to having had palpitations, 'mental trepidations' and strange sensations. He said that he made use of the magnetic resonance of his voice in combat to give his men confidence, and held the belief that spirits 'also fought, both in bodily and in disembodied form'.[42]

THE INFLUENCE OF THE APRA IN THE SANDINISTA MOVEMENT

Among the diverse ideological currents that converged in the *Sandinista* movement, the study of which is necessary in order to understand the significance of the role of the Communist International, one of special importance was that represented by the APRA, the 'American Popular Revolutionary Alliance',[43] an organization formed in 1924 by a group of Peruvian political exiles led by Victor Raúl Haya de la Torre. It sought to establish sections throughout Latin America, and enjoyed great prestige among the intellectual of the continent at that time.

It seems true to say that Sandino's relations with the APRA dated from the first months of his campaign. The APRA was active in organizing demonstrations in support of the Nicaraguan cause from the moment of the first landing of US Marines in Corinto in 1927. The Marines moved into Nicaragua on 6 January of that year, and on 13 January the *Apristas* held a mass rally in Paris, in the *Salle des Fetes* of the Societé Nationale d'Horticulture de France. On that occasion, Romain Rolland sent the Paris section of the APRA a message in which he expressed his solidarity with the protest against the invasion of Nicaragua, which he considered part of a grand design by the United States to gain control over the whole of the American continent. He mentioned that although the crime being committed in Nicaragua was not the only one of its kind, as China, Syria and other countries were in a similar situation, the case of Nicaragua was, he thought, that which had most urgently to be denounced.[44]

It would be reasonable to expect that as soon as Sandino's decision to continue fighting against the American invaders was made public the various anti-imperialist organizations should make contact with him, and the APRA was among the first to do so. Indeed, in the first manifestos of Sandino, from 1927, one already sees the appearance of the terminology that was in common usage in *Aprista* circles, which laid emphasis on 'Indoamericanism' and addressed itself to the intellectuals, the workers, artisans and the 'Indohispanic Race' (*Raza Indohispana*) as a whole.[45]

In his first political manifesto, of 1 June 1927, Sandino categorized himself as a worker from the city, an artisan, and stated that the bond of nationality gave him the right to assume responsibility for his actions in the affairs of Nicaragua, of Central America and of the whole of the continent 'of our language'. He went on to defend, in the manner typical of the APRA, the internationalist aspirations of his struggle. It should be noted that this internationalism of Sandino was not a proletarian internationalism, but rather an 'Indohispanic' internationalism, even though in some documents he might speak of the liberation of the worldwide proletariat.[46] Through a number of articles written by leading figures of the APRA in that period, the ideas of the movement had been schematized into five fundamental points: action against yankee imperialism, support for the political unity of Latin America, for the nationalization of lands and industries, for the internationalization of the Panama Canal and for solidarity between all the oppressed peoples and classes of the world. Time and again they declared that one of the most vital steps needed for the achievement of these objectives was the establishment of an anti-imperialist United Front, which would bring together all the forces that in one way or another found themselves in opposition to imperialism.[47]

In outlining this United Front, in which there would be room for men of all tendencies and beliefs, the *Apristas* referred by way of a model to the Chinese Kuomintang, though they affirmed that they would seek to establish a body that was broader, more solid and better organized.[48] All these aspects of the APRA found fertile ground in Sandino, albeit that they would be adapted to the particular *Sandinista* universe.

The first of the five points, action against yankee imperialism, was the very *raison d'etre* of the Sandino movement, though it was not conceived by Sandino with the same complexity as it was by the APRA, which at that time was seeking to resist not just the US military, but also American economic penetration which they believed impeded the growth and development of the national bourgeoisies of the Latin American countries.

Nevertheless, the APRA was in agreement with Sandino in seeing the armed struggle to force the expulsion of the US Marines from Nicaragua as a necessity in which the interests of the whole of Latin America were involved. It was for this reason that the APRA decided to name the Honduran Froylán Turcios, Sandino's semi-official representative outside Nicaragua, an honorary member of their organization, and their own representative in Honduras. Through the pages of his magazine *Ariel* Turcios had been carrying on a constant propaganda campaign in favour of Sandino and his movement, at the same time as he undertook to ensure that news of the struggle reached other information media in Latin America, becoming the principal channel through which statements and information from Sandino reached the outside world. In his letter conferring honorary membership on Turcios, Haya de la Torre declared to him that in his view this press campaign against Yankee imperialism had been based in the most sacred principles of Latin American unity, which they shared, and that his work revealed the identity of convictions that existed between Turcios and the 'United Front of Manual and Intellectual Workers of America',[49] as the APRA was also sometimes known.[50]

Even more, the APRA also decided to fight alongside Sandino, and designated some of its leading militants for the task. Haya de la Torre wrote again to Turcios on 5 January 1928 that the Peruvians driven into exile by the tyranny of Augusto Leguía, who was placing their country upon the same path of indignity down which Adolfo Díaz had already taken Nicaragua, should consider the cause of this small country to be theirs also, and follow the course of its struggle against imperialism with the anxiety of one who saw the dispute as his own. It was for these reasons that they had agreed, Haya told Turcios, to give more substance to their solidarity with Sandino, by offering him, by means of this same letter, unconditionally, their 'contribution in blood', placing themselves at the orders of the Liberation Army of Nicaragua in order to fight in its ranks. They had taken this decision, he went on, because they were convinced that Nicaragua was defending the whole of Latin America, and no one could remain indifferent before this struggle.[51]

In fulfilment of this resolution the *Sandinista* Army was joined in Las Segovias by the Peruvian Esteban Pavletich,[52] who Haya de la Torre called 'the Benjamin' of the Peruvian exiles, and who held an important position within the APRA.[53] He rapidly came to occupy a senior position also in the Sandinista High Command, and when Sandino travelled to Mexico in 1929, accompanied by his principal lieutenants, Pavletich went with him.

There exists a particular documentary record of Pavletich's stay in Las Segovias in the form of a letter sent by him on 8 June 1928 to Joaquín García Monge, dated as being written from 'the camp of the Liberation Army'. In this letter Pavletich described the difficulties of the journey that he had to undertake in order to reach Las Segovias and join the Liberation Army, and he extensively eulogized General

Sandino, stating that, in spite of the tendentious stories about him that had been circulated by American imperialism, it was in Sandino in whom the new generation of the continent would find a great man of achievement, and Central America its greatest leader. He declared that Sandino had in him a lot of Trotsky and something of Saint Francis of Assisi, and that he was the man who would be able to lead these nations towards their liberation, although he was incapable of much in the way of analysis or sociological conclusions. He recounted the details of two combats he had witnessed, and said that they had constituted the clearest possible confirmation that violence placed at the service of justice, even though it were the instrument of scarcely a handful of men, was stronger than the organized and highly technologically sophisticated violence in the service of slavery and conquest. 'In Nicaragua,' Pavletich concluded, 'we are turning back with the rifle and the machete the arrogant insolence of the most powerful army in the world.'[54]

For Haya de la Torre, too, Sandino was the most glorious figure produced by Nicaragua since the Indian rebels of the time of the Spanish conquest.[55] Haya declared that Sandino was a symbol and an omen, and deserved the full support of the Indoamerican peoples, because he was a liberator.[56] According to US archives, at the same moment when Sandino's sympathizers had succeeded in paralysing the port of Corinto with a strike, Haya de la Torre took his admiration for Sandino into the field of action, by organizing agitation among the poorer classes of the Nicaraguan city of León in January 1928.[57] This cannot be correct, given that, although Haya de la Torre had in effect had the intention of entering Nicaragua and joining Sandino's guerrillas, the obstacles that the Honduran authorities put in his way obliged him to change his plans.[58]

In all, though, we can say that the APRA made Sandino's struggle against US military intervention its own, and took an active part in it, and that the Communist International would have to struggle against this influence in its efforts to establish its own presence in the movement.

With regard to the theses on the political unity of Latin America that were put forward by the APRA, numerous declarations in defence of this unity were made by Sandino. On 2 June 1928 he said in an interview, when questioned on the limits of the Republic of Nueva Segovia, that is, of the territories occupied by him, that the fatherland for which he was fighting had no frontiers in Spanish America, and that although in the beginning he had only been concerned with

Nicaragua, with the confidence gained in combat he had begun to think in terms of a Central American Republic. On another occasion, when referring to the unity of Latin America, Sandino said that he called himself the son of Bolívar, because he would never betray the Latin American cause.[59]

On 10 June 1928 he said to Froylán Turcios that in speaking of the Monroe Doctrine, people in the United States always said 'America for the Americans', but the imperialists interpreted this Doctrine as 'America for the yankees', whereas he reformulated the phrase as follows: 'The United States of America for the yankees; Latin America for the "Indo-Latins" (*Indolatinos*)'. He told Turcios that it would not be surprising for him or his army to be found in any of the countries in Latin America in which the invaders had established themselves with the attitude of conquerors, because 'Sandino is Indohispanic (*Indohispano*), and there are no frontiers for him in Latin America'.[60]

In the message the General sent, through Turcios, to the members of the Latin American governments on 4 August 1928, he asked if they perhaps believed that the yankees would be content solely with the conquest of Nicaragua, and if they had forgotten that six republics (Panama, Puerto Rico, Cuba, Haiti, Santo Domingo and Nicaragua) had already lost their independence to become colonies of yankee imperialism. He stated emphatically, 'We are ninety million Hispanic Americans, and we should only be thinking of our unification.' Referring to the governments that attained power with the support of Wall Street and the bankers, he said, 'Tyrants do not represent nations, and liberty is not won with flowers.'[61]

Sandino denied that his movement was *excessively* nationalistic, and maintained that over and above the nation was the idea of a continental federation, and that his movement was laying the foundations for making a reality of Bolívar's dream of a unified Latin America.[62]

Regarding the canal route through Nicaragua, Sandino adapted to the conditions of his country the *Aprista* thesis of the internationalization of the Panama Canal. He maintained that the canal through Nicaragua should be built with capital from the entire world, but that at least one half of the project's value should be undertaken with capital from Latin America. The United States, in his opinion, should only be allowed to participate by the amount given to Nicaragua under the Bryan–Chamorro Treaty: three million dollars.[63] The United Front, too, and more in its *Aprista* version than the Communist model, was also supported by Sandino, who considered it to be the best means of containing the advance of the United States in Latin America. He wrote to the Nicaraguan journalist Alemán Bolaños on 9 September 1929 that, 'Neither extreme right, nor extreme left, but a UNITED FRONT is our slogan. This being the case, it is not illogical that in our struggle we seek to obtain the cooperation of all social classes, without classifications into this or that "ism".'[64]

As for the nationalization of land, when Sandino was asked about his project for the colonization of the Río Coco, to which he dedicated himself after the signing of peace, the General stated that he was in favour of land being the property of the State. Sandino did not propose an agrarian reform, but rather a process of internal colonization. On one occasion, in 1934, he said that it made him laugh to hear talk of people without work, as there was a wealth easily within the reach of everyone, and all that had to be done to get it was to go to the mountains.[65] Lastly, it is of interest to point out that on one occasion the Salvadorean philosopher Alberto Masferrer, in a declaration of his *Aprista* beliefs in the magazine *Repertorio Americano*, said that he served in the same ranks as many notable figures in Latin America, and cited among them as a militant of the APRA – alongside Juana de Ibarborou, García Monge and Froylán Turcios – Augusto César Sandino. Curiously, neither Turcios, García Monge or any other of Sandino's sympathizers wrote in to rectify this statement, although it was common for the magazine to publish relevant commentaries or clarifications in succeeding issues.[66]

The close relationship between *Sandinistas* and the APRA would become evident, as we shall see, in the Second Congress of the League Against Imperialism in Frankfurt, when the delegate from Sandino, José Constantino González, refused to support the motion for the expulsion of the APRA from the Congress.[67]

APRA's presence in the movement and Sandino's political activities implied a simultaneous tension in two different directions: on the one hand, a complete openness to all those who sought to combat American imperialism, and in particular its military intervention in Nicaragua; on the other, a marked tendency to restrict the movement, to limit it in its social and political significance. The first tendency facilitated joint action with the international Communist movement, which was undertaking a determined and uncompromising struggle against the imperialist presence in the area; the second opened up an eventual breach, in that the final objectives, which in the last analysis were of interest to the International and its agents, were left indefinitely postponed. Hence, the *Sandinista* movement offered to the International only the possibility of political collaboration similar to that established in China with the Kuomintang (which by that time, 1927, had already failed and broken down) but with much greater limitations in terms of the worldwide significance of the conflict, the size of the populations involved and the remoteness of the scene of events. Moreover, if to this is added the American decision not to build a canal through Nicaragua, supposedly for technical reasons, the potential for conflict with other imperialist powers, particularly Britain, disappeared, and with it the at-one-time major international political significance of the *Sandinista* campaign.

The APRA, which could have brought out and reaffirmed the great importance of Sandino's movement in Nicaragua for Latin America and for its continental vision of the anti-imperialist struggle, did not have the political or the material resources needed to do so. As a result Sandino found himself, at a crucial point in the history of Nicaragua, without the assistance of either one group or the other. The rise of Sandino, ostensibly on the backs of the APRA on one side and the international Communist movement on the other, did not ultimately have any more real support than his own soldiers and officers recruited in Nicaragua. Ideologically weak and abandoned at the worst moment, Sandino's courage and shrewdness were not sufficient to make up for his naivety in the field of foreign political and cultural ideas which, in constant debate around him, denied the Nicaraguan the implementation of his own, indigenous alternative. What the International wanted, as we shall see, was to transform Sandino's national liberation movement into a social revolution, and thereby modify the real nature of the revolutionary process that was taking place in Sandino's Nicaragua.

3 Nicaragua, a Profitable Episode for the International: From Sandino the Hero to Sandino the Traitor

THE ROLE OF THE LEAGUE AGAINST IMPERIALISM: ITS CONGRESSES AND DECLARATIONS

The Executive Committee of the Communist International published a manifesto titled 'Against the Imperialist Offensive of the United States', on 5 February 1927. It called upon all anti-imperialist forces to support the Nicaraguan people. The liberation struggle of the peoples of America, it said, should meet with the support of the proletariat, and it ended emphatically, 'Down with the imperialism of the United States! Long live the liberation struggle of the oppressed peoples against imperialism! Long live the international solidarity of the workers, peasants and subject peoples against the common enemy.'[1]

On 9 February a new, more developed version of the same manifesto was issued, which added, 'Every struggle by an exploited people against no matter which imperialism can count on the active solidarity and support of the III International. It calls upon all the anti-imperialist forces to sustain the small nation and people of Nicaragua in their resistance to their attempted strangulation by American imperialism'. It concluded, 'Comrades: the same militant solidarity that inspires you in your support for the independence struggle of China and India should now inspire us to act against the brutal crushing of the peoples of Latin America by American imperialism.'[2]

The League against Imperialism of the Americas had been in operation since the end of 1925, in accordance with the recommendation of the V Congress of the Comintern, which had laid down that Communists should work together with other groups and parties of the American continent towards the objective of establishing an anti-

55

imperialist association for the whole area, the purpose of which would be to organize propaganda against Yankee imperialism in Central and South America.[3] It had branches in several countries in the continent, and its Secretariat was made up of representatives of each one of these sections.

At the beginning of 1926 the members of the Secretariat were: for Cuba, Julio Antonio Mella; for Puerto Rico, Jaime N. Sager; for Colombia, Juan de Dios Romero; for Mexico, Enrique Flores; for Ecuador, Juan F. Karolys; for Venezuela, Gustavo Machado; for Brazil, Eduardo Mattos; and for the United States, Manuel Gómez.[4]

The First International Congress against Imperialism and Colonial Oppression, organized by the League against Imperialism and held in Brussels from 10–14 February 1927, was attended, as delegate for the League against Imperialism of the Americas and Federation of Agricultural Workers of Mexico,[5] by the Cuban Communist leader Mella, who at that time was active in the Mexican Communist Party, and a member of its Central Committee.

More than a hundred delegates from the colonial and semi-colonial countries were present at this Congress, which was also attended by social-democratic groups from several countries, and representatives of a variety of nationalist tendencies. The APRA was also represented in Brussels. The leader of the organization, Haya de la Torre, together with another APRA delegate took an active part in the discussions, as did the Latin American intellectuals José de Vasconcelos and Carlos Deambrosis-Martins.[7]

Among the most important of the resolutions that were approved was one that was presented jointly by the Kuomintang and British delegations, headed, 'The breakdown of imperialism has begun. The working class and the masses of the oppressed peoples are its grave-diggers.'[8] The delegations from proletarian organizations present at the Congress declared that their support should not be limited to demonstrations in sympathy with the fighters for colonial emancipation, or protest demonstrations against the acts of violence of the imperialist aggressors, but should include mass actions that would have a practical effect on the development of the struggle, such as strikes and boycotts.

The Latin American delegations, for their part, drew up a joint plan for defence against United States imperialism, along the lines of an economic and political federation for Latin America.[9]

In the final manifesto issued by the Brussels Congress, titled 'Against Imperialism. For National Liberation!', specific mention was made of

Nicaragua. It stated, 'The example of the little republic of Nicaragua demonstrates that sustained opposition is possible even against the most gigantic imperialist powers, thanks to the propaganda that is spread about this resistance among a great number of more powerful peoples that are interested in defending their own independence.'[10]

A large number of national-revolutionary organizations had been invited to the Congress, some of them of an openly petit-bourgeois nature. The broadly-based composition of the League against Imperialism led to mixed opinions within the Communist International. Willy Münzenberg, the German Communist and later, in 1933, Reichstag deputy who was then Secretary of the League, openly opposed Zinoviev, who had called the League 'a toy'. Münzenberg argued that this position was not Leninist, and that the true Leninist approach to this question was to 'sustain, within the League, a certain number of classes and groups of proletarian revolutionary orientation, and invigorate their influence in the League'.[11]

At that time the League maintained the very best of relations with the Calles government in Mexico, which needed its support in its own conflict with American imperialism.

In December 1927 the first ordinary session of the Council of the League was held, once again in Brussels. This Council was composed of fifty members, politicians, economists and figures from the world of the arts and culture, ascribed to very diverse parties and ideologies, but all, according to Münzenberg, 'linked by an awareness of the need for the organization of the liberation struggle of the oppressed peoples and for the establishment of a great bloc bringing together the revolutionary parties of the oppressed peoples and the proletariat of the imperialist countries'.[12]

By this time the Kuomintang had already carried out their 'betrayal', and the British delegate who had signed the joint declaration with the Chinese in February, George Lansbury, had accepted the Chairmanship of the Labour Party. In view of this, it was decided that the first task of the League would be to demand that all of its sections fulfil its resolutions. Nevertheless, in an article written on that occasion Münzenberg claimed that the League was powerful, and that its foundation was the event that had had the greatest impact since the foundation of the Communist International itself. The manifestos of the League, he wrote, were translated into twelve languages, and were received 'as much by the dispossessed black proletarians of Africa, as by the Indians of the Mexican plains . . . The Brussels Congress had had a particularly powerful impact in the countries of South and Central America.' He mentioned the Mexican section of the League as being one of the best organized, with its own newspaper, offices, and so on, and also referred to sections of the League that existed in other countries of Central America.[13]

In this second Brussels conference a unanimous declaration was approved addressed to all the sections of the League, calling on them to make a great effort to interest the millions of workers and peasants in their countries in the work of the organization, 'in order that it should maintain a strictly revolutionary line, avoiding any kind of deviation, so that the League may assist the national revolutionary movements to broaden into proletarian revolution':[14] a recommendation that sums up the strategy that the Comintern would attempt to apply, via the League, in Nicaragua.

At the VI Congress of the International, in July 1928, Münzenberg engaged in a polemic with Bukharin, reproaching him with having belittled the activities of the League, which according to the former had not only organized in Brussels one of the largest and most important expressions of opposition to imperialism yet seen, but also already possessed the embryo of a significant organization. 'Bukharin complains that not one Communist Party has taken an interest in the struggle in Nicaragua,' Münzenberg said. 'He should have spoken of what the League has done in Mexico. This has been one of the strongest mass movements that Mexico has ever seen. There is no doubt that the League is not a Communist organization, but it is a great organization of workers and national-revolutionary groups that deserve our support.'[15]

Also at the VI Congress, on 31 July 1928, Wallace, of the United States, proposed in the name of the US delegation and of those from the Latin American countries to send a telegram to Sandino. The text of the message, which was approved unanimously, was as follows:

The VI World Congress of the Communist International sends fraternal greetings to the workers and peasants of Nicaragua and to the heroic army of national emancipation of General Sandino, which is sustaining courageous and constant battles against the imperialism of the United States.

The imperialism of the United States is becoming more and more aggressive; with the help of the power of its capital and the aid of its armies it is subjugating the republics of Latin America, which it wishes to make into its economic 'hinterland'.[16]

The struggle to liberate the republics of Latin America from the yoke of imperialist capital is the common cause of all the exploited workers and peasants of the world. In the front ranks of this struggle against United States imperialism should be the workers of the United States and the workers and peasant workers of the republics of Latin America.

The VI World Congress of the Communist International invites the Communist Parties, all workers' organizations and the proletariat of every country to support the emancipation struggle of the workers and peasants of Nicaragua. Down with the war of pillage of the United States!

Hands off Nicaragua! Long live the coordinated struggle of the Communist Parties of Latin America and the United States against the common enemy: American imperialism. Down with imperialist war! Long live international solidarity![17]

The VI Congress saw an end to the good relations between the International and the *Aprista* movement. One of the US delegates, Wolfe, said in a speech that in Latin America one also found dangerous *arrivistes* like Haya de la Torre, who had, however, attended the V Congress of the Comintern, with the status of fraternal delegate, and been a full delegate to the III Congress of the Red International of Labour Unions. Now, however, he was accused of trying to draw the veil of communism over a non-communist movement.[18] In the same statement in which he attacked the APRA, Wolfe put forward the Nicaraguan struggle as an example of the forces of resistance to Yankee imperialism in Latin America. 'In that country,' he said, 'the guerrillas have for more than a year confronted the army of the United States. It has not been able to defeat them, and their feat has set in motion a process of unification of the revolutionary and anti-imperialist forces in Latin America. This makes it a factor of greater importance than ever, which affects the whole of the Communist International.'[19]

The Mexican delegate, Contreras, stated in his intervention that:

It is now a year and a half since Sandino, at the head of 300 peasants and miners, declared an anti-imperialist war in Nicaragua against American capital and its local agents. The League against Imperialism of America has immediately taken up the defence of the Nicaraguan cause and has begun an international campaign in solidarity, collecting money to assist Sandino and his soldiers as well as to pay for doctors and pharmaceutical products. In this movement the League against Imperialism forms a united front, in the continental sense of the term, and has occupied the position of vanguard in all the anti-imperialist movements of the Continent. The Communist International, with the League against Imperialism of Brussels, should give more attention to these movements and urge the Communist Parties to organize, under these slogans of a united anti-imperialist front, movements in those countries where anti-imperialist organizations do not exist. It is only under the direction of the Communist Parties that the anti-imperialist movements can follow the correct policies against imperialism.[20]

The factional dispute that was then going on between the delegates of the United States Communist Party was also reflected in the discussions on Nicaragua. One delegate, Dunne, accused the official organ of the Party of having published an openly social democratic and pacifist manifesto, which had laid emphasis on the idea that the United States had declared war without consulting Congress, rather than on the imperialist nature of the action.[21] Bertrand Wolfe criticized Dunne in turn for not mentioning that this manifesto had been published before the most recent conference of the CPUSA, and that this position had been corrected at the conference. He also pointed to other faults that he said had not been corrected, such as the sabotaging of the US 'Hands off Nicaragua' Committee and the substitution of it by a committee of the Red Cross; the use of the slogan 'Enlist with Sandino, join the Red Cross'; and the recommendation given to supporters by the head of the US League against Imperialism to plead guilty before the courts if arrested for demonstrating in front of the White House. Wolfe claimed that this was not mentioned by Dunne because those responsible, the members of the left wing of the Party, were also present at the Congress.[22]

Nevertheless, despite these errors, the US section of the League against Imperialism, based in New York, did in fact carry out a wide-ranging campaign to publicize the *Sandinista* cause.[23] Its primary effort was directed towards making the American public understand that the actions of the movement were not directed against them, but against the imperialist policies of the government. Sandino's brother, Sócrates, who lived in Brooklyn, took part in several meetings organized by the League.[24] Both the League and the US Communist Party openly called upon the Marines to desert and join Sandino's army.[25]

That said, the conflicts between tendencies within the American Party undoubtedly did partially obstruct the work of solidarity with

Nicaragua. According to Wicks, if this campaign was not all it should have been, this was due to the incompetence of the leadership of the League in the United States.[26]

In the report that Münzenberg presented to the session of the League Secretariat held in Berlin following the VI Congress of the Comintern, it was stated that the Mexican section of the League already possessed thirty groups in operation.[27] This section had been founded in 1927 by members of the Mexican Communist Party, with the collaboration of the Venezuelans Gustavo Machado and Carlos Aponte and the Cuban Julio Antonio Mella. It published a newspaper, *El Libertador*, which announced itself as the organ of 'All the Sections of the League against Imperialism of the Americas.' It was edited by the painter Diego Rivera, with the close collaboration of Mella, and administered by Gustavo Machado.[28] In his report Münzenberg claimed that at that time *El Libertador* was regularly publishing five thousand copies.[29]

Münzenberg also mentioned the 'Get Out of Nicaragua'[30] campaign as 'the first great movement of the Mexican workers in an anti-imperialist spirit'.[31] The weight of this campaign was borne by the Mexican 'Hands Off Nicaragua Committee',[32] organized by Gustavo Machado on instructions from the League in January 1928.

This Committee, which was directly subordinate to the League and the Mexican Communist Party, was intensely active in working to publicize Sandino's struggle. Its General Secretary was Jacobo Hurtwits, who represented Latin America in the Conference of Anti-Imperialist Youth that was held in Frankfurt am Main in mid-1929,[33] and was also a member of the Mexican section of International Workers' Aid.[34, 35] The Hands Off Nicaragua Committee had its own Central Committee, which also included Machado, Diego Rivera and Julio Antonio Mella.

In the same report to which we have been referring, Münzenberg also quoted various resolutions of the Executive Committee of the worldwide League, and noted that 'the Executive Committee of the League has similarly received knowledge of the discussion that has taken place in the recent Congress of the III International on the League against Imperialism'. He commented that 'the League is not a Communist organization'.[36] However, in spite of this resolution of the VI Congress, the reality was that in practice the different sections of the League were more and more being left solely in Communist hands. As we have said, it was precisely through the League against Imperialism and the Hands Off Nicaragua Committees that the Communist International handled its relations with Sandino.

Gustavo Machado, who, as we have seen, was one of the most prominent figures in the League and the Mexican Committee, went personally to Las Segovias, with the mission of delivering to Sandino the results of the solidarity campaigns carried out in Mexico. Machado wrote from Las Segovias in 1928:

We, Venezuelan fighters are obliged to lend Nicaragua – in this hour of intense tragedy – the aid and solidarity that we ourselves have requested from our brother peoples . . . In Nicaragua the imperialist forces that are the oppressors of the Latin American peoples and the forces of liberation that defend the sovereignty of the whole of Latin America are in combat . . . Nicaragua is a symbol and a warning. General Sandino and his army of peasants and miners have proven the military possibility of combating and defeating the invading forces. The Colossus of the North has been humiliated in a multitude of battles. Whatever may be the final result of the struggle, Nicaragua has shown us the practical route that our peoples should follow if they wish to liberate themselves from imperialist oppression. Latin America has demonstrated in many ways the existence of a Continental consciousness.[37]

In June 1929, in an article in preparation for the Second World Congress of the League, which was planned to be held in Paris in the following July, but which finally took place in Frankfurt, Münzenberg pointed to 'the magnificent example of Sandino who, for years, has fought with a small group of badly armed guerrillas against considerably superior forces, and revealed to us all the tenacity with which the struggle for the independence of the Latin American States is being engaged'. He also said that the programme drawn up in Brussels had been put into effect in everyday practice. The central idea, he went on, had been to bring together in the League all the anti-imperialist groups in the world, without any differentiation between political or labour organizations or according to their precise political position. The objective was to unite the two formidable currents of the contemporary liberation struggle: the national-revolutionary movement in the oppressed countries, and the great movement of the proletarian masses in the imperialist homelands. 'The League cannot fulfil its role, if it does not also succeed in the future in incorporating into the struggle the best national-proletarian organizations and groups, together with the broad proletarian masses of the capitalist countries, and reinforcing this community of struggle with the group of honest anti-imperialist intellectuals, such as Henri Barbusse and hundreds of others like him.'[38] This was considered to be the historic role of the League.

The second Congress of the League revealed important differences in attitudes within the organization between the Communists and the various national-reformist organizations and nationalist movements. Accounts were given at the Frankfurt Congress of the reorientation to the right of the dominant factions in the national bourgeoisies of the oppressed countries, and denunciations were made of their counter-revolutionary role in the struggle for national and social emancipation.[39] A conflict arose on this question in the Congress between the Communists and the group of James Maxton, of the British Independent Labour Party. This led to talk of a split in the League. A conflict also developed when Sandino's representative, José Constantino González, refused to support the Communist motion to expel the APRA delegation from the Congress.[40] This, as we have seen, was easily explicable, since the APRA was so closely linked to *Sandinismo*, and even after the League had repudiated the organization, following the discussions at the VI Comintern Congress, representatives of the International and the APRA continued to coexist at Sandino's headquarters, as the first breach between Sandino and Farabundo Martí and the International would not come about until September 1929, as we shall see.

It is interesting to recall here that the APRA had always made much of its similarities with the Kuomintang, which was no longer in the League, going so far as to compare itself directly with the Chinese movement. In an interview given to the *Canton Tribune* at the end of 1926, Haya de la Torre had declared that 'the only United Anti-imperialist Front similar to the Kuomintang is the APRA. Like the Kuomintang, we are a united front of students, workers, peasants, intellectuals, soldiers, etc., against Yankee imperialism and in support of the sovereignty and freedom of our countries.'[41] This supposedly created the basis for the establishment of a united front between the APRA and the Communist movement. However, this would not be the case.

In the Manifesto issued following the second Congress, Münzenberg wrote that:

in the Frankfurt Congress the League against Imperialism has taken all the measures necessary for the achievement of its historic role of creating an alliance in struggle of the national-revolutionary wing of the petit-bourgeoisie and the national bourgeois sectors with the masses of the international proletariat. In certain countries that are important from the point of view of world political developments, such as India, the Arab countries, particularly Syria and North Africa, and Latin America, there already exist, in effect, national-revolutionary organizations that desire genuine national emancipation. Compared with that of Brussels, the Frankfurt Congress marks an important step to the left. The centre of gravity of the League is no longer represented, as in the period of its foundation, by intellectuals and liberals, but instead consists of the broad worker and peasant masses of the oppressed peoples. This development has had the unanimous support of anarchists, syndicalists, anti-militarists, socialists, communists and revolutionary socialists.[42]

This, in his judgement, indicated that it had been a complete success.

In this same Manifesto, in addition, calls were made to the peoples of the colonies and the oppressed countries for them to fight in a powerful worldwide, revolutionary, anti-imperialist front; for the mobilization of the worker and peasant masses; for a radical improvement in the living conditions of the working class; for the creation of revolutionary organizations of peasant workers; against war with the USSR, and for the energetic defence of the latter; against social-imperialists; and against social democracy.[43]

In spite of the fact that the Kuomintang was no longer in the League while the *Sandinista* movement did continue to be affiliated, the League's Congresses had enabled some contact between them, and it was for this reason that the portrait of Sandino appeared on the standards of several units of the Kuomintang Army when it entered victoriously into Beijing in 1928. One unit of Kuomintang troops that was seen by US Marines in China was called the 'Sandino Division'.[44]

In 1929, following the affiliation *en bloc* of the USSR trade unions to the League, emphasis began to be laid on the proletarian nature of the organization and on the need to ensure that it should strive, whether in Mexico or in North Africa, to put into practice the anti-imperialist programme of Brussels with proletarian and revolutionary tactics.

Nevertheless, in December 1930 *La Correspondance Internationale* still published a commentary on the League that insisted that it was an organization outside of parties, that desired to and in effect could bring together all the forces that were fighting against imperialism. It emphatically denied the claim that the League was a Communist organization or an instrument subordinate to the policies of any one party. The fact that the Kuomintang and the Calles government of Mexico, like the left-wing social democrats, were no longer in the League, the article said, was not its fault, but due to the pro-imperialist positions of these groups.[46] However, the fact is that the League and its sections were becoming steadily more composed exclusively of Communists.

THE PRINCIPAL REPRESENTATIVES OF THE COMMUNIST INTERNATIONAL SENT TO SANDINO

Before this had happened, and during the period of good relations between the International and Sandino, the League against Imperialism not only undertook solidarity campaigns in his support throughout the continent, but also sent some of its best cadres, experienced militants of the International, to Sandino's headquarters. The two most important representatives of the Communist International with Sandino's staff were Carlos Aponte and Agustín Farabundo Martí.

When Carlos Aponte, a cadre of the Venezuelan Communist Party, arrived in Las Segovias in March 1928[47] he already carried with him the experience provided by participation in two insurrectionary movements: one in 1917 in his homeland against the tyrant Juan Vicente Gómez, and another in 1925 against the dictatorship of Gerardo Machado in Cuba.

It was during his stay in Cuba, in the period in which Julio Antonio Mella, Rubén Martínez Villena and others were founding the Cuban Communist Party, that Aponte established deep bonds of friendship with these men and other revolutionary leaders of the continent. Also in Cuba at that time was his compatriot and fellow-communist Gustavo Machado, with whom he would be reunited a few years later in Las Segovias, and who would eventually come to be General Secretary for life of the Communist Party of Venezuela. The Cuban dictator Gerardo Machado expelled Aponte to Mexico, where he once again met up with Mella and entered the Hands Off Nicaragua Committee. In February 1928 the Committee sent him to Nicaragua to join the *Sandinista* army, which he reached the following month.

Two documents exist that were sent by Sandino to the Committee that from the way in which they are written appear to have been reports on the work of Aponte. The first of them, dated 5 November 1928, typewritten and with Sandino's own signature, announces the appointment as Lieutenant Colonel of the Army of the 'Venezuelan citizen Sergeant Major Carlos Aponte Hernández' and states that orders given by the latter should be respected in accordance with his rank, for the purposes of greater efficiency in the organization of combat against the Yankee invasion of Nicaragua. It also states that he was confirmed in the rank of Sergeant Major provisionally accorded him on his first entry into the *Sandinista* forces, and that these dispositions would be made known to the Army in the general orders for that day. Thus, scarcely eight months after his enlistment and after having given unquestionable demonstrations of his worth, Aponte was already a Lieutenant Colonel and one of Sandino's closest aides.[48]

There is also a second document, that of his release from the army, which we reproduce in its entirety:

> The undersigned, General and Supreme Head of the Army in Defence of the National Sovereignty of Nicaragua, using the faculties conferred upon him by this same Army, makes known: That Lieutenant Colonel Carlos Aponte Hernández, a Venezuelan citizen, has given service in our Army since 4 March of last year in the struggle sustained by our forces against the Yankee invasion, distinguishing himself in many of the combats in our liberation campaign, and that on this date he is withdrawing from our ranks *since to do so is in the interests of the Cause of Latin America in its opposition to Yankee imperialism.*[49]

> (Headquarters in El Chipotón, Nicaragua, 1 February 1929.)

Aponte's return to Mexico 'since to do so is in the interests of the cause of Latin America in its opposition to Yankee imperialism' was no doubt due to an order from the Hands Off Nicaragua Committee, or the Mexican Communist Party, of which all the Communist exiled in Mexico were also members. It was precisely at this time that the Military Committee of the Venezuelan Revolutionary Party was being constituted, the purpose of which was to undertake a military operation in Curaçao to obtain arms with which to invade Venezuela, and hence his return would have been urgent.[50]

Sandino also wrote to Mrs Socorro Hernández, Aponte's mother, informing her of the latter's departure for Mexico. In the letter he said, 'Since our cause is a continental one, Colonel Aponte Hernández will continue his activities in other areas of the struggle for the freedom of our Latin America, and recently left our Army with the aim of reaching Mexico. Our Army retains the best memories of Colonel Aponte

Hernández, as he was able to show us the best and finest examples of self-sacrifice and valour in resisting the Yankee invasion forces.'[51]

In one of the letters that Aponte sent to the Hands Off Nicaragua Committee in Mexico during his time with Sandino, written in El Chipotón and dated 22 March 1928, he wrote that he had witnessed several bombing raids by American aircraft, and wanted to give them his impressions:

> After searching for something like three hours the infernal machines bombed all the houses of the defenceless peasants, no doubt killing women and children, as happens in every case of this kind, the spirit of destruction and evil is the only banner of peace and progress that they bring to our unfortunate America . . . Till when will we be the slaves of the sellers-out of their countries and the invaders? Wherever we go all the men and women come out of their hiding places to meet us whose only sin is to be at the side of this Army, headed by the man who has seen how to give a lead to all honourable men onto the path of duty, making them feel the need to awake from their deep sleep of indifference towards their trampled and exploited homeland . . . In my previous letter I said to you that the rest would depend on you, that is, the press and the funds you can collect, as they are very necessary, and quite urgent. The General and his comrades in arms congratulate you, in union with all those who feel within them this just struggle that will serve as an example for the peoples of America.[52]

Aponte was an individual of extraordinary courage, who devoted the energy of his youth to fighting imperialism in various countries of Latin America. The Cuban Pablo de la Torriente Grau said of him, 'what was greatest in him was his instinct of struggle against the North; he was the image of a compass in the face of imperialism'.[53]

In 1934, in his constant search for a place in which to fight, Aponte joined up with the Cuban revolutionary Antonio Guiteras, of whom he said, 'This is another Sandino!'[54] He was shot dead alongside Guiteras on 7 May 1935 while fighting the dictatorship of Batista, on the eve of one more journey to Mexico, where he was to have joined another group of Latin American anti-imperialist revolutionaries.

It was through men like this that the International wished to cultivate and develop the *Sandinista* movement, to the point of converting it into a proletarian movement, as could be seen from the resolutions of the Congresses of the League. From his temperament,

Aponte's contribution would seem to have been above all of a practical and military nature. Without underestimating his political capacity, his ideological preparation or his links with the Communist International through the League, his reports tend to emphasize, in a manner that goes beyond understandable considerations of propaganda or indignation, the specifically military aspects of the operations undertaken in Las Segovias.

A much more political and ideological role does, on the other hand, seem to have been played within the *Sandinista* movement by the other representative of the International, Agustín Farabundo Martí. Born in El Salvador, Farabundo Martí was one of the founders of the Central American Socialist Party, established in Guatemala City in 1925. He had begun his political activities in 1920, when the then President of El Salvador, Jorge Meléndez, sent him into exile for taking part in a demonstration over the right to stay in the country of a group of exiled Guatemalan students.[55] He then went to Honduras, and from there to Guatemala, where he took part in the foundation of the Socialist Party. Later he was in Mexico, where he met Esteban Pavletich, of the APRA, with whom he became friends.

In the spring of 1928, following a police raid on the offices of the League against Imperialism in New York, Martí was arrested there. In May of that year, he travelled from New York to Mexico, and from there to Cuba and from Cuba to Jamaica. He then entered Guatemala via Belize, and from there took a boat to Honduras. Once there he had meetings with Froylán Turcios, Sandino's personal representative in the country,[56] and, in the town of Danlí, Department of Paraíso, with José Idiáquez, who acted as an agent for Sandino for the transmission and despatch of correspondence, munitions and supplies. Whichever of these two channels was used, the result was that Martí presented the *Sandinista* movement with his credentials as a revolutionary, which were accepted, and he left for the encampment in Nueva Segovia.

Everything seems to suggest that both Martí and Pavletich, before travelling to Las Segovias, had made contact with the 'United Front Hands Off Nicaragua Committee'[57] in Mexico. It was from Mexico that Martí had left for New York, and on his return he passed through the country once again. It is probable that on his arrival in Honduras to present himself to Sandino's agents he brought with him letters of recommendation from Gustavo Machado, who had been in Las Segovias the previous April and by 20 May was already back in Mexico.[58] Machado's presence in Mexico by that time can be inferred from a letter that was sent to him in Mexico City on that date by

Sandino, requesting that he assume the role of official representative of the *Sandinista* movement before the Mexican people.[59]

In March 1928, when Martí was in Mexico – as too was Pavletich, until his departure for Nicaragua – Machado was working closely with Sandino's representative in Mexico City, Dr Pedro José Zepeda, with whom he attended fund-raising meetings.[60] Martí's precarious monetary situation, in his position as an exile, must have meant that both the journey to New York and his return and subsequent journey to Honduras via Mexico, Cuba, Jamaica and Guatemala, were financed not by him but by the League against Imperialism and, through it, the Communist International.

In June 1928, scarcely two months after the arrival of Esteban Pavletich in Nicaragua, Martí wrote from the camp in Nueva Segovia:

> We arrived in the camp of our Supreme Leader, General Augusto César Sandino, on 22nd June, becoming members of the Army in Defence of the National Sovereignty of Nicaragua. Our war against the invaders of Central America has been formally engaged. The liberation struggle of the Americas has been initiated in Nicaragua, and we await the combined action of the oppressed peoples of the continent to sweep away Yankee imperialism to its last vestiges.[61]

We are inclined to believe that if from the moment of his arrival in Las Segovias Martí occupied a position on Sandino's staff, and was even appointed his personal secretary, this was due to his position as an envoy from the Communist International, via the League against Imperialism. This representative status and his theoretical preparation, added to the fact that he took part successfully in guerrilla action,[62] rapidly won him Sandino's confidence.

According to the writer Javier Campos Ponce, it was Martí who was originally intended to have taken the American flag captured by the *Sandinistas* to the Frankfurt Congress of the League, where it was put on display. He could not do so, though, this author claims, because he had been arrested in El Salvador.[63] However, while Martí may initially have been chosen as the delegate, the reason for his absence could not be that given by Campos Ponce since, as we shall see, on the dates when the Second Congress was being held (July 1929), he was in Mexico with Sandino.

The most important statements issued by Sandino in the year in which Martí and Pavletich were with him in Las Segovias, the letter to the members of the governments of Latin America, to which we have already made reference, and the letter to the President of Argentina Hipólito Yrigoyen, of 20 March 1929 (in which he proposed that a Latin American conference be held in Buenos Aires, with Sandino himself participating), are like his communications with his comrades and representatives in that one does not find the esoteric vocabulary that we have previously examined, and which would appear in his declarations and communiqués following his return from Mexico in the latter half of 1930. On the contrary, one notes a higher level of political sophistication at this time. When Sandino travelled to Mexico in June 1929, exactly one year after the arrival of Martí in Las Segovias, both the latter and Pavletich were members of the party that went with him.

In a letter sent by Sandino to Alemán Bolaños from Mexico on 9ʻ August 1929 he informed the latter that Martí would shortly be leaving for Central America and would bring him fully up to date on the latest decisions taken by the *Sandinista* high command in Mexico.[64] Ten days later in another letter to Alemán Bolaños of 29 August he again wrote that it would be Colonel Martí who would give him details of everything.[65] On 8 September the General wrote that they were only awaiting the arrival of some other comrades for Colonel Martí to depart.

Alemán Bolaños, for his part, had sent Sandino the text of a manifesto, which was published in Mérida, Yucatán, on 6 September, and was nationalist in content, calling upon Nicaraguans to continue the struggle against the invader. From what one can deduce from Sandino's words, the intention of this declaration was not to lose contact with the patriots 'of limited intelligence'.[66]

FROM SANDINO THE HERO TO THE TRAITOR OF LAS SEGOVIAS

Surprisingly, on 9 September, only a day after his previous letter to Alemán Bolaños, and in the same letter in which he wrote that 'Neither extreme right, nor extreme left, but a UNITED FRONT is our slogan', Sandino sought to put Alemán Bolaños' mind at rest by assuring him that this and no other was the orientation of his thinking, and informed him that 'it would no longer be Colonel Martí who would be charged with going to Central America, because at present he is ill in a sanatorium in this city'.[67]

It is clear that some serious disagreement must have occurred between Sandino and Martí, or more correctly between Sandino and the Communist International, to bring about such a sudden and what would normally be an important change of plan. Anderson has found in the US National Archives an outrageous version that claims that the breach was due to Martí having told Sandino that the Mexican government was trying to poison him, which caused the General to lose patience and expel Martí from among his followers.[68]

What is on record is that the Mexican government of the period, led by Portes Gil, was adopting a repressive attitude towards popular organizations. In June 1929 agents of the Cuban dictator Machado shot dead the Cuban Communist leader Julio Antonio Mella in the streets of Mexico City, with the complicity of the head of the Mexican police, who was a trusted associate of Portes Gil. In May, Guadalupe Rodríguez, a Mexican Communist from Durango, had been condemned to be executed on orders from the Ministry of War. Portes Gil himself personally ordered the closure of *El Machete*, the newspaper of the Mexican Communist Party.[69] Precisely at that time Sandino was receiving two thousand pesos a month from the government of Portes Gil for the support of himself and his entourage.[70] There can be no doubt that neither the Mexican Communist Party nor the International could regard this situation favourably, most of all when one could foresee a complete break off of relations with the Soviet Union, which eventually occurred in January 1930.[71]

The object of Sandino's stay in Mexico had been to obtain armaments and other resources necessary to continue the struggle against the US forces. Sandino hoped also to receive these resources from the hands of the Portes Gil government, the same one that was crushing the Mexican Communist movement. One can imagine that neither Martí or the Communist International could be in agreement with Sandino's prolonged residence in Mexico, nor with the state of financial dependence in relation to the Mexican government in which he and his men were living.

Whichever may have been the precise circumstances, the undeniable fact is that while Sandino was still in Mexico, on 4 January 1930, an announcement appeared in *La Correspondance Internationale* under the title 'Sandino goes over to the Imperialist Camp', which stated, in full, 'Sandino, the former leader of the Nicaraguan insurgents, who has led the struggle against the military intervention of the United States, has allowed himself to be bought for 60,000 dollars. He has agreed to abandon his concern for the revolutionary movement in Nicaragua and take up residence in the Mexican State of Yucan [*sic*].'[72] The note, which was not signed, was published in the days immediately preceding one of Sandino's most important meetings with Portes Gil.

On 9 January, Sandino made public a statement 'with the intention of refuting attacks that have been made in the press against the dedication to its ideals of the Army in Defence of the Sovereignty of Nicaragua'. In it he said that he proposed to publish documents that would demonstrate the morality of his actions and his loyalty to the principles of Latin American brotherhood. He recounted the events of his years of struggle, and included a paragraph in which an attentive reader can detect a desire to improve his relations with the International. The paragraph read:

> Undoubtedly these four years of war of liberation have also given me more experience, as well as (an awareness) of the need better to understand the necessity that exists for all of our peoples in Hispanic America to expel United States citizens and capital completely from our native soil, since they are in reality nothing else than a permanent danger for the nationality that innocently accepts them in its midst, and, similarly, of the need to develop our industries and our trade, making every effort to achieve the alliance of all our brothers in Hispanic America.[73]

Sandino's meeting with Portes Gil took place on 29 January 1930. Four days earlier the General had written to Dr Zepeda, expressing to him his doubts and reservations with regard to the possibility of a betrayal on the part of the Mexican representatives who had promised to help him. He also let Zepeda know that his army did not support the foreign policy that the Mexican President-elect, Pascual Ortiz Rubio, was expected to put into effect on occupying the Presidency, since he had been seen to 'flirt' with the US government, the common enemy, Sandino wrote, of all the 'Indohispanic' peoples. Sandino considered the attitude of Ortiz Rubio in this regard to be contemptible, and suspected that once President he would recognize Moncada as President of Nicaragua, giving a slap in the face to the *Sandinista* army.[75]

In international affairs one of the most important indications of the Mexican government's attitude at that time, referred to by Sandino, was the withdrawal of its ambassador from the Soviet Union. The justification given by the Mexican government for this action was 'the report on Communist demonstrations that have been carried out against our Embassies in some capitals of the American continent, on the pretext of protesting against measures that have been taken here against certain foreign agitators who have been interfering in our internal affairs and seeking to subvert public tranquillity'.[76] The 'foreign' agitators to which this referred were in reality Mexican Communists, but among the group there was one foreigner: the Peruvian Esteban Pavletich, who had come to Mexico with Sandino.[77]

In his letter of 25 January to Dr Zepeda mentioned above, written several months after Martí's supposed illness, Sandino mentioned the latter as 'my secretary, citizen Colonel Agustín Farabundo Martí'.[78] This reference, together with the statements that have just been quoted, makes it reasonable to suggest that there had been a temporary reconciliation with Martí and the International. Further evidence of this was given in the Manifesto issued by Sandino on 26 February 1930, in which he declared that his departure from Nicaraguan territory had not implied a truce in the struggle against the common enemy, Yankee imperialism, but instead had been a prolongation of that struggle, in the sense that it had been directed towards attracting new contingents into the 'Hispanic American' Union Confederation.[79]

Sandino stated that up to that time his Army had received the support of sincere revolutionaries, 'but that, with the intensification of the struggle, brought on by the Yankee bankers, the waverers, the timid ones, because of the character the struggle has taken, are abandoning us, because only the workers and peasants will go to the very end, only their organized strength will achieve victory'. He concluded by issuing a call to all Nicaraguans and all those who were still without organization and outside the Hispanic American Union Confederation, exhorting them, 'In the name of the heroic soldiers of the Army in Defence of the National Sovereignty of Nicaragua, we cry to you: Organize! Your place is in the ranks of the Hispanic American Union Confederation, the only union organization that defends the interests of the working class!'[80]

This fervent proclamation from Sandino in support of the Latin American Union Confederation[81] constituted a kind of reparation on his part in order not to lose the support of the International. The Latin American Union Confederation was the first step toward the establishment of a continent-wide workers' organization as part of the Red International of Labour Unions. If the work actually undertaken by this Confederation was admittedly very limited,[82] it nevertheless still fulfilled an important role, as we shall see. And, in effect, on 23 April 1930, in the same days in which Sandino was returning to Las Segovias to rejoin the armed struggle, Willy Münzenberg and V. Chattopad-haya, members of the International Secretariat of the League against Imperialism, published for their part some emphatic declarations in *La Correspondance Internationale* with the title 'The Slanders against General Sandino'. In their statement and in the name of the League Secretariat they declared that the reports accusing Sandino of having sold himself to imperialism for 60 000 dollars were slanderous and had been put into circulation by the imperialists themselves. They stated that Sandino was at that time a member of the Executive Committee of the League against Imperialism. It was also said that both the League and Sandino himself had asked the Mexican section of the League to carry out an investigation of the accusations. It had done so, and the inquiry had shown that the charges were totally without foundation, and that Sandino was innocent.

The statement also said that Sandino had declared 'that he was not only determined to continue his struggle against United States imperialism, *but also against all the Latin American governments that are just so many more instruments of imperialism, including among them the Mexican government, which has turned into a government that is frankly counter-revolutionary*'.[83]

The League's statement included a call for a far-reaching mass campaign of solidarity with Sandino, directed above all at the League against Imperialism of the Americas and its sections. In addition, in case there remained any doubt about the reconciliation, they added:

> The oppressed peoples see in him and in his freedom army sincere combatants who, faithful to the programme of the international organization of the League, will continue the struggle against imperialism not only in Nicaragua, but also in the other countries of Latin America, with the aim of achieving the unity in struggle and action of all the oppressed of the colonial and semi-colonial countries, a unity that is absolutely necessary for the victorious conclusion of the struggle that has been initiated against the imperialist bandits.[84]

Nevertheless, when Sandino returned to Las Segovias, Martí still did not accompany him. He remained in Mexico until May or June of 1930, when he was expelled by the Mexican government and left for El Salvador, accredited with the status of representative of International Red Aid to the Section of the latter organization that was operating in the country. The return of Martí to his homeland took place at a critical moment in the social conflicts of El Salvador, which would culminate in the massacres of 1932.

The reconciliation with the Comintern, which was largely formal in nature, did not last long. The *New York Times* published a despatch in May in which it was reported that the Mexican Communist Party had already accused Sandino 'of having betrayed the cause of world anti-imperialism' and of 'having sold himself to the highest bidder'. It mentioned a statement by the Mexican Party in which it was claimed that Sandino, after accepting Communist money and agreeing to undertake a world propaganda tour against imperialism, had obtained funds from another source and returned to Nicaragua 'to resume his struggle, together with small groups of bourgeois, to subjugate the country'. It was asserted that the United States wanted the conflict to continue, in order to 'keep alive the threat of a Sandino victory over the government of Moncada, or to enter into agreements with Sandino if he were to obtain sufficient power'.[85]

Nevertheless, almost a year later, in a letter to his lieutenant Pedrón Altamirano of 30 March 1931, Sandino made use of a class-based approach in examining their position, telling him that only the workers and peasants of Central America could defend their countries, and declared, 'Our movement for Central American Union would become *detached* (*desligado*)[86] from the bourgeois elements, who at every point have wanted to oblige us to accept the humiliations of the Yankees, since to do so would be more favourable to their bourgeois interests.'[87]

In another letter, to José Idiáquez, of 26 April 1931, Sandino also spoke of a Central American Union, to have the name 'Central American Communes' (*Comuneros*), and said that 'only the Central American workers and peasants' could reestablish a federation of Central America. However, he also anticipated that Nicaragua would provide the primary motive for the outbreak of the next world war, in which 'the great oppressive magnates' would be destroyed and 'the oppressed people' would rise to the fore.[88]

A document of great importance is the report that Farabundo Martí sent to International Red Aid, on 22 February 1931. In it he wrote the following with regard to Sandino: 'In Nicaragua power is held by Moncada, an agent of Yankee imperialism, who we fought against from Las Segovias, when Sandino was supported by the revolutionary anti-imperialist organizations, before Sandino betrayed the world anti-imperialist movement to become a petit-bourgeois liberal caudillo[89] with aspirations to govern Nicaragua with bourgeois semi-feudal and semi-colonial moulds.'[90]

Sandino, who on one occasion said that he regretted the split with Martí 'as much as the loss of a battle',[91] would later write, in a document that is of extraordinary political significance for the definition of the nature of his movement:

> On several occasions attempts have been made *to distort this movement of national defence, and convert it into a struggle more of a social character.*[92] I have opposed this with all my strength. *This movement is a national and anti-imperialist one.*[93] We are keeping aloft the banner of liberty for Nicaragua and for the whole of Hispanic America. Other than that, *in the social field, we advocate a progressive movement in (the satisfaction of) social aspirations.*[94] We have had coming to see us here, to influence us, representatives of the International Federation of Labour, of the League against Imperialism, of the Quakers ... *We have always responded with our determined view that this was a nationalist struggle. Martí, the propagandist of Communism, saw that he could not overcome with this programme, and withdrew.*[95]

Martí, for his part, declared minutes before being shot by firing squad in El Salvador, on 1 February 1932:

> I wish to testify to the moral integrity, to the absolute purity of General Sandino. I am personally aware that in Mexico he repeatedly received offers of considerable sums of money for him to abandon his struggle in Las Segovias, and that these offers were refused by the General with the most noble indignation. My breach with Sandino did not, as has sometimes been said, arise out of a divergence of moral principles, or opposing standards of conduct. *I refused to follow him back to Las Segovias, because he did not wish to embrace the Communist programme that I supported. His banner was solely a banner of independence, a banner of emancipation, and he did not pursue goals of social rebellion.*[96] I am interested that these points should be clarified, to establish the historical truth. And in order to die, two steps away from execution, I solemnly declare that General Sandino is the foremost great patriot in the world.[97]

It should be mentioned here that when Sandino himself said that he was a communist, this declaration had very special connotations, that should not confuse us. In May 1931 he explained this point by saying that since Nicaragua, under the Spanish conquest, had never been settled by any nobles belonging to the privileged families of Europe, there had only ever been one class, the common people (*la clase común*), and that, this being the case, he and his followers, rather than simply Liberals, were all more or less '*communists*' (*comunistas*).[98] Later, he would say to Dr Humberto Barahona that while the latter recoiled from calling himself a communist, he, Sandino, would proclaim it to the whole Universe, with all the strength of his being, because he was a 'rationalist communist'.[99] He also used the term 'communize' (*comunizar*) as a synonym of 'fraternize' (*fraternizar*), and proposed humanitarian schemes for the benefit of the worldwide proletariat.[100]

On 27 August 1932 Sandino said that he was preparing to take power with his army in order to organize the workers and peasants of Nicaragua, who would exploit the country's riches for the benefit of the Nicaraguan family as a whole.[101] On 16 March 1933, he reproached Alemán Bolaños for apparently not having understood his motives for signing peace. Sandino said that with the ending, even if only in appearance, of armed intervention in Nicaragua, the mood had cooled, because though the people suffered the effects of political and economic intervention they did not identify it, and, what was worse, did not believe in it. This situation placed him in a difficult position.[102] In that message to Alemán Bolaños, one can see clearly that, although Sandino was aware to some degree that the problems of Nicaragua had not ended with the departure of the Americans, he considered, in his isolation following his break with the International, that to continue fighting would not produce any positive results.

In the same month J. Gómez, of the Mexican Communist Party, published an analysis of the *Sandinista* movement in *La Correspondance Internationale* which he titled 'Sandino's Betrayal'. A painstaking effort has been made to consign this article to oblivion, but it is necessary to examine it in detail, as it expresses what was then the official opinion of the Communist International on Sandino. It began by describing the historical context of the invasion, and the development of resistance. 'Groups of workers of revolutionary tendencies, and above all peasants, together with some elements of the petit-bourgeoisie from the cities, went to the mountains of Las Segovias, where the insurgent High Command was situated,'[103] wrote Gómez, exaggerating the real level of worker participation which, as we have seen, could not be very great in an underdeveloped and dependent country in which industry did not exist. 'It was not only Nicaraguan workers, but also others from Mexico, Guatemala and El Salvador, who arrived to swell the numbers of the insurgent army,' Gómez claimed.[104] This was no more true, as the majority of the foreign elements found in the *Sandinista* army came from the petit-bourgeoisie, with the exception of the contingent of Honduran agricultural workers who crossed the frontier and joined Sandino in 1931, after they had suffered repression following a wave of agitation against the United Fruit Company. We do not know the size of this group. The prevailing economic conditions and the level of organization of the working 'masses' in the countries mentioned by Gómez at that time make it impossible that large numbers could have moved to join Sandino's forces. 'The role played by the Mexican proletariat and by the working masses of Mexico, with the Mexican Communist Party,' Gómez went on, 'was particularly important.'[105]

He stated that the Communist Parties of Central and South America had presented the *Sandinista* movement to the working masses of the continent as an anti-imperialist movement directed against United States imperialism, which had been correct. However, he continued, the Communist Parties had forgotten to explain to the working masses 'in a well-grounded, Leninist manner, in whose hands, from the point of view of class, the anti-imperialist movement in Nicaragua lay, and in whose hands it should be placed, for it not to be betrayed, for it to continue as a genuine revolutionary struggle against imperialism and its "national" lackeys, for it to defend the fundamental demands of the working masses'. Gómez then added:

> From the beginning 'General' Sandino[106] put himself at the head of the movement. He was a petit-bourgeois chieftain, the incarnation of the typical *caudillo*, a little boss-dictator, incapable of accepting that anyone should interfere in his affairs and in the measures taken by him, making all decisions by himself alone, entirely out of his own head. The struggle against American imperialism was limited by him to a struggle against the armed intervention of the United States. His sole demand was simply for the withdrawal of the American Marines from Nicaragua, with absolutely nothing being said about the struggle against all the forms of imperialist domination in these countries, for a full and genuine independence for Nicaragua in the face of American imperialism, or for the confiscation of the industrial enterprises and plantations owned by American capital . . . Sandino has not declared war on the dominant classes, the allies, the agents of American imperialism. He has not called for a struggle against feudalists, for an agrarian and anti-imperialist revolution,

but only for a struggle for the withdrawal of the American Marines from Nicaragua, for the external independence of the country. The wealthy undertakings owned by American capital in the regions where the insurgents led by Sandino are active, remain virtually intact (where this rule has not been observed, this has been due to the work of the insurgents themselves, and not to instructions given by Sandino).[107]

This last statement was not correct, as the taking of the Bonanza mines and the mines of the Luz and Los Angeles company, both of them US-owned, as well as the attack on the fruit company installations on the Atlantic coast on 11 April 1931 and several other guerrilla actions against American-owned companies, were all carried out on orders from Sandino. Gómez went still further, in order to present a picture of a Sandino fearful of violating American property:

A petit-bourgeois boss-figure, without a coherent revolutionary line, Sandino had inevitably to reach the point of betraying the movement . . . It is beyond all doubt that the withdrawal of the American naval forces from Nicaragua was agreed with Sandino, as was his 'subsequent struggle'. All his 'anti-imperialism' has blown away like a soap bubble, as soon as the last American Marine has left Nicaragua. And worse still, not only does he believe it useless to continue the struggle against American imperialism, but he considers it necessary to 'invite' American capital to come to the country. In the manifesto published by him on 2nd February of this year he declares, without any attempt to dissemble, 'I have no ill will towards the Americans. Let them come here and work.'

This latter claim, again, we believe to be false, as one can find no documentary confirmation of it, nor would it be inferred from subsequent events. However, Gómez, continuing his line, then went yet further again to claim that, in order to avoid the possibility that his army – made up of working people, labourers – might continue fighting after his betrayal, Sandino had declared, 'If the troops that have removed themselves from under central control offer unforeseen resistance and continue the insurrection, I will place myself at the disposition of President Sacasa, and will come to his aid to force them to follow my example.'[108]

Gómez added ironically that the example of Sandino was in effect highly demonstrative, above all for Central and South America, where the petit-bourgeois elements sought to occupy the leadership of revolutionary movements, and where the Communist Parties themselves had not freed themselves from petit-bourgeois influences, which affected both their political line and their day-to-day activities. He claimed that these Parties had still not sufficiently realized that there was a difference between 'the leadership of the revolutionary movement by the working class, exercising its hegemony, as the only class capable of having a consistent revolutionary line, and the vacillating, unreliable leadership of the petit-bourgeoisie. And still less had they explained it to the masses.' He then added, 'Only the proletariat, led by the Communist Party, can lead the working masses to victory.'[109] Gómez said that Sandino had served to clarify all of these questions, because the movement would have continued 'if it had been seen to be fighting for complete political and economic independence for the country, for the confiscation of the enterprises owned by the imperialists, for the confiscation and redistribution among the peasants of the land held by the great landowners allied to the imperialists, and if at its head had been the vanguard of the proletariat, its Communist Party'. He accused the Communist Parties of Central and South America of not having made sufficiently clear the indecisive, hybrid nature of the *Sandinista* movement.

Gómez extended his argument further, saying that:

one should point out another error of the Communist Parties of Central America – and most of all, of those of Honduras and Mexico – that they have done nothing to create Communist cells among the Nicaraguan insurgents, which would have been able to oppose the will of the petit-bourgeois General Sandino with that of the workers, and would have been able to force him to continue the struggle . . . or alternatively, if there were renewed vacillations, or resistance on his part, take the leadership of the struggle into their own hands, placing the revolutionary proletariat at its head.

It is of interest to note here that the US Captain Evans F. Carlson, in command of a police unit in Managua, reported that on 22 February 1932 he had 'searched the houses of ten persons suspected of being agents active in the organization of communism in Nicaragua', and detained twenty people, 'for having been found in the possession of subversive literature, or under suspicion of being connected with the communist movement'.[110] However, from Gómez's article one would conclude that there was no degree of genuinely Communist organization in existence in Nicaragua at that time.

Gómez drew attention to the point that 'the struggle for the hegemony of the proletariat in the revolutionary movement is the struggle for it to be led by the Communist Party, the vanguard of the truly revolutionary class, of the proletariat'. He then concluded, 'The betrayal by this former hero constitutes a lesson in life, which demonstrates that, to obtain victory, the working masses represented by the Communist Party must take the direction of the struggle into their own hands.'[111]

In another Communist document, an official pamphlet published in 1933 by the Communist Party of the United States, it was stated, in referring to the *Sandinista* movement, that in Nicaragua the struggle of the workers and peasants against American imperialism had taken on the form of open warfare. For years, Sandino's armies had heroically resisted the US armed forces.

However [the pamphlet went on] this battle was limited with regard to objectives due to the petit-bourgeoisie leadership of Sandino. Instead of combating the landowning bourgeoisie and the national bourgeoisie that acted as agents for American imperialism and fighting for the needs of the workers and peasants, Sandino asked only for the expulsion of the US Marines, as if their presence constituted the sum total of imperialist oppression. When the Marines left Nicaragua, Sandino capitulated. But the brutal exploitation of Nicaragua did not change.

This document also mentioned what it described as a more genuine blow against the imperialist domination of Nicaragua that had occurred in April 1931, when the armed struggle had been extended to the banana plantations of the Standard Fruit and the Steamship Corporation. In the clashes that followed eight American employees of the company had died, and the pamphlet concluded, 'It is these workers of the banana plantations in the East, of the mines and of the railroads, who, allied with the peasantry, will carry forward the heroic struggle for the complete and genuine national independence of Nicaragua.'[112]

We should point out here that these attacks against Standard Fruit and other American companies of the Atlantic coast were undertaken by *Sandinista* guerrilla forces under the command of Pedro Blandón, one of Sandino's most loyal lieutenants, and undoubtedly in accordance with orders issued by the General.[113]

Another document exists that also fully confirms our hypothesis with regard to the attitudes of the Communist movement and moreover further demonstrates the way in which it was hoped to transform Sandino's national liberation movement into a movement for proletarian revolution. The Costa Rican section of the League against Imperialism published a statement, before the signing of the peace treaty by Sandino, which declared that in his campaigns the General had detached the anti-imperialist struggle from that against capitalism, from the struggle against the Nicaraguan landowners and bourgeoisie who were 'the allies yesterday, today and forever of the pirate invaders'. Although they regarded him, according to the statement, as unquestionably a guerrilla fighter for liberty, a determined and valiant warrior, they accused Sandino of not having a clear, precise idea of the way in which to make this struggle truly, decisively effective, since as long as it was not put forward in terms of class, with demands of land for the peasants and for the control of the government and economy of the country by the workers, he would continue to operate without attaining meaningful results. 'His few hundred comrades,' they said, 'would today be thousands upon thousands, if to his just, but limited slogan of YANKEES OUT, he had added others: The land for those who work it, the government for the workers and peasants, no more of the shackles of the exploiters in alliance with outside imperialists.' The members of the Costa Rican section of the League were still waiting for a definition of his position in this regard from Sandino. Still hopeful, they asked themselves, 'Will Sandino come to adopt this class-based position?', and ended with a declaration of their best expectations: 'We who admire the determined will to fight of Sandino, would wish that the Nicaraguan guerrilla leader, realizing that the anti-imperialist struggle must be linked to proletarian action, would establish his position once and for all as being within the ranks of Communist militants.'[114]

A month later, when Sandino had already signed the Peace Treaty with the Liberal government and all illusions about transforming him into a proletarian leader had been lost, the Communist Party of Costa Rica made further declarations in the same vein as those of the US Party mentioned previously. They began by asking, 'What's more, in what way have the working masses benefited from Sandino's struggle? Now that he has disappeared from the theatre of conflict, what benefit will the exploited masses of Nicaragua gain from it?' They went on:

As before, the landowners will remain in the countryside, the traders and manufacturers in the city, exploiting the labour of the workers and peasants, enriching themselves at the cost of the workers' hunger. For the workers of Nicaragua and for all the peoples under the capitalist regime, this bitter experience should be useful. *Their struggles should always be under class banners, with class ideals, responding to class needs.*[115] In the specific case referred to, the sacrifice of the thousands of soldiers of the Liberation Army fallen under imperialist shrapnel would have had some compensation, if at the end of this struggle their class comrades, their children and their descendants had obtained any tangible improvements in their situation.[116]

As one can see from the events that have been described and the documents that substantiate them, the policy of the Communist International in Nicaragua was oriented in a clearly visible direction, which corresponded to certain strategic theses that had been approved by the Comintern.

These theses, which had already been presented, in a totally contradictory manner, in the II Congress of the International, were based around the idea of giving support to the national-revolutionary movements in the countries subjected to imperialist domination. However, at the same time they also implied the necessity of stimulating and accelerating a reorientation of purely nationalist movements towards more socially- and class-based positions, in such a way that would make it possible to propose not only a revolutionary struggle against imperialism, but also the creation of the conditions necessary in order to pass over the uncompleted stages of the bourgeois-democratic revolution and bring forward the establishment of a soviet-style system. Clearly, the politico-governmental instrument at the centre of this process was to be the worker–peasant government, which, in spite of the criticisms that had been made of Zinoviev's ideas, continued to be understood as a synonym for proletarian dictatorship.

With regard to the Party, the policy of the International was not able to contemplate the creation of any kind of independent political organization in Nicaragua. *Sandinismo*, as a national and patriotic movement, absorbed all its attention. It seems more that what was attempted was the conversion of the movement's leader, Sandino, directly to Communism, an attempt that was destined for failure not only in view of the nature of the conflict and the level of social and political development in Nicaragua at that time, but also due to the mystical sensibilities and esoteric tendencies of the General, adapted via his strong personality to the purposes of the conflict in which he found himself.

This method, moreover, was the same as had been applied in China with Chiang Kai Shek, and would later be used with Castro in Cuba, resulting in failure in the first case and success in the second.

The Communist International not only failed to establish any kind of Communist Party in Nicaragua through its policy, but was also incapable of sustaining and encouraging the national liberation movement of General Sandino enough for it to go to its ultimate consequences. Their narrowness of political outlook, which oscillated between two poles, positive and negative, according to whether one did or did not declare oneself to be proletarian and communist, regardless of the international and historical significance of the conflict, particularly for the colonial and semi-colonial countries, prevented the International from formulating a clear and positive strategy, once their markedly sectarian efforts had failed to achieve the conversion of the Nicaraguan patriot leader.

The importance of the *Sandinista* movement was not seen as simply that of a movement directed towards rescuing a people from imperialist domination, an example that would have been of unquestionable significance for the rest of the colonial and semi-colonial world. Also very much in mind was the expectation of an Anglo-American confrontation, which in the Comintern was then given to be almost a certainty, as a result of a number of different disputes between Britain and the United States which, together with the other European powers, were in contention for markets and influence in the whole of Latin America.

Outside Nicaragua, the abandonment of Sandino and his condemnation as a traitor led to the international political isolation that weighed so much on his morale, as can be seen from the letter to Alemán Bolaños already mentioned. On an internal level, they were ultimately the determining factor that decided him upon the unsound policy that would lead him to his death. This policy did not just arise out of his personal character but reflected the particularly difficult situation in which he was placed, given that no effective, serious and well-rooted political work had been carried out among his soldiers or the populations of the areas controlled by him. All of these circumstances facilitated Anastasio Somoza's death blow not just against Sandino, brutally murdered by Somoza, but against the whole of the insurgent movement.

With the *Sandinista* movement at least partially liquidated, the subsequent skirmishes that occurred did not signify a resurgence of the national liberation struggle, but were more just rearguard combats. Somoza had succeeded in installing himself in power through murder, terror and corruption. It would be well into the 1950s before there would be a serious and organized revival of the struggle against his despotism. All of which leads us to the conclusion that the strategy and tactics of the Communist International, conceived on the basis of schematic formulae that were incapable of grasping the essential elements of the national liberation struggle, constituted an important factor in the temporary but prolonged failure of the resistance against the American domination of Nicaragua, and the tyranny of Somoza.

What makes this failure still more serious, like that which would be suffered in El Salvador in 1932, which would put back any kind of real democratic change in that country for more than four decades, is that it took place when the International already had before it the experience of the revolution in China.

The Communist International was incapable of rationalizing and applying effectively in Nicaragua all the wealth of experience they had obtained from the Kuomintang period of the Chinese revolution, before the so-called betrayal by Chiang Kai Shek in 1927. Their efforts were limited to repeating the approach followed in China, of trying to 'educate' the leader. When this attempt failed, the house they had built up collapsed much more easily than it had been raised. Moreover, this demonstrates that the errors made were not personal mistakes by agents of the International. They were errors in political policy, which, once again, clearly decided everything in a revolutionary process. It was impossible to apply an effective United Front policy in Nicaragua, while dogmatically trying to force the leader to label his national-revolutionary movement as communist and proletarian.

As a result, the real contribution of the International to the *Sandinista* struggle was in the field of propaganda, through which it publicized in every corner of the world the actions, unquestionably audacious, heroic and of great political significance, of Augusto César Sandino. Little Nicaragua occupied a prominent place in the attentions of the intellectual community that was influenced by the Communist movement or, in Latin America, by the APRA. However, this contribution, without doubt a major bulwark of the resistance against the American presence in Nicaragua, was later overshadowed by the campaign unleashed by the International to destroy the image of General Sandino that they themselves had helped to create. Nevertheless, the figure of Sandino was able to remain as a symbol of resistance against the tyranny of the Somoza's and become part of the history, legends and epic past of an entire people. Sandino played the part that it fell to him to play and managed to go well beyond the limits that his background and existing conditions sought to impose upon him. The Comintern did not. Because, despite having been responsible for a fundamental socio-historical error through its inability to unravel the harsh realities of the colonial and semi-colonial situation of these countries, an error that had occurred in spite of it having assigned men of excellent abilities as its representatives, the Communist International ignominiously and unjustly sought to wipe away the record of Sandino. Labelling him a 'traitor' meant in effect to deny the Nicaraguan people the mystique and regenerative impulse that his memory would stimulate from then on, in spite of the gross slanders thrown against the hero of Las Segovias. In so doing the Comintern not only failed to satisfy the political and historical responsibilities of that particular period, which it claimed to have assumed, but also abandoned the revolutionary future of the Nicaraguan people, for decades and without justification, into the hands of its acknowledged adversary – imperialism.

4 Historical and Political Origins of the Salvadorean Social Revolution of 1932

EL SALVADOR IN THE 1930s: A COLONIAL INHERITANCE

The Communist International maintained contact with Sandino's movement in Nicaragua by means of the Anti-Imperialist League. In El Salvador, it did so principally through another of its front organizations: International Red Aid.[1]

These organizational channels were not chosen casually, and reflect different perceptions of the social characteristics of each country and of the character of its revolution. The theoretical dualism seen in the work of the II Congress of the Communist International took on its fullest implications, with a high degree of tragedy, in the case of Central America.[2]

It was as a representative of International Red Aid to its Salvadorean section that Agustín Farabundo Martí returned to his homeland in 1930, after having fought with Sandino in Nicaragua.

The situation in El Salvador at that time was extremely difficult, with a population of 1 722 579 inhabitants in an area of only 20 877 square kilometres, given over as a first priority to the cultivation of coffee, its principal export product, which bound it completely to the fluctuations of the world market.[3] The consequences of the world crisis of 1929 were felt severely in the country, and the social situation that Farabundo Martí found on his return was explosive.

In Nicaragua, US companies owned large landholdings, and their banana estates, together with timber and mining concessions, played an important economic role. In El Salvador it was not the land that was in the hands of these companies. They dominated transport, with the International Railways of Central America; energy, with the San Salvador Electric Light Company; and banking, through the Occidental Bank and other branches of American banks. The Central

American Mines Ltd had a concession, in which its workers were exploited to an incredible degree, but it did not possess large areas of land. Total foreign investment in El Salvador at that time came to around forty million dollars.[4]

The coffee growing bourgeoisie maintained a total dominion over the country, whose economy and socio-political structure they had moulded entirely in accordance with their most immediate class interests. The machinery of the State had always been in their hands, and was used in a direct and effective way to produce the greatest benefit as conceived in the light of the short-term interests of this dominant elite.

Coffee made up 95.5 per cent of exports. Imports amounted to around US $20 000 000, the most important items being foodstuffs and cotton. This gives an indication of the social and political effects for a country such as El Salvador in the crisis of 1929, which would reduce exports to a minimum and contribute decisively to making imports, particularly food, prohibitively expensive.

The coffee growers, whose relations with the great powers were carried on through the world market in coffee, exported their product and in turn imported all the consumer goods and foodstuffs they needed. The obvious consequence, as in Nicaragua and other countries of the Third World, was the non-development of a national industry and the growth of an agriculture dependent on a single export crop, to the detriment of others necessary for the feeding of the population.

With the economic crisis of 1929 neither the small-scale industries, nor the remains of the agrarian petit-bourgeoisie still in existence, could survive, so that the pre-eminence of the agro-export sector and the proletarianization of large sections of the population were encouraged still further.

The years between 1880 and 1912 in El Salvador had seen the final absorption by the great coffee growers of the *tierras comunales* (lands belonging specifically to Indian communities) and the *ejidos* (municipal common lands), and the disappearance of the majority of small landholdings. The cultivation of coffee was imposed in El Salvador by means of a series of government measures, the most important of them being the building of railways to the ports, in order to carry the crop efficiently to the place of embarkation (at a very high cost that made it necessary to resort to foreign loans); and the already mentioned elimination of the communal lands. The latter was because the Indian communities did not use such land to grow coffee, and also, because it was not profitable for the big producers–exporters to have to buy coffee from a large number of small growers when they could use their power to gain full legal control over the land. Closely associated with this measure was the introduction of laws against vagrancy, which sought to ensure the large coffee growers a supply of cheap labour, all of these measures being in turn directly allied to the immediate repression of the least outbreak of discontent that occurred in the countryside. In this way the coffee-growing bourgeoisie (organized from 1930 in the Asociación Cafetalera de El Salvador for the purposes of facing the shocks of the crisis united), continued to hold complete control over the country. They had, nevertheless, to submit to the presence of an American Customs Inspector, who passed on only 25 per cent of receipts to the government, reserving the remaining 75 per cent for the creditor banks as service for their loans, which in 1930 amounted to a little more than eighteen million dollars.[6]

In their control of the country's internal affairs, the dominant Salvadorean coffee-growing sector did not suffer, as had occurred in the case of Nicaragua, from strong competition on the part of American companies, nor was there a direct US military presence, so they enjoyed greater power and autonomy than their Nicaraguan equivalent. This power was exercised in a brutal manner over the great mass of peasants, who lived in a situation even worse than that suffered by the peasants of Nicaragua.

In El Salvador, the racial factor played a much more important role than in Nicaragua. The coffee growers, for the most part direct descendants of the Spanish conquerors, had, since independence, continued and intensified their exploitation of the indigenous races that had inhabited the ancient Cuzcatlán, the modern-day territory of El Salvador. This added to the social conflict, already acute in itself, an important racial, historical and cultural element.[7]

The fact, moreover, that the country had a density of fifty inhabitants per square kilometre, with a substantial itinerant unemployed population, had permitted the landowners to pay wages that were extraordinarily low, something that would be aggravated still further by the world economic crisis.

In 1932, the normal wage for a working day of over eight hours, and in extremely severe conditions, came to around eight American cents. On many states the labourers were virtually paid only in kind, with minimal rations of maize tortillas and beans. Where this was not the case, the method used was a little more sophisticated, that of the so-called *tienda de raya* or company store,[8] in which the labourers were obliged to obtain their food and other goods they needed and pay with tokens that the landowners gave them as wages. These tokens were minted on the haciendas themselves and their circulation was limited to the estate.

The workers were thus left bound to the land by the debts run up in the store, as the tokens were always insufficient for their own and their families' needs, and so they could not leave to work on another estate. If they died before paying off the debt, which, since it went on progressively increasing, happened quite frequently, this debt was passed on to their descendants as an inheritance, and so the landowners ensured themselves a permanent supply of labour almost for nothing.

The mass of peasants found themselves in utter poverty, with a diet that was scarcely enough to survive, sleeping in the open air, and even having to pay the landlords for the water they consumed on the estates, in a situation of virtual slavery. 'The labourers obtain the greater part of their vitamins,' wrote William Khrem, 'from wild herbs, and by chewing flowers that grow by the side of the roads.'[9]

The coffee growing bourgeoisie of El Salvador, meanwhile, were building vast mansions, with comforts of every kind,[10] on their estates, though they lived on them for only three months of the year, at the time of the harvest; once the latter had been gathered in they went away to Europe, to live the life of the great cities until the next crop was ready. The children were left in English and French schools, so that they could acquire a European education. When they returned to their own country, these young people continued amongst themselves to speak the language they had learnt in school, which separated them still more from other sections of the population. Their cosmopolitan habits led them to import large quantities of canned foods, and in the food shops of the upper classes one could obtain articles of the most sophisticated kinds. A single tin of canned food cost the equivalent of the wages of an agricultural labourer for a week. Nevertheless, several million dollars were spent annually on importing food from the United States.[11]

THE EXPROPRIATION OF THE INDIAN COMMUNAL LANDS

Despite this, it was not just the abrupt contrast between their misery and the opulence of the small number of landlords that continued to feed the resentment of the peasants. This anger was rooted in a very powerful factor: their awareness that the land had been the property of their ancestors, and that the current masters and their families had acquired it through a blatant and brutal act of seizure, concealed behind a legal façade. The Law for the Abolition of Native Communities, enacted on 26 February 1881, and the Law for the Abolition of Common Lands of March 1882, had ensured that the the great mass of peasants fell from being joint owners of the land to a situation of semi-slavery. These laws, however, were no more than the culmination of a long process, that would continue until 1912, through which the estate owners had gradually taken complete possession of the land, and broken up the Indian communal properties.

The coffee growers had initiated this process when coffee was first planted in El Salvador. The process of converting the *tierras comunales* into private property passed through an initial period in which they were rented out, priority in the granting of leases being given to those who intended to plant coffee. The natural result of this was that they were largely appropriated by a few, an effect that was further compounded by the inability of the municipal authorities to control the process. The sole criteria against which any claim for the use of the communal land could be judged was the planting of coffee and, to a lesser extent, of cocoa and other export crops. This was also the only deciding factor that enabled a lessee to become the owner of the land. The estates that had been the property of the State – a legacy from the Spanish Crown – were also transferred into private hands. In 1874 a coffee grower from the town of San Vicente made an analysis of the country's agricultural situation and commented that the existence of common lands dedicated to subsistence agriculture was not profitable, both because they were barred thereby to the production of coffee, and because the peasants, being able to satisfy their immediate needs with the produce of the communal lands, did not then feel any urgent need to work in the plantations, which led to a shortage of labour. He also argued that there were large areas of common land that were left uncultivated and that could be planted with coffee; and concluded by asking for a decree that would made it obligatory to plant coffee in at least a half of the communal lands, and increase the hours of work of the labourers so that they could cope with the harvests. These points were accepted by the government and became an integral part of its policies.[12]

The coffee growers had already begun effectively to take over the communal lands long before the Law for the Abolition of Common Lands, either by charging the peasants high rent for their use, by using them as pastures, or by putting them forward as security for loans. There was even one landowner who let out 4500 acres of communal land at twenty pesos a year.[13]

By means of this law and the other decrees that accompanied it, a process was consummated through which a form of landholding that had been established in the area for centuries was destroyed, and the seed was sown for future rebellions. For the legal sanction given to these actions did not succeed in quelling the anger of the members of the old communities, who saw coffee taking over the land where they had previously grown maize, the basis of their diet, and other primary necessities, while they themselves had to go to work on the coffee estates, by now monopolized by the major landowners, for starvation wages.

It should be mentioned here that among the villages most affected by the disappearance of the communal lands were Ahuachapán, Sonsonate and Juayúa, which would be important centres of the rebellion of 1932. The last of these three would, together with Izalco and Nahuizalco, be the scene of the brief experiment with the soviets that were created during the insurrection. Juayúa had been a small community surrounded by its own communal lands, which had been transformed, by the process already described, into one surrounded by private coffee plantations. One coffee grower, General Francisco Salavarría, had such extensive estates there that in 1858 President Gerardo Barrios wrote to him saying that when the crop was ready for harvesting he would have to be called 'Count of Salcoatitlán' or 'Marquis of Juayúa'.[14] The coffee estates of Salavarría were, naturally, planted on land that had been communally owned.

The abolition of the communal lands was accompanied by other new decrees, the object of which was to force the recently dispossessed campesinos to work on the plantations and become day labourers. In each village Jueces Agrarios or 'agricultural magistrates' were appointed, whose task was to draw up a list of men that were able to work and organize the pursuit and capture of those who left the estates without having paid off their debts and other obligations. From time to time they also had to visit the different estates to ascertain their needs with regard to labour. The army, demonstrating to the full its nature as an instrument of established interests, assisted them assiduously in these tasks.[15]

This long-drawn-out process led to a number of conflicts of greater or lesser importance. The most significant, however, was the rebellion of the pure-bred Pipil Indian Anastasio Aquino, of Santiago Nonualco, a community in the Central area of the country, towards the South. Aquino was an agricultural labourer who in 1833 succeeded in raising thousands of Indians of the region in armed rebellion, causing the government to totter. Independence from the Spanish Crown had signified a still worse deterioration in the living conditions of the indigenous population. Since the latter could not, due to their terrible poverty, pay taxes to the government, their contribution was charged in the form of forcible military service. Anastasio Aquino first rebelled against this system, which placed his community in a position of total inequality, and went on to demand land and social and economic rights for his people. He managed to bring together a sizeable force, but nevertheless the military superiority of the government still led to his failure. Aquino was hanged and his head exhibited in a cage, as a lesson to the rest of the Indian communities.[16] Nevertheless, further revolts broke out in the same region in 1872, 1875, 1880, 1885 and 1898. In the figure of Feliciano Ama, leader of Izalco, of Felipe Neri, of Nahuizalco, and of thousands of peasants descended from the tribes that had inhabited El Salvador at the time of the Spanish Conquest, the war-cry of Anastasio Aquino would be raised once again in this century, transformed by now into a call for social revolution.

The world economic crisis of 1929 seriously affected the Salvadorean landowners, who saw coffee prices fall precipitately.

The result of this was that many producers did not wish even to harvest the crop, thus avoiding the expense of the wages, and left it to rot on the plant. This had a terrible effect on the agricultural labourers, who saw unemployment in the countryside increase to a still greater level.

Socially, therefore, there was in El Salvador a double-faceted situation, which would become explosive with the arrival of the crisis of 1929; on the one hand, a historical legacy of exploitation, subjugation and dispossession ever since the beginning of Hispanic domination, which had provoked bitter anger and hatred against the leading families descended from the conquerors; on the other, a policy of extreme liberalism in the economic field, promoting the development of a system of property distribution that entailed, firstly, the dissolution of the communal and common lands that produced the basic necessities of the indigenous population, and secondly their total concentration in the hands of a few families of Spanish origin who held real power in El Salvador.

As if these factors were not enough to create the social conditions necessary for a revolutionary or insurrectional outburst, which could already call on such important precedents as that of Anastasio Aquino, they were compounded by the policy followed by the great coffee planters in the crisis of 1929.

THE CRISIS OF 1929 AND THE SALVADOREAN POPULAR MOVEMENT

In effect, the action of the landowners in saving themselves the miserable wages they paid, among a population with the serious demographic problems of that of El Salvador, had the result that the mass of peasants doubly resented the dispossession and land seizure of which they had been the victims. Without these lands, they had only their wages, however meagre, on which to survive. With the crisis, even this was denied them, as the harvest was left to go to waste on the coffee plants. Hunger, the inevitable consequence of such a situation, revived old injuries and hatreds, gave a renewed vividness to the still relatively recent memories of the abolition of the common lands and made it possible to create, with a mixture of atavistic community sentiment and Marxist collectivist vocabulary, the social foundations for the by then unsurprising Salvadorean insurrection of 1932.

The political situation was also affected by the crisis. In 1930, the Presidency was held by a Liberal lawyer, Pío Romero Bosque, who had introduced measures that were to some extent directed towards improving the situation of the poorer classes, such as the Law for the Registration of Workers and Trade Associations, the Decree for the Creation of Conciliation Boards, charged with arbitrating in disputes between workers and employers, and the Law on Working Hours, through which the eight-hour working day had officially been made obligatory.[17]

The political generosity of Romero Bosque came to an end when the rural organizations became too big, spurred on by the unbearable conditions in which the peasant masses were forced to live following the crisis. His liberalism, which had even led him to allow his Minister of War to officially receive Sandino when the latter was on his way to Mexico in 1929, did not include the possibility of entering into a conflict with the landowning bourgeoisie, to which he himself belonged. It was for this reason that in his speech of 1 May 1930, having seen for himself the size of a demonstration that was attended by 80 000 people, the vast majority of them peasants, he declared that he was not prepared to permit union organizations among agricultural workers.[18] There was an immediate intensification in repression, and two decrees were published, on 12 August and 30 October, the object of which was to check the growth of the popular movement. Meetings of workers and communist agitation and propaganda were prohibited, together with the printing and circulation of any kind of press by the workers' movement, and the Post Office was authorized to inspect the correspondence and printed mail of union organizations from home or abroad. The Penal Code was modified to include prison terms and fines for communist agitators. It was also stated that workers' and peasants' organizations that wished to hold meetings should first have to request permission from the police.[19] Nevertheless, the mass mobilization of 1 May 1930 was the first indication that the long process that we have earlier described was once again about to explode.

The virtually complete non-existence of industry in El Salvador, already mentioned, meant that there were no groups of factory workers, but rather craft workers, who with the agricultural workers made up the majority of the Salvadorean population. These sectors had attained a considerable level of organization, and by the 1930s already had behind them several years of struggle and militancy. Let us examine these antecedents.

There had been a major strike of railway workers in 1919, and a tailors' strike in 1920. In 1921 there had been the first mass strike of shoemakers, in demand of better wages and against the mistreatment and arbitrary dismissal to which they were subject, which ended successfully, and was one of the first victories of the organized craft workers of El Salvador. In the following years a number of individual strikes had been organized, and by 1924 there already existed several unions that were referred to as being of 'general trades' (*Oficios Varios*) which brought together shoemakers, building workers, carpenters, plumbers, tailors, bakers, mechanics and other craft trades.

On 21 September 1924 the El Salvador Regional Workers Federation (Federación Regional de Trabajadores de El Salvador, FRTS) had been formed, as a branch of the recently created Central American Workers' Confederation (Confederación Obrera Centroamericana, COCA), which also included similar organizations in Guatemala, Honduras and Nicaragua.[20]

In the following years the Regional Federation maintained relations with a variety of tendencies in the international workers' movement.[21] In 1927, the FRTS sent a shoemaker named David Ruiz to represent it in the Congress of the Pan-American Federation of Labour, affiliated to the II International, which was held in the United States.[22]

In 1928 the Regional Federation was represented at the Congress of the Mexican Workers' Confederation (Confederación Regional Obrera Mexicana, CROM), by a shoemaker, Gumersindo Ramírez, and by the carpenter Raúl B. Monterrosa.

In 1929, the Federation took part in the Latin American Labour Congress held in Montevideo, Uruguay, on 18 May of that year, represented by the mechanic Serafín G. Martínez and the carpenter Luis Díaz.[23] This Congress, in which Argentina, Brazil, Bolivia, Venezuela, Guatemala, Colombia, Costa Rica, Cuba, México, Paraguay, Perú, Panamá, Chile, Uruguay and Ecuador were also represented, was attended in addition, by delegations of the League for Union Propaganda in the United States, the French Confédération Générale du Travail Unitaire (CCTU), and the Red International of Labour Unions (RILU).[24] The main point of the agenda was the building of a Latin American Union Confederation, which had been agreed by the RILU in its meeting held to commemorate the Tenth Anniversary of the October Revolution, with the objective of unifying the Latin American union movement.

In the tenth session of the Executive Committee of the International, Ramírez, the Mexican delegate, mentioned the Montevideo Congress stating that it had served to clarify the minds of Latin American workers on the need to win hegemony in the workers' movement.[25] This was immediately put into practice during the Fifth Congress of the FRTS, held after the return of Serafín Martínez and Luis Díaz. The communist sympathizers among its leaders quickly displaced reformists and anarchosyndicalists from the leadership.[26]

Ramírez had also indicated that in Montevideo it had been demostrated that the majority of workers who were attracted to revolutionary unions in Latin America were rural labourers, and that it was necessary to combat anarchosyndicalism with the massive support that the rural areas provided.[27]

Other important issues discussed in the Congress of Montevideo were the struggle against imperialism and war, that against the Pan American Federation of Labour and the Amsterdam International, and the means to promote the organization of the indigenous proletariat. As a result of the contacts made in Montevideo, publications from the Communist International began regularly to reach the FRTS: the bulletin of the Caribbean Bureau, pamphlets by Lozovsky, and *El Machete*, the Mexican Communist Party newspaper.

Among the most important tasks of the FRTS was the formation of peasant leagues and agricultural unions, which grew from day to day.

The organization of the massive parade of 1 May 1930 was also undertaken by leaders of the FRTS.

Another activity used by the Salvadorean Regional Federation to attract new members and build up its cadres was the so-called Popular University, a programme of education through which university students, progressive intellectuals and other members of the liberal professions gave talks to workers, peasants and other groups among the poorer classes.[28]

This programme was carried out effectively in Ahuachapán, Izalco, Juayúa and other towns and villages. The content of these talks was anti-imperialist, and at one point specifically pro-Sandinista, since Sandino's struggle enjoyed widespread sympathy in El Salvador. The Popular University was not, though, a clearly class-orientated institution.[29]

It is important to point out that education was one of the most urgent needs of the ordinary people of El Salvador, and something that had not been given any encouragement by the landowning classes. They openly declared that it was not wise to give too much instruction to the masses, since they could then cease to serve as agricultural labour and might develop a wish to exercise liberal professions. 'If the education of the masses has been deliberately limited to a few fundamentals, this has been to avoid the tendency, so harmful in other parts of Central America, to adopt liberal professions at the expense of the needs of agriculture,' wrote Dana Munro with total frankness.[30] The masses, however, were highly interested in learning much more than a few simple 'fundamentals', and both the sessions of the Popular University and those called upon by the individual unions were always heavily attended.

The central focus of action of the Regional Federation for the rural sector was the struggle for an agrarian reform that would give land to the peasants, destroy the latifundios, eradicate feudal forms of exploitation and provide peasant farmers with credit, technical assistance, fertilizers, seeds and tools.[31] In April 1930 the FRTS succeeded in obtaining 50 000 signatures for a petition demanding a law that would guarantee agricultural contracts and institute a minimum wage in the countryside.[32] Since these were among the most deeply-felt and long-standing demands of the peasant communities, one can understand why it was that the Federation was able by this time to gain influence over some seventy five thousand people.[33]

To respond to the wide-ranging organizational work that such a vigorous mass movement originated, the Regional Federation could look to the moral and material support of the Latin American Union Confederation. They also had the help of leading militants of the international communist movement, such as Jorge Fernández Anaya, a member of the Mexican Communist Youth from the age of fourteen, with a great deal of experience in the organization of agricultural unions in his own country; the already mentioned Ricardo Martínez, a member of the Venezuelan Communist Youth and a militant already hardened in union and organizational work for the International; and also, initially, some members of the APRA, such as Jacobo Jorowics, who gave classes in political economy to the leaders of the FRTS and clarified their ideas on some fundamental theoretical concepts; and Esteban Pavletich, previously seen in Nicaragua.

With regard to this point, it is important to note what has been said by Miguel Mármol, who played a major part in the conflicts of those years in El Salvador. Mármol states that, conscious of their political and ideological weaknesses and their inability to orient the education of their cadres in a revolutionary direction, the leaders of the Federation looked abroad. 'If the system of oppression and exploitation is international,' he asks, 'why should the workers be so stupid as to rely only on their own national resources?'

This is important because several independent authors and leading communists have sought to deny or minimize the participation of outside elements in El Salvador at this time. In some cases, by outright denial; others, like Thomas Anderson, by giving the presence of Fernández Anaya and others a purely individual or regional character, as if they had not had any contact with the Communist International.[34] On the contrary, it was following the arrival of the militants mentioned above, and the return shortly afterwards of Farabundo Martí, that the communists founded their party and linked themselves definitely to the Communist International as we shall see.

It is interesting to note here that following the Labour Conference of Montevideo, the First Conference of Latin American Communist Parties was also held in 1929, in Buenos Aires, and delegates from the Communist Parties of El Salvador and Guatemala were there. In reality, the participation of the latter was as nominal as was its very existence. This was not so in the case of El Salvador, which, due to the particular complex of contradictions that existed within its small territory, had seen the growth in a very short time of a significant mass movement, without parallel in the history of Central America.

THE STORM APPROACHES: TOWARDS THE PEASANT UPRISING OF 1932

To recapitulate, we can see, then, that there was in El Salvador a hub of contradictions, which were made acute by the world economic crisis. There was, first, the traditional and hereditary racial divide, which meant that beneath the form of domination established for centuries there still smouldered the ancestral conflict between conquistadores and the conquered; second, the contradiction between the indigenous population in their position as a proletarianized peasantry, and the descendants of the families of aristocratic origin in their capacity as agro-exporting landowners; third, the contradiction originated by the American companies that were placed in key points of the country's economy; and, added to this, the process of acute proletarianization and impoverishment suffered by the artisan and petit-bourgeois sectors of the population, aggravated by the abrupt change that followed the crisis of 1929.

Nevertheless, in El Salvador the main weight of these contradictions was primordially oriented towards the traditional internal forms of domination. Unlike in the case of Nicaragua, in El Salvador the internal social conflict appeared to the eyes of the mass of peasants, Indians and proletarianized artisans, to be the most immediate contributory factor in maintaining their terrible conditions. In Nicaragua, in contrast, the difficulty had lain in comprehending the direct connection between United States intervention and the internal forms of domination, a difficulty suffered by Sandino himself, in the survival of the traditional liberal–conservative conflict within his essentially anti-imperialist position.

In El Salvador the internal social conflict was made more acute by the element of external imperialist domination. The predominant form of relations, the manner in which imperialism had penetrated the country, and the relatively recent expropriation of the indigenous communities by capitalists of European descent who had a monopoly over land, production, trade and political power, all led the peasants and craft workers to direct their anger in a very immediate way towards this latter landowning class. The foreign presence could thus seem more distant, particularly because of the indirect nature of the control that it exercised over the coffee-growing country, where native capitalists dominated production at a local level and their dependency only became manifest at that of the world market.

There was in operation in El Salvador, then, a form of under-developed, dependent capitalism, with a strongly colonial tone, headed by the Salvadorean ruling class, landowning and often absentee, but with direct control over production, trade, political power and the land. The presence of American capital in vital sectors of the economy, or that of an irritating customs agent, were not matters that would seriously worry the complacent ruling minority. What the great mass of the population, on the other hand, felt the most was the domination of these local landowners, their most recent expropriators and those who had benefited directly from the repressive policies of the State.

If to this is added the worsening of the social and economic situation in the towns and countryside and the frankly irresponsible measures taken by the landowners, together with the volume of population, which was unusual for that time and in the conditions of Central America, it is understandable that the struggle put forward would attack directly the domination of the great bourgeosie of El Salvador.

Although this was considered, in the minds of the movement's leaders, to be a struggle against imperialism, its most immediate manifestation for the broad mass of peasants was as a battle against the confiscation of communal lands, against repressive laws, against the measures that forcibly obliged them to work for the great landowners, and so on. There was no economically and socially important bourgeoisie to whom support could be given in their struggle against imperialism, nor anything remotely like it, but rather just the contrary.

This meant that in the eyes of the Salvadorean revolutionaries, driven forward by the pressure of the mass of peasants and workers impoverished by the crisis, their struggle would be to carry out tasks that the bourgeosie could not undertake since it was itself, directly, the sector that most benefited from and made use of the existing order – the latifundio form of landholding, slave-like conditions of exploitation, and so on. It would have to be the workers, understood in the broadest sense of the term, together with the peasants, who would bring about the bourgeois-democratic revolution, not only without the bourgeoisie but in opposition to it, and hence the eventual proposal of a Soviet-type form of organization. Despite the fact that they did put forward some conventional bourgeois-democratic demands, the movement also acquired an orientation that went beyond this limited framework and sought from the beginning to transform the bourgeois-democratic process into a socialist revolution.

It is highly symptomatic that the front organization of the International that was involved in the events in El Salvador was not the Anti-Imperialist League but International Red Aid, so closely linked to International Workers' Aid. This indicates that for the militants of the International operating in the country the principal and predominant contradiction, and certainly the most acute, was that between the tiny minority of Salvadorean landowners and the proletarianized urban and rural masses. Only through this intervening factor could the fundamental contradiction with imperialism be discerned.

The social and economic conditions of El Salvador, thrown into effervescence by the world crisis of 1929, brought together all these contradictions in a tight knot. But they did so in such a way that they launched the different forces into a desperate conflict. On the one hand, the dominant conqueror was clearly identified. On the other, there was the rebellion of a vast mass of peasants who fought for a radical agrarian transformation, against a handful of near-feudal landowners. The agitation of the impoverished craft workers was intensified, as in the worsening process of proletarianization they saw themselves without any possibility of becoming a vigorous working class, given the absence of any industry capable of absorbing them. And all this took place within the context of the structural dependency of the rural society of El Salvador in relation to the United States and the world capitalist market, shaken to its foundations by the crisis.

The Salvadorean crisis occurred precisely because of the indissoluble link between the country's economy and the 1929 crisis. However, this revolutionary crisis did not have behind it a social base capable of giving it unity, nor the ideological and economic strength sufficient to convert it, with the mass support of the peasants, into a successful revolution.

It was, ultimately, a peasant insurrection, and so suffered from the failings characteristic of movements of this kind, lacking the solidity that could only have been given, in this context, by the classes with a genuine will for power: the bourgeosie or the working class. In El Salvador the peasant insurrection went directly against the bourgeoisie. As for the working class, it had scarcely taken its first steps, and the sector that did predominate, outside agriculture, was an agglomeration of artisans and craft workers that had been ruined by the economic crisis. The intermediate sectors, on the other hand, were socially and economically irrelevant. All these factors placed the movement in a situation where it had to formulate goals that could mobilize the insurrection, but which would also put forward, without real possibilities of success, objectives that corresponded to another type of revolution.

The tactics of the International and its strategy based on the Russian revolutionary example of the transformation of a bourgeois-democratic revolution into a socialist revolution was ever present.

In the midst of a revolutionary upsurge that had originated in centuries-old conflicts, on the one hand, and the crisis of the world capitalist system on the other; with a massive and spontaneous peasant movement, but without a strong working class with a tradition of organization and political and ideological solidity, the revolutionary crisis that was approaching in El Salvador in the early 1930s could not be transformed into a Revolution, and much less into a victorious Revolution.

Perhaps it may be useful here, following the habit of the International in drawing analogies, to risk the following comparison. In Russia the absence of a working class capable of overthrowing Czarism had led in the middle of the nineteenth century to the creation of a whole current of thought and action. Lermentov expressed his frustration in his novel *A Hero of Our Time*, a biography of the youth of his time. Herzen, a thinker and revolutionary, withdrew to Europe to sound his 'Bell' for the freedom of the Russian people. In El Salvador, in contrast, Martí and Luna, in desperate conditions and pushed forward by an impressive number of followers, chose to emulate the path of the French Communards, which Marx characterized as 'an assault on heaven'. The consequences were different though, and the mythology that developed in the case of the Commune was absent. They were driven towards death by unrealizable strategic slogans, based on just and legitimate immediate demands. The repression of the vanquished by the victors was followed by irresponsible criticism, defamatory epithets and a consignment to oblivion from those who had been the intellectual promoters of the tragedy and, supposedly, the movement's firmest allies.

5 Farabundo Martí and the Communist International: Hunger in the Fields

THE COMMUNIST PARTY: PRESENCE OF THE COMMUNIST INTERNATIONAL IN EL SALVADOR

The Communist Party of El Salvador arose out of the communist group that had taken control of the FRTS in 1929, and was formally constituted in March of the following year, on the arrival of Jorge Fernández Anaya, who was at that time its contact with the International.[1]

The meeting to found the new party was attended by those militants who had most distinguished themselves in earlier popular struggles, which led Miguel Mármol to affirm that the Communist Party of El Salvador was a genuine product of the working class, contrary to what had been the case in other countries of Latin America, where the Party was first formed among groups of intellectuals and students.[2] In reality, it could not be a product of the working class because the latter, scarcely in the first stages of gestation, was practically non-existent, as has been said. As in other cases, the Communist Party was more the product of the groups of craft workers and of the peasants of El Salvador. A carpenter, Luis Díaz, who had been a delegate for the Regional Federation in the Latin American Labour Congress in Montevideo, was elected General Secretary. The Secretary for Organization was a teacher, Víctor Manuel Angulo, as was the Secretary for Propaganda, Juan Campos. (Where Mármol is correct is in affirming that the intellectual elements that gave the principal support in the theoretical field were well-prepared and experienced cadres of the international communist movement,[3] revolutionary militants directly connected with the International, such as Fernández Anaya, Agustín Farabundo Martí and Ricardo Martínez.) This same constituent meeting also proceeded to elect the leadership of the

103

Salvadorean Communist Youth, which was made up of two printing workers, three shoemakers and a carpenter. One of the shoemakers was Miguel Mármol, whose testimony, combined with other material, has served to throw light on events that had remained obscure up to the present day.

Relations between the new Communist Party and the Third International were maintained through various channels. One of them was the contact the Salvadorean labour movement had with the Latin American Union Confederation and the Red International of Labour Unions (Profintern), the V Congress of which in 1930 would be attended, as we shall see, by two Salvadorean delegates. Secondly, those relations were highlighted by the presence of the Latin American cadres of the International, who participated actively in the theoretical preparation of the Party's militants and collaborated in the organization of the masses. Thirdly, the most important intermediary was International Red Aid, represented by Agustín Farabundo Martí. And, finally, the still weak Caribbean Bureau also send them ideological and informative material and news of experiences in other regions.

During the preparation for the V Congress of the Red International of Labour Unions, which was to be opened in Moscow on 15 July 1930, the International sent an invitation to the youthful Communist Party of El Salvador, which had scarcely been in existence a few months, by means of Jorge Fernández Anaya. The delegates chosen were a farmworker, Modesto Ramírez, and Miguel Mármol, both of them leading militants of the Salvadorean popular movement with many years' experience in the conflicts of the country.

In this Congress, which was attended by representatives of 61 countries, particular stress was laid on the presence of new members in a meeting of the worldwide workers' movement, and El Salvador was put forward as an example.[4]

The Congress defined the most important task for all the colonial and semi-colonial countries: to overcome imperialism and establish the democratic and revolutionary dictatorship of the proletariat and the peasants under the hegemony of the working class.[5] Lozovsky, the General Secretary, mentioned the importance of organizing the workers on the colonial plantations of coffee, sugar cane and rubber, who up to that point were not organized in the majority of countries.[6] It would be these workers from the coffee plantations who would bear the main weight of the insurrection of 1932 in El Salvador.

The Congress made declarations of militant solidarity with the weakest groups of the world proletariat and called for close alliance of the colonial slaves with the proletariat of the capitalist countries and the USSR.[7] Importance was also given to work among the Indians of Latin America and with the struggle of blacks against white chauvinism.[8] Two delegates from Guatemala were present, Antonio Obando, a carpenter, and Luis Chigüichón, a baker, both of whom had previously been in El Salvador and had friendly relations with the Salvadorean delegates. There was also a delegate from Honduras named Valdés.

In the debates of the Congress the Colombian delegate Canot expressed his opinion that the question of the organization of the agricultural proletariat had not been dealt with in sufficient depth. He believed that this was a question of the first importance and that the strikes by agricultural workers in Europe and Latin America had proven that this 'category of workers' had a special place in the revolutionary firing line.[9]

It was also agreed that in the colonial and semi-colonial countries a good deal of attention should be given to organizing and gaining the adherence of the semi-proletarian sectors, the small craft workers who did not employ wage labour. This was done, most effectively, by the Salvadorean Communist Party, due to the non-existence of a factory proletariat.

The Congress agreed, in addition, that the red labour unions and the members of the revolutionary union opposition in the more advanced countries should fulfil the following duties with regard to the union movement in the colonies: the provision of material aid, assistance in the education of cadres, the sending of militants to contribute to the building of the revolutionary union organizations, the sending of documentation, the creation of offices in the ports, together with clubs close to the frontiers, the organization of solidarity campaigns to oppose any imperialist intervention in these countries, the efficient organization of work among the proletarians that had emigrated from the colonial countries, and the denunciation of manifestations of white chauvinism, and unremitting struggle against them.[10]

It seems that in the case of El Salvador many of these tasks were undertaken not by the United States communist movement but by that of Mexico. That was possibly due to a variety of reasons, among which must have been language, proximity, the probability that its delegates would be more rapidly accepted by the masses, and the greater possibility of passing unnoticed by the police. Fernández Anaya, who had the appearance of a Salvadorean Indian and even learnt to speak with the characteristic accent of the country, is an example of this.

Assistance at points of entry, though, was provided by the United States Communist party and its organizations. When Agustín Farabundo Martí was deported to the United States, in December 1930, he was met by members of the International Labour Defence Organization, Jorge Mauren, Emma Butler and the Spaniard Juan Vilariño, who gave him their assistance. American Communists also undertook organizational work among the Latin American workers in the United States, particularly through the Anti-Imperialist League.

The resolutions passed by the Congress on Latin America incorporated a concrete programme for the Latin American bourgeois-democratic revolution. That programme included the following points: the confiscation of the land usurped by the great landowners and its redistribution among the peasants, the nationalization of foreign companies, the socialization of estates where there were unions capable of administering them effectively, the nationalization of the banks, and the promotion of industrial development.[12]

At the suggestion of the Salvadorean delegation a resolution was approved that would be of fundamental importance, and have unsuspected consequences. This resolution maintained that in Latin America a communist party that was small but which had prestige and a real hegemony of leadership over the masses could initiate the revolution and then continue the struggle, via the direct seizure of power, and taking into account the objective conditions in each country, until the achievement of final victory. However, Mármol has stated that the Salvadorean delegates did not entirely understand problems of strategy and tactics, but that instead they were acting on the level of slogans for agitation and propaganda that were usual in communist congresses and their resolutions. But Mármol made these speculations many years after the armed insurrection of 1932. At the time it was precisely the content of this resolution that encouraged the Salvadoreans to prepare the insurrection.

It should be pointed out that in the new Executive Bureau of the RILU, named by the Central Council of the organization at this time, Ricardo Martínez was included in the representation of Latin America. Following the Congress, some special conferences were held, among them the International Workers' Conference, the International Youth Conference, and that of the Labour Unions of Latin America.[13]

The latter was attended by the delegates from El Salvador, together with those of fifteen other countries. That Conference was thought to be as successful as that of Montevideo the previous year, and the delegates believed it would give a great impulse to the Latin American Union Confederation.

The Conference had two sessions. In the first of these the problems of organization in the rural areas were the sole subject for discussion. An argument arose over whether it would be beneficial for the revolution if the tenant farmers and the small independent peasant farmers were allowed to join agricultural unions. The proposition that eventually won was that which limited the agricultural unions exclusively to wage labour. This pleased the Salvadoreans, who, due to the large number of agricultural day labourers in the country, and the relatively small number of independent peasants, had already followed this criteria in their own rural organizations. It was agreed that the unions, both in the cities and in the countryside, should be solidly composed of the working class.

In the second session some of the questions debated were the character of the revolution in the Latin American countries, legal and illegal forms of organization, and the different methods of struggle. Manuilski gave an extense talk to the delegates on these topics. All were agreed in that the type of revolution that should be put into practice in Latin America was the bourgeois-democratic revolution, with the content that has already been indicated.

Before returning to El Salvador, Mármol requested four grants to enable members of the Communist Party of El Salvador to study in the USSR. His request was answered favourably, but only two of these grants were made use of, due to the political situation that existed on his return to the country. Nevertheless, two members of the Communist Youth, Aquilino Martínez and José Centeno, travelled to the Soviet Union for this purpose. Neither of them, though, rejoined the Salvadorean revolutionary movement. The former was arrested in Berlin on his return journey and submitted to intense torture by the Nazi police, until he went insane. When he was deported to El Salvador the government placed him in an asylum. Centeno completed his studies in 1934, and due to the difficult conditions that existed in El Salvador at that time took up residence in Cuba, nothing more having been heard of him.[14]

On their return from Moscow the Salvadorean delegates passed through Paris, where they had a meeting with Gustavo Machado, who was living in the city studying for a doctorate in medicine. They obtained money for their return from the representative of the International in Paris at the time, Gustave Herclet. On their arrival on Central America, the Salvadoreans gave an account of the resolutions of the Congress to the members of the weak Guatemalan communist group, as their own delegates had still not returned. They stayed in Guatemala for a month, in close contact with the few communists in the country, since they could not travel immediately to El Salvador as an order had been issued for their arrest. Mármol returned to El Salvador on 30 December 1930, and Ramírez shortly before – one year before the insurrection, which would be launched on 22 January 1932.

The new General Secretary of the Salvadorean Communist Party was a baker, Narciso Ruiz. Martí was not a member of the Central Committee but worked very closely with it, in his position as representative of International Red Aid. So too did the intellectuals Alfonso Luna, Mario Zapata, Moisés Castro Morales and Max Ricardo Cuenca.

The leadership decided that Mármol should inform the mass base of the Party of his experiences in the Soviet Union, for which purpose he wrote an extensive report, that was lost in 1932, but which he had previously read in a number of public meetings, some of them legal and others held in secret, in Ilopango, Santa Tecla, Ahuachapán and elsewhere.

Mármol soon had to go into hiding completely, as the police were searching for him intensely,[15] as they were for other leaders of the CPES. The social and political situation was worsening more every day. There was hunger in the fields and the workers were already on the point of eruption.

Major R. Harris, United States Military Attaché for Central America, visited El Salvador at this time and his observations are highly eloquent. He explains that he was surprised to see that in the streets of El Salvador there were only luxury cars, such as Packards and Pierce Arrows, which belonged to a nucleus of thirty or forty families who were the owners of virtually the entire country, and lived in regal splendour, with a great many servants. 'There is practically no middle class between the very rich and the very poor,' he pointed out, 'of the rest of the population it may be said that they have nothing.' He compared El Salvador at that time with pre-revolutionary France and Czarist Russia, and concluded that the situation was ripe for a communist offensive. According to him, the communists had already discovered this, since on 1 December 1931 there was 3 000 pounds in weight of communist literature in the El Salvador Post Office which had originated in New York, and which had been seized in the preceding months. In conclusion, he made a prophecy: that a socialist or communist revolution in El Salvador could be delayed for some years, perhaps ten or twenty, but that when it did occur it would be a bloody conflict.[16] Nevertheless, the confrontation was soon to follow, and the large numbers who were injured or imprisoned due to official repression were given assistance by the Salvadorean Section of International Red Aid, which had been founded on the same day as the Communist Party of El Salvador, for internal defence and 'as a means of responding to international obligations'.[17]

INTERNATIONAL RED AID: THE OTHER FACE OF THE COMINTERN

International Red Aid was an organization that had been founded on 12 August 1921 to assist the population in the Russian famine of that year, and provide relief for the forty million people that were threatened by hunger.[18] It soon broadened its field of action, and in the Fifth Congress of the Communist International it was defined as a 'neutral' organization, that sought to sustain revolutionary militants and their families materially, morally and through the giving of legal assistance, and was one of the most important instruments of the united front. Communist parties were advised to create branches and sections of International Red Aid in each country, and to support them and give them special attention in propaganda. It was decided in this Congress to proclaim 18 March, the anniversary of the Paris Commune, to be International Red Aid Day.[19] It was repeatedly emphasized that Red Aid was a neutral organization, which united large masses of workers, peasants and white-collar workers, without distinction of party, bringing together all those who suffered the exploitation of capitalism and national oppression and who were struggling for the victory of labour over capital.[20]

In the Fifth Plenum of the International it was declared that Red Aid was the most practical means of making a reality of the slogan 'Workers of the World, Unite', and also the most practical way to advance the political education of working people.[21]

Of particular interest is the resolution on Red Aid that was adopted in the Second Plenum of the International Peasant Council, in 1925, which called for the conversion of International Red Aid into a school for the preparatory education of peasants in the spirit of international revolutionary solidarity. The Council committed itself to attracting the millions of peasants in the capitalist countries and the colonies to Red

Aid, and to the creation of peasant and Red Aid organizations in every region.[22] Organizationally the national sections of Red Aid, like those of the Red International of Labour Unions, were directly subordinate to the Executive Committee of the International, as had been made clear in the Sixth Congress.[23]

When Mármol and Modesto Ramírez attended the V Congress of the RILU a conference was held for the delegates on the subject of International Red Aid. In the Plenum of the Congress itself the Soviet representative Stassova had referred to Red Aid, and had underlined that it was not a charitable institution but one whose purpose was international revolutionary education. The role of International Red Aid, she explained, was to assist the victims of the bourgeois law and white terror, and in the case of strikes to give help and support to those who had suffered any kind of harm due to political activities, such as arrest or injury.[24] The Cuban delegate Vinagel also intervened to argue that the Executive Committee should give particular attention to the Caribbean Secretariat of Red Aid, so that it could develop a productive level of activity in the countries of Central America and the West Indies.[25]

It was precisely at this time that Agustín Farabundo Martí was named as representative of the Caribbean Secretariat of International Red Aid in El Salvador. As has been shown, the mass of peasants in the country were already in motion, and repression was intensifying, and this appointment was a response that pointed not only to events that were then taking place but also to what was ever more imminent: an insurrection.

Those in charge of Red Aid in El Salvador were José Ismael Hernández, a shoemaker, and Balbino Marroquín, a bricklayer. The organization distributed international aid and solidarity within the country, together with that given by the Salvadorean people for those who suffered due to the repression. The Caribbean Secretariat, based in New York, sent a letter to the Salvadorean Section on 14 October 1930, signed by Jorge A. Vivó[26] and addressed to Octavio Regueira, one of the pseudonyms of Farabundo Martí,[27] in which it enquired about the costs of organization, propaganda and prisoners' aid, in order that it could send them a monthly subsidy. In another letter of 26 February 1931, the Caribbean Secretariat informed the Executive Committee of Red Aid in El Salvador that it had received a message, presumably from the headquarters of International Red Aid in Moscow, advising them that from January of that year the Salvadorean Section would be sent the sum of fifty dollars each month. The letter was signed by

R. Gómez.[28] Some writers have used this document to minimize the links between the Salvadoreans and International Red Aid, since, as the subsidy was small, they deny that the connection can have been of any importance. Nevertheless, independently of the amount of money that was declared, what is certain is that there was constant communication between the Salvadorean Section and the Secretariat, through Martí. This is what is really important, leaving aside the possibility that the aid supplied may have been greater than that which was actually recognized.

The Statutes of the Salvadorean Section of International Red Aid had been drawn up in May 1930, with the following slogans as a statement of principle: 'The defence of the victims in the irreconcilable struggle of the classes and the anti-imperialist movement; in defence of the social revolution, any fighter who succumbs does so for the good of all. For the victims of reaction and imperialism!'[29]

In these statutes a very revealing calendar of special events was established. It read as follows: a week dedicated to Julio Antonio Mella, Lenin and Rosa Luxemburg, from 10–21 January; 18 March, the anniversary of the Paris Commune; 1 May, a day of action against capitalism, white terror and fascism; 4 May, the Anniversary of the beginning of the struggle against the US Marines in Nicaragua; 1 August, the International Red Day of Action against War, which was to be prepared at least two weeks in advance; 23 August, the anniversary of the murder of Sacco and Vanzetti, the day of anti-imperialist action, and against white terror and fascism, throughout the American continent; 21 September, the anniversary of the foundation of the FRTS; and the 7 November, anniversary of the October Revolution.[30]

It was on the occasion of the celebration of the International Day of Action against War, on 1 August 1930, that the repressive decrees of Romero Bosque were published, and hundreds of demonstrators were imprisoned. Red Aid immediatly went into action, defending those arrested and organizing solidarity campaigns. As a result of this activity, Martí was himself arrested several times and was deported to the United States on 20 December 1930. On his return, in February 1931, the situation had deteriorated still further. Landowners set fire to the fields of the small and medium-sized peasants, let their stock loose in the maize plots of the tenant farmers and share croppers, and laid off their day labourers en masse. A climate of terror existed, and the bodies of dead peasants were continually being found.[31] At the slightest accusation from a landowner the police inflicted merciless punishments on the peasants. In February, before the return of Martí, a demonstration organized to protest against his expulsion was mown down by the forces of the government, leaving eight dead, fifteen wounded and more than eighty workers under arrest.[32] In this same month President Romero Bosque handed over government to Doctor Arturo Araujo, the victor of the elections of January, and a leading landowner of reformist tendencies. The coffee growing oligarchy did not have confidence in him, and Araujo did not provide them with sufficient guarantees at a time when the crisis, as they saw it, demanded a much firmer hand. However, the Minister of War was Maximiliano Hernández Martínez, whose inflexibility in confronting popular movements was more to the liking and style of the Salvadorean dominant elite.

The local section of Red Aid formed the Liga Pro-Luchadores Perseguidos, the Secretary of Finances of which was Rafael Bondanza, one of the closest associates of Agustín Farabundo Martí, who would also play an important part in the insurrection of 1932.[33] The Liga was something of a sub-section of Red Aid, and its actions were seen as part of the work of the latter.

The fact that Farabundo Martí was the representative of International Red Aid, while other members of the Salvadorean Communist Party held the executive posts in the local branch of the organization, encouraged total confusion between the CPES and the Salvadorean Section of Red Aid. Because of this confusion, which the International believed could reduce the radius of action of Red Aid, the Caribbean Secretariat felt obliged to issue a circular to clarify the non-communist character of International Red Aid, the role of which, it said, was to be an instrument for aiding the victims of fascist and imperialist reaction, bringing together all workers, both in the cities and the countryside, the small peasant proprietors who found themselves forced to work for the big landowners in order to live, the anti-imperialist students and intellectuals, etc., so that, therefore, it was necessary not to confuse Red Aid with 'the Communist Party of El Salvador, a Section of the Communist International'.[34] Shortly afterwards, the March 1931 edition of the newspaper *Opinión Estudiantil,* published by Salvadorean university students, carried a special supplement explaining what International Red Aid was, and including an application form for membership. It began by stating clearly that Red Aid should not be confused either with the Communist Party or with the Anti-Imperialist League, though it admitted that 'the greater part of the public, through ignorance' believed that International Red Aid was the same thing as the Communist Party. It went on to say that 'since imperialist oppression demands from semi-colonial governments, such as that of El Salvador, a brutal repression against those workers who attempt to liberate themselves, International Red Aid takes charge of defending those who are imprisoned, persecuted or driven to exile, the victims of such servile acts'. It also stressed that a number of highly renowned lawyers, themselves members of a variety of political parties, had joined in the work of Red Aid and 'lent their services for the defence of those imprisoned as victims of imperialist oppression'.[35]

This intended clarification, however, was of no great relevance at the time. The contradictions in the country were sufficiently acute for this distinction (valid at times of less class differentiation and when the tasks being faced were of a different order) no longer to have much meaning in the case of such a head-on collision of social classes as that which was developing in El Salvador.

Martí periodically informed the Caribbean Secretariat of his work. He wrote one such report just after his return to the country in February 1931, following the election of Araujo, providing a copy for the FRTS. In it he recounted what had happened since his deportation, and declared that the activities of the Salvadorean Section of Red Aid were committed to a struggle against both the outgoing 'agent of yankee imperialism', Pío Romero Bosque, and the incoming Arturo Araujo. The mass organization of workers and peasants, he went on, would continue fighting to unmask Araujist, labourite and Masferrerian demagogy.

This reference to the philosopher Alberto Masferrer may be explained by the support that the latter gave to the regime of Araujo. Masferrer, whom the landowning bourgeoisie considered little less than a Communist, propounded an ideology that he had named 'minimum vitalism', and which was based on the hope that, without the need for social conflict, the rich would divest themselves of that which they did not need, to give it to the poor, while they, for their part, would be content with the minimum needed to live. He was a member of the APRA, though he sometimes concealed his relations with this party to avoid conflicts with the Government.[37]

THE REVOLUTIONARY UPSURGE AND THE COUP D'ÉTAT OF GENERAL HERNÁNDEZ MARTÍNEZ

In early 1931 a meeting was held by the workers' union on the Asuchillo estate, in the Department of La Libertad, to discuss the problems caused by the economic crisis. In response to a call from the local landowner the National Guard went to the site and fired on the rally, leaving several dead. Martí came out of hiding, where he had been since last returning to the country, and went for a meeting with the President. However, not only was no agreement reached but instead there was rather more of a confrontation, the result of which was that Martí was sent to prison, where he declared himself on hunger strike for twenty-seven days, after which he was finally released.[38]

On 20 March 1931, following directives from the Latin American Union Confederation, the Regional Federation organized a demonstration for Unemployed Workers' Day in La Libertad Park in San Salvador. The slogans that were shouted were 'bread and work', and social insurance for the unemployed, to be paid for by the State and the employers. The demonstration was prevented from proceeding by the Guard, who arrested a large number of the participants. The National Police again arrested Martí, and put him on trial before a civil court, accused of being a communist agitator and the principal instigator and organizer of the communist demonstration hindered by the Guard. The following month, on the 13th, he was released though only for a short time; he would soon once again be in prison.[39]

On 17 May there was a mass rally in Sonsonate in support of Martí, who had begun a second hunger strike. Cavalry from Santa Ana and troops from the Registry in Sonsonate intervened, causing twelve deaths and leaving dozens of people seriously wounded or beaten, in addition to making a great many arrests.[40]

It was following these arrests that it began to be suggested among the mass of ordinary workers and peasants that it was necessary to take part in the elections of the municipalities and the Chamber of Deputies, which were to be held at the end of that year. These sections of the people still had hopes of the electoral system, since the achievement of power in the institutions of local government could ostensibly provide complete control over the different localities, including the local Municipal Police forces, court officials, and so on.

The response of the Salvadorean Communist Party to this was contained, initially, in a resolution passed by the Central Committee that prohibited the Party's militants from making any statement in favour of the elections, and reminded the masses that what they were engaged in was an economic struggle, and should not be made 'political'. The Regional Federation, the Communist Youth and the Communist Party itself, all dedicated themselves to attempts to calm the workers, in an effort to dissuade them. However, they were unsuccessful in convincing the great mass of the population that they should not take part, and in October the CPES agreed to participate in the elections of December, with the object of making known the programme of the Party and taking advantage of the occasion to accelerate the work of the organization. This agreement to participate was accompanied by another resolution: that to prepare simultaneously a national strike of coffee-estate workers for higher wages. With the aid of the imminent electoral campaign, the Party would seek to convert it into a mass political strike that would, it was hoped, be supported by workers in other sectors of the economy. The whole of the discussions that took place within the Central Committee on the elections and the strike were reported to the Caribbean Bureau of the Communist International, but they were never sent any reaction on the subject.[41]

A further meeting of the Committee was called to reconsider these accords, at the request of the cabinetmaker Carlos Castillo. He, with good reason, considered that the Party was not in sufficient condition to lead the people in an insurrection intended to take power, and believed, correctly, that the results of the elections (which would undoubtedly be obtained fraudulently) would be used by the oligarchy to prevent the victory of the CPES, and would immediately lead to violence. He cited the case of Ahuachapán, where the population had already prepared a plan to assault the local police barracks if they were denied victory by fraud. However, in spite of the contrary opinions of Castillo, and the declarations of Miguel Mármol to the same effect, the decision to participate in the elections was confirmed.[42]

The entire structure of the Party and its secondary organizations was immediately dedicated to the work of intensive agitation and propaganda with the aim of achieving the highest vote possible. The base organizations of the Party, which consisted of local committees made up of differing numbers of people, normally varying between eight and twenty but capable of growing without any limitation, were subordinate to a central body in each Department and to the national leadership. The CPES did not function on the basis of the Leninist structure of cells, but instead through local committees, which were better adapted to the conditions and needs of its rapid and massive growth. It is clear, in addition, that this also reflected the nature of the Party, the majority of which, as we have seen, was composed of craft workers and peasants.[43]

The fact that it was organized on a basis of broad committees and not the Leninist cell structure partly indicates what was a decisive element in the political and organizational contradictions of the Salvadorean Communist Party. On the one hand, its declaration that it was the local Section of the Communist International, a Marxist–Leninist organization and a party of the working class, gave it a well-defined formal identity as a class entity: the political revolutionary vanguard of the Salvadorean working class. On the other, the following elements modified that formal condition: its peasant–artisan composition and its broadly based committees that were susceptible to being indefinitely extended in each locality; and the social and political situation, in which no other real form of participation in the political system existed. The latter, in such circumstances, was converted simply in an aim and aspiration for the future, and the organization was transformed into a multi-class mass party, overwhelmed by events, and in the difficult situation of trying to promote a radical social transformation, which included the creation of a Soviet system and the utilization of Marxist–Leninist vocabulary and international directives, in the midst of a process that did not contain the real conditions necessary to propose such goals.

In November, the Central Committee of the CPES received news of the possibility of a coup d'état, to be led by the Minister of War, Maximiliano Hernández Martínez.[44] Some militants proposed that they should anticipate the coup by bringing out the masses in a nation-wide insurrection, since it appeared evident that the rise to power of Hernández Martínez, who was directly responsible for the recent massacres, would signify a hardening in the apparatus of the State. Farabundo Martí, however, opposed this, saying that the CPES had very few real possibilities of preventing the coup, and that a national insurrection was too high a price to pay to avoid the installation of a dictatorial government. According to Mármol, Martí cited Lenin, and maintained that the Salvadorean Army was still not sufficiently discredited in the eyes of the people, although, he believed, the landowner-politicians like Araujo already had lost their prestige. His opinion was that, instead of confronting the coup d'état head-on, what the Party had to do was protect its organizations, ensure the preservation of its influence over the masses in the new circumstances and build up its strength.[45] On the night when this was being discussed, the Central Committee also heard that 900 peasants had surrounded the police barracks in Ahuachapán, prepared to put an end to the arbitrary treatment they suffered from the military. The communists managed to pacify the peasants momentarily, but eight days later another 700 peasants laid siege to the police headquarters of the same district. Throughout the region, a great many people were already virtually in arms well before the election.

The Communist Party had made an intense effort to gain sympathizers in some sections of the officer corps of the Army, as well as among lower ranks in the barracks of El Salvador – corporals, sergeants or ordinary soldiers – and some of these contacts communicated to the CPES that the government's plan to permit the holding of elections, and allow the participation of the Communist Party, was basically a military plan through which it was hoped to eliminate the Party's leaders and militants. It should be pointed out that in order to vote, it was necessary to inscribe one's name and that of the party to which one belonged in a register held in the local Municipality, which gave the authorities the material for potentially wide-ranging control over political groupings.[44]

On 2 December Hernández Martínez's coup took place, but despite this, the elections were not suspended. The communists continued their pre-electoral work with even greater enthusiasm, opening local halls in Ahuachapán and Sonsonate, and, according to Miguel Mármol, in the rural areas of these latter two Departments the Party's militants moved about as if the estates and plantations already belonged to the people, so great was the mass support they enjoyed.[47] Militants took part in public meetings at which the speakers were intellectuals and leaders of the Party such as Alfonso Luna, Mario Zapata, Farabundo Martí and others. The number of copies printed of the Party's newspaper, *Estrella Roja*, also multiplied. It is logical to suppose that, for the ultra-conservative landowners, all this activity must have seemed like an open declaration of war, in itself enough to justify their barbarous repression, to which the coup of Hernández Martínez was only the preamble.

The municipal elections were to be held on 5 January, and those for the Chamber of Deputies the following day. On election day, while the candidates of the landowners gave away drinks and tamales, the communists sang at the top of their voice 'The Red Flag', 'Red Cavalry' and the 'Internationale'. The Army, for its part, placed machine-gun nests in all vantage points, ready to prevent any kind of disorder. Nevertheless, the elections went off calmly, though the government did suspend them in several villages where the CPES was strong. On 6 January the elections for Deputies were held, and from that morning there was already clear evidence of the size of the support for the communists. The government suspended voting, and although results had been published in *La Prensa* that gave the victory to the CPES in the Department of El Salvador, the authorities kept silent until 21 January, when the official government gazette published a list of the successful candidates who, of course, were not those of the Communist Party.

In Ahuachapán, the election was suspended when it was seen that the queue of peasants waiting to vote for the communist candidates amounted to some five thousand people. The National Guard surrounded and threatened them, forcing the peasants to withdraw and go back to their work. However, they then agreed to begin a general strike in protest. The centre of the strike was the 'La Montañita' estate, whose owners called upon the Guard to intervene. They did so, and shot dead the peasant leader Alberto Gualán, a leading militant of the Communist Youth who was much liked among the local people, and wounded several others, including women and children. The strikers replied in turn, and fourteen National Guards were killed. The landowners were alarmed and called for more reinforcements, and the repression rapidly gained force in the whole of the western part the country, principally in Santa Ana, Ahuachapán and Sonsonate. In an attempt to halt this repression the communists requested an audience, in the name of their Central Committee, with General Hernández Martínez. This request was conceded; however, it was the Minister of Defence who received them and told them that nothing could be done.

After this failed visit to the President, on 7 January 1932, the Central Committee of the CPES met again, and agreed to carry out an armed insurrection on 16 January 1932.[48]

6 The Rebellion of the Flower-Eaters: El Salvador, 1932

THE INSURRECTION OF 1932: THE CATASTROPHE IS PREPARED

After it had been agreed to proceed with an armed insurrection, a decision that was influenced by the fact that the CPES had reason to believe that, if it did not assume leadership, the masses would launch themselves into a revolt spontaneously, the Central Committee was charged with the military preparation of the rising. Its members undertook, with a space of scarcely eight days before them, to carry out the essential tasks of strengthening their contacts within the Army, acquiring arms and other necessary material, organizing communications, and incorporating other social sectors into the struggle.

The country was divided into zones, and each member of the Central Committee was given responsibility for one of them. The Committee also proceeded to appoint the 'Red Commandants', who would be the leaders of the commissions that would operate at the level of sub-zones, work-places, and so on. It was agreed that, once the insurrection had been initiated, the Red Commandants would fulfil the role of a Captain at the head of his batallion, while the subcommissions would, in addition, be charged with the work of organizing within the Army, together with such tasks as searching for arms, carrying out sabotage, and controlling the railways and other means of transport.

With regard to the Party's contacts with the military, it was taken for granted that the entire garrisons of Sonsonate and Ahuachapán would join the insurrection, and also that a good many troops from that of Santa Tecla, together with two companies of cavalry, some soldiers from the Regiment of Artillery and the garrison of the air base at Ilopango, would be equally sympathetic. They also expected to receive the support of two companies of soldiers from the Regiment of San Miguel, in the east of the country, under whose orders would be placed seven hundred men whom the CPES had been organizing for some time as a popular militia. These contacts with groups of officers in the different Army posts were carried on personally by Farabundo Martí.[1]

It was decided that the leading elements among the petit-bourgeois intellectuals, with whom Martí also maintained contact, would only be called upon at the moment of constituting a government.

These plans were moving forward, when it was proposed to postpone the rising until 19 January, in order to see whether the First Regiment of Infantry could be incorporated into the movement. This proposal had the support of Martí, who was the most prestigious figure of within the CPES and its real General Secretary; hence it was approved. Later there was a further postponement, until 22 January. However, with each day that passed the government acquired more information, and on this basis decided to break up the insurrection, commencing by attempting to arrest its leaders. On 18 January[2] Martí and the students Alfonso Luna and Mario Zapata were captured in a hiding place in San Salvador. On hearing this news, the Plenum of the Central Committee met again and discussed the possibility of suspending the insurrection, since many leading militants were in prison, and the government had declared a State of Siege in the whole of the central area of the country.[3] They agreed, nevertheless, to continue with the rising, because the workers were already practically in arms in many parts of the country.

According to Mármol, until the last moment the CPES treated the insurrection simply as a mass political movement, and did not draw up any specific military plans, failing to appreciate the vital importance of these in such circumstances.

They proceeded as if a national uprising was a more advanced form of union work, or of the mass action of the Party. In many places, the Army provoked the people into action outside of the plans prepared by the CPES, and open repression had already intensified even before 22 January.[4]

The CPES had decided to proceed with the insurrection with the object of carrying out the bourgeois-democratic revolution, for which it had drawn up a programme (undoubtedly very similar to the one already mentioned that was presented at the V Congress of the RILU, attended by Miguel Mármol), certain as they were of finding themselves in a genuinely revolutionary situation.

A Manifesto issued by the Central Committee of the Communist Party of El Salvador, dated 21 January 1932 and addressed to the working classes of the Republic, began by stating that the Communist Party was the leader of the proletariat towards final victory, which could only be achieved with the elimination of hunger, unemployment, and all the other forms of slavery to which the rich and imperialism condemned the working people. It recalled that the Communist Party had carried on a bitter struggle against the government and the great landowners, and analyzed the inhuman conditions in which the agricultural workers and the ordinary soldiers had to live, as well as the killings of workers, children and elderly people that had occurred in Santa Tecla and Sonsonate, Zaragoza and Ahuachapán. Referring to the election of Municipalities and Deputies, it declared that the action of the government and the rich in ignoring the election result in spite of the fact that the Communist Party was the largest and most disciplined grouping in the country, had demonstrated that until the rich fell from power by force the workers would always continue to be slaves. In view of this, the Central Committee of the Communist Party, representing the opinion of all the workers of the Republic, trusting in the moral and material support of the workers of the whole world, and under the direction of the Communist International, ordered all workers and peasants to arm themselves, constitute the headquarters of the Red Army in El Salvador and continue the general uprising of the workers until the formation of a government of workers, peasants and soldiers.[5] The echoes of the resolutions in conferences and congresses, of the subjectivism and voluntarism of the 'international Lozovskys', joined with the terrible situation of the Salvadorean masses to precipitate a tragedy that is only understandable within the retrograde and brutal structure of power in El Salvador.

The members of the CPES proposed to carry out the directives of the Communist International for Latin America, bringing forth the bourgeois-democratic revolution in El Salvador, but under the direction of the Communist Party, self-defined as the vanguard of the proletariat, by means of the immediate constitution of a Red Army, the capturing of the arms held by the forces of the government, and the installation of soviets of peasants, workers and soldiers.

The masses who took part in the revolt were very large in number, but they did so in disastrous conditions for combat, since the majority had scarcely a machete as their only armament, and lacked all military experience.

In spite of their marked military and technical inferiority, the dismemberment of the leadership of the CPES and the preparedness of the government, which was ready to suppress the insurrection even before it had begun,[6] the courage and spirit of the Salvadorean people, who, since they owned nothing, had nothing to lose but their lives, enabled the rebels to gain short-lived victories in the western part of the country. In Juayúa, a town of some 3000 inhabitants, situated in a valley between the Izalco volcanoe and the mountain Apaneca, and surrounded by coffee plantations established as has been described, on old Indian communal lands, the revolutionary movement was very strong. The principal leader in the locality was the Secretary of Finances of the local section of the FRTS, Francisco Sánchez, a poor peasant, but who was recognized as the chief of the town and enjoyed great respect among the other peasants of the community. He had been arrested in December, and again on the day of the municipal elections, but had later been released. The insurrection broke out on the night of 22 January, as planned, although the news that a plan existed to carry out an uprising on that date had even appeared in newspapers on 21 January. The great mass of peasants, the majority of them illiterate, did not have access to this means of communication, and therefore could not have realised that the government was fully aware of what they were doing.

On 22 January Alberto Marín, delegate of the Departmental Executive Committee of the Red Army in Juayúa, issued a circular to 'all revolutionary class organizations', in which he declared that their struggle was one of life and death, and that all sections and companies should be duly organized,with their respective Red Commandants. The rising, he announced, would be launched at midnight that night, with simultaneous attacks on the police post and the town hall.[7]

The peasants did indeed take the police barracks, cheering for Red Aid and Farabundo Martí,[8] on the night of 22 January; they declared the constitution of a soviet government, and for three days the red flag flew over the town next to that of El Salvador. During the first days the rebels believed that the operation had been successful in the whole country. At half past six on the morning of the second day an aeroplane flew over Juayúa, joyfully received by the people in the town, who thought that the air force was controlled by the CPES. The bomb that was thrown down into the crowd, however, sowed the first doubts of the likelihood of total victory, and plans began to be made for the defence of the town.

In Tacuba, an assault was made on the barracks of the National Guard under the command of Abel Cuenca, the brother of Max Cuenca (an important figure in the Central Committee of the CPES), and the soviet was installed that would resist the forces of the government the longest. As the insurrection was progressively overrun in other towns and villages, the peasants withdrew to Tacuba, with the result that eventually five thousand people were concentrated there.

In Tacuba there was more time to form the soviet government, and it was Abel Cuenca, who was barely twenty years old, who took charge. The Tacuba soviet obliged the landowners to make a number of concessions to the rebels in respect of the redistribution of land and wealth to the peasants, but it also had to confront, in addition to other political and military problems, the problem of having to feed five thousand extra people, for which it was evidently not prepared. Afterwards, following the defeat of the movement, the landowners took revenge on the Cuenca family, killing the elderly father and several others, including a younger brother.[9]

In Izalco and Nahuizalco, the communists could count on the valuable support of the chiefs Feliciano Ama and Felipe Neri, whose prestige among the population was indisputable.[10] The authority of the chief or cacique was not officially recognized by the government, but instead functioned in a de facto manner that was on the margins of existing legal institutions, but which had very strong foundations in Indian traditions. Of all the caciques the most important and the most widely recognized was that of Izalco. In 1932, Feliciano Ama was also the leader of the most powerful of the local religious brotherhoods, that of the Holy Spirit, an association whose activities mixed together Catholic ritual and indigenous ceremonies, and which had great influence in the community. Ama had joined the Communist Party determined to end the existing order in El Salvador. The Regalado family, one of the richest coffee-growing families in the country, had dispossessed him of his land and had him beaten and hung up by his thumbs. In his community, moreover, the memory of the seizure of the communal lands was still very fresh.[11] Ama had initially supported Dr Alberto Gómez Zárate, the defeated candidate in the election that had been won by Araujo. However, when Gómez Zárate wrote to him in the middle of 1931, warning him that he should not work with the communists, Ama replied that he no longer wished to have any correspondence with an arrogant and exploiting bourgeois.[12]

A contingent of two thousand peasants, led by Feliciano Ama and other communist leaders, took the town of Izalco and held it for three days and nights, installing a local soviet. After then, however, the air force bombed the town and the government regained control, in the same way that it would in other towns and villages. Feliciano Ama was publicly hanged, his death being witnessed by the children from the local school, who were taken there to see it so that they 'should not forget what happens to communists who dare to raise themselves up against their employers and the established authorities', as an official statement declared.[13]

Nahuizalco was also taken by a group of some five hundred insurgents, who, to the cry of 'Long live Red Aid', dominated the town for a time, under the command of the cacique Felipe Neri and the national leaders of the CPES Tomás González and Juan Isidro Pérez.

The rebels also entered Colón, shouting 'Long Live the Soviet Republic', but for an even shorter period of time. The same occurred in Ataco, Salcoatitlán, Turín and San Julián.

Neither Santa Tecla or Ahuachapán could be taken. And they only partially entered in Sonsonate.

THE CRIMINAL REPRESSION OF THE 'MACHINE-GUN PHILOSOPHER'

The government crushed the rebellion with the full force of the Army and the air force. The sympathizers within the Army on whom the organizers of the insurrection had counted had been detected and eliminated mercilessly. Once the revolt had been stamped out, the authorities went on to undertake the most bloody repression carried out in Central America in this century. While the numbers of deaths caused by the rebels during the rising scarcely reached a hundred,[14] estimates of the number of peasants killed (the majority of them after the revolt had been defeated) vary between twenty and thirty thousand.[15] In the first week the troops killed 4800 peasants, this being the figure that was reported by Colonel José Tomás Calderón[16] to the US warship *Rochester* and the Canadian ships sent by the British government, the *Skeena* and the *Vancouver*, which had rapidly taken up position off the Salvadorean coast, ready to intervene in the case of the slightest possibility of a victory for the insurgents. To prevent any disembarkation of foreign marines,[17] Maximiliano Hernández Martínez intensified the repression, giving the United States and Britain[18] proof that he was self-sufficient in the maintenance of internal order. The international scandal that was caused by the message from Colonel José Tomás Calderón obliged the latter to attempt a rectification, pointing out that, though he had referred to 'bolsheviks [that had been] liquidated', this did not necessarily mean that they had been killed. The real figures, however, were even higher.

Hernández Martínez, like Sandino, declared himself to be a theosophist, but whereas the latter had used his beliefs to justify his struggle for revolution and national liberation, Hernández Martínez used his to justify his terrible methods of repression, which led him to be given the nickname of the 'machine-gun philosopher' (*filósofo ametrallador*). Referring to the massacre of 1932, this theosophist calmly explained that this was a matter of 'souls [that had been] liberated' or 'purified', and said that it was more of a crime to kill an ant, which would not be reborn, than a man, because the latter would be reincarnated.[19]

His criminal personality, given to all kinds of superstitions and excesses, helped, through repression to perpetuate the closed character of the Salvadorean social and political system. He forced the Indians to cease speaking Pipil, because to do so constituted a passport to the prison or the cemetery. He broke up every social organization through which the demands of the Salvadorean population could have been expressed. And he was, in all these actions, the obedient instrument of an absentee and unmerciful ruling class that had been installed in power since the time of the Spanish Conquest. Furthermore, conditions were favourable for carrying out this repression, moreover, in particularly favourable circumstances. International public opinion, and that of Central America in particular, lacked the least information necessary to be able fully to comprehend the real dimensions of the tragedy and so offer a protest against these acts of genocide. Shortly after the bloodshed, the Salvadorean government initiated a public relations offensive in the region, supposedly to make known Salvadorean culture by means of its artistic creations. As one of its cultural ambassadors, the government sent a famous marimba group who played a song called 'The Stammerer', an ironic allusion to the machine-gun, which had been the principal weapon used in the mass extermination of the Salvadorean peasants.[20]

THE HISTORICAL RESPONSIBILITY OF THE INTERNATIONAL: THE REVOLUTION DENIGRATES ITS HEROES

The decision taken by the CPES to carry out an insurrection had good foundations in, and was framed in the light of, the directives of the Communist International. The relative weakness of foreign domination in the country; the recent rise to power of a *de facto* government that still did not enjoy international recognition; the desperation of the popular classes, aggravated by the effects of the world economic crisis; the discontent that existed among the bureaucracy, whose salaries the government had just reduced by 30 per cent; and the hope of finding the support of important elements within the Army, all led the Salvadorean communists to the conclusion that the moment was right for an insurrection. They also anticipated that, if they were successful, and subsequently imperialist intervention occurred, they could look to the support of the repeatedly offered practical and moral solidarity of all the Communist Parties in the world and in particular of the Soviet Union. It was as a result of these considerations that they attempted to bring into reality the slogan of a bourgeois-democratic revolution, led by the proletariat, in alliance with the peasants, and undertook the immediate constitution of soviets as the local organs of the new revolutionary power.

Inexperience, lack of coordination, the leaking of vital information due to the open structure of the Party, the lack of a real military structure and the fact that the rapid and powerful presence of the British and Americans had not been taken into account, conditioned the failure of the insurrection.

The Communist International and its sections, which, if not directing the revolt in an immediate physical sense had undoubtedly had a determining influence on the decisions taken by the small and recently created CPES, threw themselves into a round of intense criticism of the latter Party. This was done at a time when it was completely decimated, its leadership almost entirely liquidated and its principle base of support, the Indian peasants, largely crushed, with the survivors terrorized and scattered.[22]

The communists Penelón, of the Argentinian Communist Party, and Siqueiros, of the Mexican, strongly criticized the CPES. They pointed out that less serious events had prompted American imperialists to invade Nicaragua, and that the United States would not allow twenty-four hours to pass before militarily invading El Salvador if the masses did take power. If this happened, they also stated, the communists would not have the capability to oppose the troops, well-equipped and disciplined, and so in such circumstances the insurrection was an adventure.

La Correspondencia Internacional referred briefly to the existence of the Civic Guard, an organization of paramilitary nature that was formed by the landowners of El Salvador among themselves to assist the Army in its work of repression,[23] but the insurrection as such was not deemed to merit commentary of any kind.

The Latin American Confederation, for its part, published an article in its official newspaper *El Obrero del Caribe,* in which it was stated that the Salvadorean Regional Federation had not linked the insurrection to the struggle for immediate demands, such as the eight-hour day, a minimum wage, social insurance, and so on, which would have broadened the basis of the struggle, reinforcing the proletarian sector in the countryside by forming a common front with the poor independent peasants, through the demands for the confiscation and redistribution of the land, and the other directives of the 'anti-imperialist revolution'. What this expressed was a complete ignorance of the character and reality of the conflicts faced in El Salvador[24] on the part of the critics of the insurrection, and was a poor way of eluding their own political responsibility for the events.

In the organ of the Caribbean Bureau, *El Comunista,* O. Rodríguez attempted (in a more respectful though maybe too optimistic a manner) a political analysis of the Salvadorean insurrection. He stated that the insurrection had been a mass movement of workers and agricultural labourers against the unbearable conditions caused by the crisis, and against the intolerable oppression from the landowners and the capitalists, allied to foreign capital. He went on to say that the insurrection had revealed an accumulation of revolutionary energy and a readiness for the struggle among the mass of workers and peasants, under the banner of the Communist Party, and a growing revolutionary upsurge. He added:

> The workers and peasants of El Salvador have written an imperishable and glorious chapter in the history of the worldwide revolutionary movement, and have proved to the struggling masses that in the next stage, with a stronger Communist Party, and with the more powerful revolutionary unions and peasant leagues that will be created in the course of the daily struggles for the immediate demands of the workers and peasants and for the application of the principles and tactics of Leninism, victory must and will be for the masses.[25]

At no point was any mention made of the objective of the CPES of carrying out the bourgeois democratic revolution, nor of the constitution of soviets. Nor was any indication given of the extent of the subsequent slaughter, which would make it impossible for the Salvadorean revolutionary communist movement to recover until 1956–7, when the Communist Party would once more exist in reality and not simply on paper.

The Red International of Labour Unions, for its part, reprinted the commentaries of the Latin American Union Confederation and the Caribbean Bureau and added its own lofty criticisms of the Salvadorean movement. After applauding the increasing influence of the red unions in El Salvador, it stated that the influence of the revolutionary organizations would have been more substantial if they had been less leftist, less sectarian in their daily struggles, if they had known how to formulate better the immediate demands of the workers and agricultural labourers, and if they had remembered that the revolutionary struggle in El Salvador, as in other countries of Latin America, should always have as its first stage not the proletarian revolution, but the anti-imperialist agrarian revolution.

The version of the insurrection given by the various communist bodies was substantially at variance with reality. It was said that it had been carried out because the communists had found themselves forced to build up armed resistance against a massacre of communists that was being prepared by General Hernández Martínez. It was also stated that the insurrection had been a success until Hernández Martínez had received the aid of the Mexican and British navies, as half of the Army of El Salvador had refused to fight against the workers and peasants.[26]

The irresponsibility of the analyses made by the European communist leaders was exposed precisely by L. Deval, the author of the criticisms of the Salvadorean movement published by the RILU. After having explained that the nature of the revolution in Latin America was agrarian and anti-imperialist, this same L. Deval claimed, in an article dedicated to analyzing the attempt made in Chile to create soviets of peasants, workers and soldiers, that these events in Chile, which took place five months after the insurrection in El Salvador, showed that the working class of the Latin American continent was beginning seriously to emancipate itself from the influence of its class enemies and to struggle for the early triumph of the revolution; and that the experience of the Chilean soviets, in particular, would undoubtedly contribute to their future re-constitution within the revolutionary movement in Chile.[27]

He added that the Chilean comrades had been perfectly correct in launching the directive to create soviets, and putting it into practice in a number of localities, as this signified that they had understood that the internal conflict in the camp of the latifundist bourgeoisie, and the powerful movement of the masses, created the opportunity for a rapid intensification of the revolutionary crisis and its transformation into a revolution, provided that they first organize these masses fully in the struggle for power, in order to be able to establish the revolutionary democratic dictatorship of workers and peasants.

He also wrote that the Chileans were correct in dedicating themselves to the creation of soviets, which alone were capable of bringing together the whole of the working masses and preparing them for the struggle for the triumph of the popular anti-imperialist revolution, which only the proletariat, allied with the peasants, could carry out, because the bourgeoisie were no longer capable of doing so. After all these categorical and grandiloquent declarations on the virtue of having created soviets, Deval admits openly that he does not have much information about them, since they were crushed after a brief period of existence, 'principally because they had not managed to gain sufficient influence in the Navy and the Army'.[28]

Hence, the *a posteriori* criticism of the Salvadorean movement, and the avoiding of any reference to the creation of soviets within it, in view of the bloodshed that followed the insurrection, occurred at the same time as praise was given to the soviets formed in the same period in Chile and Cuba,[29] which, in turn, also failed.

Even in 1933, in a joint declaration by the Cuban Communist Party and the Cuban Communist Youth published in *La Correspondencia Internacional* in September of that year, it would still be stated that only a government of workers' and peasants' soviets could liberate Cuba from the yankee imperialist yoke and that of its local agents, the message ending with a 'Viva' for the anti-imperialist agrarian revolution.[30]

The criticisms of the CPES, accusing it of sectarism and ultra-leftism, were made, therefore, after the International itself had put forward, at that precise moment, the slogans of class against class and of the transformation of the bourgeois-democratic revolution into a socialist revolution, through the hegemony of the proletariat in the former, and by means of the revolutionary-democratic dictatorship of the workers and peasants. Defamatory labels were thrown after the Communist International had declared that the theory of the revolution in one country was universally applicable, and that with the aid of the countries where the proletarian dictatorship had already been accomplished, the capitalist stage of development could even be passed over. The Communist International dissociated itself from the CPES after it had proposed as an objective for the whole of Latin America the creation of workers', peasants' and soldiers' councils, and the orientation of the political process of the continent towards the formation of a federation of soviet, worker–peasant and anti-imperialist republics. In consequence, such criticisms only denote the grave confusion and lack of seriousness, theoretical rigour and respect that existed within the Comintern, with regard to its national sections and on the strategy and tactics of the revolution in Latin America. This was directly related to the absence of a clear economic, political and social analysis and understanding of the realities of these countries, which would have made it possible to determine, in concrete terms, the tasks that should be attempted by the local political movements that, due to a variety of historical circumstances, had gained real support among the masses as was the case with the armed insurrection in El Salvador. This insurrection, confused and frustrated, was the first attempt, with mass support, to put into practice the class- and soviet-based strategy and tactics recommended by the International in Central America, on the basis of a peasant rebellion that had its deepest roots in the Indian and colonial past of El Salvador.

After the failed attempt to transform Sandino's national liberation struggle into a social revolution, there followed an attempt by the Communist International to convert an indigenous and peasant insurrection into a soviet revolution. The so-called betrayal by Sandino, which Farabundo Martí personally would deny courageously when before the firing squad that was to execute him, was followed by the revolutionary assault on power in El Salvador.

A repetition of history? The analogy is too evocative for us to resist the temptation of mentioning it: Chiang Kai Shek's betrayal was followed in China by the Commune of Canton. The supposed betrayal by Sandino in Nicaragua was followed by the Salvadorean insurrection of 1932. However, the members of the Chinese Commune were declared by the Communist International, in the face of the criticisms of Trotsky, to be the heroes of the world revolution. The Salvadorean leaders Martí, Luna, Zapata, Feliciano Ama and Felipe Neri, to mention only a few, meanwhile forgotten by Trotsky (then interested only in Europe and China), and representing unwelcome and compromising evidence for the leaders of the International, were given the derogatory label of *macheteros* or 'machete gangs', and were soon forgotten.

The massacre of 1932 placed in suspension the social and political problems of El Salvador, only to make them re-emerge with greater force and virulence fifty years later. For, when today the name of Agustín Farabundo Martí resounds in Salvadorean politics, it is not simply a ghost at large in the smallest country in Central America. It is the spectre of the colonial centuries, of the dispossessed mass of peasants, of outdated political and social systems, and of dominant classes that only continue to exist because the country has not recovered sufficiently to be able to relegate them to a painful historical archive, alongside the phantasmagorical soviet revolution.

Today, once again, a peasant insurrection in El Salvador, now made much more complex by an amazing growth in population, much deeper social differentiation and a crucial necessity to overcome the decayed and exhausted social, political, economic and cultural structures of the country, brings forth the monstrous figures of terror and war.

And once again, also, but this time with much more specific interests of a State and imperial nature, external forces seek to gain advantage amidst the anguish and desperation of the Salvadorean people. It is not only a question of a social conflict with profound historical roots among a brave and spirited people worthy of another destiny, but also the efforts of some to convert this small Central American nation into another arena for the East–West conflict.

The key to understanding the complex Salvadorean situation cannot be found either in the sole analysis of the political and military expansionism of the Soviet Union, nor in the reduction of the question to purely internal problems.

It is necessary to include two elements in this analysis. First, the internal component that manifests itself in obsolete and inhuman structures inherited from the colonial period. And second, the external one, the attempts from outside to turn a national conflict into a profitable propaganda episode in the struggle for world hegemony, that cannot be ignored. More than ever, the need to think for themselves and to provide original ideas, suitable for their specific needs, is one of the most urgent tasks for these peoples.

For Salvadorean experience indicates that in 1932 others provided the ideas and later the recriminations. But it was the people of El Salvador who provided the dead.

7 Costa Rica: An Original Democracy in Central America

COSTA RICA: THE FORMATION OF THE ONLY CENTRAL AMERICAN DEMOCRACY

For the purposes of this study, it will be of interest to highlight not so much the quantitative data on the economy and productive activities of Costa Rica, as the qualitative conditions in which its economic and social life has developed. This will be especially necessary in relation to the other two countries under examination.

The distinctive social and political configuration of Costa Rica, as compared with El Salvador and Nicaragua, is not the result simply of a different intellectual conception on the part of the founding fathers of the Republic, but of a whole body of different historical relations, which have determined a course of evolution that is particular to the isthmus of Central America.

As has been demonstrated by Samuel Stone,[1] in spite of the fact that they all originated from the Spanish *conquistadores*, the specific conditions in each of these countries – first internally, and then externally – brought about an evolution that has decisively influenced the structure and manner of operation of the different national political systems. The latter, in every case based almost by inevitability on the federative constitutional models of the United States,[2] clashed with the hard realities of the social and economic conditions of these peoples, and ended up being adapted, if not in the letter at least in fact, to the real and concrete practice of political life that left behind it declarations and lofty intentions.

The correlation between the factors of land, capital and labour[3] meant that the political system in Costa Rica, where these same elements were scarce, developed differently from that which evolved from the relationship between economic, social and political power in the north, above all in Guatemala and El Salvador.

In saying that there was a scarcity of land, in spite of the fact that Costa Rica is greater in size than El Salvador, this refers to land suitable for producing export crops, and particularly coffee. This crop, which has to be grown at more than 1000 metres above sea level, requires certain conditions that, in the period in which its large-scale cultivation was initiated in Costa Rica, were only found on the central plateau of the country, precisely where the vast majority of the population were concentrated. During colonial times this population had been very widely scattered, and at the end of that period was settled in a very particular system of land distribution, which, despite the attempts made to change the structure of property ownership in 1860–71 by the so-called Coffee Oligarchy, would be maintained, retaining a system of landholding that combined small- and medium-sized property with great landowners farming for profit and export.

From the point of view of the dominant elite the possibilities for expansion were continually being obstructed by the limits imposed by this shortage of land, which only with difficulty permitted the eldest sons of the class to continue in the activities of their fathers and obliged any other sons to resort to other directions such as trade, the weak and meagre financial sector, and the liberal professions, particularly law and medicine. As a result, in Costa Rica this elite found its way into the field of politics, in which it became very directly involved, in contrast to the pattern seen in Guatemala and El Salvador, where political activities were delegated to other hands – and in particular the military – as the elites could not exploit by themselves all possibilities brought about by the abundance of land and capital.

The limitations on the availability of land in Costa Rica were complemented by no less important shortages of capital and labour. This had the effect of moderating social customs, reciprocally binding the large coffee grower to the land and to the peasants, and the latter to him, in an interdependence that was mutual, though different in nature and degree. It thus avoided the danger of absenteeism and created in the coffee growers an awareness of the need to employ more than just economic mechanisms if they were to keep both the labourers and the small and medium proprietors, each of which groups they needed equally in order to work their estates and fulfil the productive capacities of their holdings. The result was a level of paternalism and a complex of social relations in the countryside that were substantially different from those that existed in the rest of Central America.

At the same time, as the heirs of the great coffee producers got involved, in a direct and personal manner, in national politics, there was strong competition between them that meant that the question of precisely to whom political power would be accorded became one of paramount importance in the formation of the State and local authorities. Again in contrast with the rest of Central America, where elections, when they occurred, were held to legitimize, for the benefit of outside opinion, a politico-military authority that had already been constituted, in Costa Rica – in spite of certain flaws that were repeatedly denounced (even after the civil war of 1948, which had as its primary motive the freedom of elections) –the electoral process was *the element through which the public authorities actually were constituted and legitimized.*[5] External recognition came as an added bonus. When this rule was violated at the beginning of the century, with the coup by the Tinoco brothers against the government of Alfredo González Flores, this coincided with the period of the non-recognition policy followed by the US government under Woodrow Wilson, which finally forced the renunciation of the *de facto* government and their replacement, in somewhat murky and unorthodox circumstances, by a 'legitimate' representative. This incident appears to have played a more significant role in the configuration of the Costa Rican electoral system that has up to now been recognized.[6]

At all events, the possibility of choice between the different 'cousins' (*primos*) – all of them descendants of the same original families from the colonial era – meant that the procedures and rules of the political process became the favoured means for settling quarrels over the possession and exercise of State and local power. Hence, it was in this way, against this background in social, economic and family relations, that the historical evolution of the electoral system and the system of parties in Costa Rica took on its distinctive shape. The electoral laws became the systematization of the rules of the political game carried on between the 'cousins', as a civilized solution that avoided bloodshed, in sharp contrast to the rigid transactions between military leaders and 'those who counted' (*los que mandaban*) in the north of the Central American isthmus.

The political differences between candidates coming from the same social strata were not overcome simply through agreements made over dinner in their social clubs, in conversations between the big representatives of the national capital, as has often superficially been suggested. Political reality was, naturally, much more complex and variable than this.

It meant an increasing openness of the system towards the incorporation of new elements coming from other social sectors.

These new actors found themselves invited to join the political arena on behalf of one or other of the cousins. Equally, their support would eventually also be sought not simply by individual candidates but by actual political groupings from among the wealthy classes, whether connected with domestic or foreign capital, or both, and on occasion, too, by the Church.[7]

This meant the configuration of a basis of social support for the various candidates that gave legitimacy to the system. But it also signified the insertion into that political system of the demands and aspirations of the new arrivals. They supported their candidates, but they expected to obtain satisfaction for their own demands as well.

The weakness of the Costa Rican political system lay, as a result, in its very strength. As it extended itself and incorporated more and more new social sectors and more and more new demands, the ruling system gained legitimacy and became firmly rooted in the national consciousness. It also broadened its base, diluted its authority and increased its collective obligations in an ever-growing and disproportionate manner. However, at the same time it remained rooted in an economy that was weak, unbalanced and subject to the shocks and oscillations of not just the world market in coffee, but also the periodic crises in 'First World' economies.

The abolition of property qualifications for the right to take part in elections, whether as a candidate or as a voter, and the introduction instead of the requirement of being able to read and write (together with the establishment of free, compulsory primary education paid for by the State), all of which were measures promoted by sons of the large coffee growers with the idea of thereby ensuring themselves a monopoly of political power, came hand in hand with the universalization of electoral participation and the introduction of the secret ballot. This had the effect of broadening the existing political panorama, under the figure of Ricardo Jiménez and, behind him, the ambivalent figure of the Costa Rican *gamonal* or chief landlord of a district.[8]

This made the system of domination more flexible, the country's political system more dynamic, and the lines of communication between the latter and social and cultural reality clearer and more sophisticated. It thus gave new vigour to a regime that, if not strictly speaking one of political parties, was liberal democratic in terms of control over State bodies, the division of powers, the independence of the judiciary, the effective exercise of individual liberties and a broad, if not unrestricted, freedom of the press, thought and expression. In the long term this facilitated the adaptation of the institutional and political structures of the country to the new challenges that its social and economic progress would impose upon it.

It was in this context in which education constituted a factor of social control as important or more so than that exerted by the armed forces, that the increasing social differentiation would occur. This process developed from the end of the nineteenth century, with the arrival in the country of the banana companies and the attempts at railway construction, and later, in 1931, would lead to the creation of the Communist Party of Costa Rica.

THE STRUCTURE OF PRODUCTION AND SOCIAL ORGANIZATION IN THE 1920s

The Costa Rica of the second and third decades of this century, with a population of scarcely 500 000 in a territory of 51 000 square kilometres, more than double the area of El Salvador, had some similarities with the cases of Nicaragua and El Salvador that have already been examined, in that all were dependent agrarian economies based on monoculture. There were, however, a number of fundamental differences in the Costa Rican case, one of which, as has been shown, was the consolidation at a political level of a juridical and institutional structure of a liberal and democratic nature, built upon a social structure that included a great deal of small and medium-sized property.

Coffee, its principal export product, had linked Costa Rica to the world market since 1844, when four million kilos were already exported annually to Great Britain (a figure which had doubled twelve years later).[10] However, in contrast to the situation that developed in El Salvador, where the cultivation of this crop was the immediate cause for the disappearance of communal property, the virtual liquidation of small property and the formation of a few, enormous *latifundios*, in Costa Rica it served to consolidate the position of small property, and thus shaped the future socio-economic development of the country quite differently from the rest of Central America.[11]

Coffee production was developed on the basis of the existing structure of property, made up mainly of either small or large properties, but with a clear predominance of the former, and thus consolidated a tendency that was already present in the traditional crops such as tobacco and sugar cane.[12] Initially the production and export of coffee remained in local hands, and this made it possible for the expansion of holdings and capital to be oriented not so much towards the simple absorption of more land for production as to the better cultivation and export of the crop. Instead of producers expanding their activities by extending the area of production and cultivation itself, creating great plantations, as in El Salvador, in Costa Rica a different process occurred, giving rise to a coffee-growing middle class, without the characteristics of the Central American *latifundista*.

The distortion of the Costa Rican economy, oriented, as in the other cases studied previously, towards the cultivation of a single crop, also led, however, to the phenomenon typical in such situations of the contraction of other economic activities, and the effects of this one-sided reduction of the productive process and of the tendency towards monoculture revealed themselves in all their crudity. In this process a series of economic activities which supplied the needs of internal consumption disappeared. Already in 1890, 'subsistence crises began to appear in Costa Rica, as a direct consequence of the displacement of the products needed for immediate and indispensable internal consumption by coffee, our only product with a lucrative position in the international market'.[13]

To the economic distortion caused by coffee would later be added that created by banana production, which was developed and controlled by foreign companies. Exports of bananas, initiated in 1883 with 110 000 bunches, reached 1 700 000 bunches by 1896.[14]

All products of primary necessity were imported. Articles of clothing all came either fully ready-made or in a partially made-up state from abroad. Costa Rica had, by virtue of its links with the international coffee trade, been converted into a single-crop economy, dependent mainly on one central economy, Britain, to provide a destination for its produce, while in the acquisition of articles for its own internal consumption it was the United States that was the predominant source of imports. In 1925, 42.83 per cent of exports went to the United States and 45.79 per cent to the United Kingdom, while 54.15 per cent and 15.62 per cent, respectively, of imports came from these same two countries.[16]

This kind of economy, built on the basis of an export–import relationship, also gave rise to the unquestionable predominance within Costa Rica of the coffee-growing, agro-exporting sector, and of a commercial sector linked to the import trade. These groups, intimately connected in power and through family relationships, were found in trade, in coffee production, in export handling, in finance, and so on, established as a dominant grouping above a substantial, but varied, mass of small agricultural producers and a relatively important body of small tradesmen, craftsmen and workers, which constituted a particular source of pressure upon the dominant class.

As in the other two countries, industry was almost non-existent, limited to a few small textile factories (which imported their raw materials), brickworks and factories making yucca starch, soap and so on. This meant there was no concentrated and cohesive working class, with a class-consciousness and capable of becoming an important adversary of the dominant grouping. The main form of wage labour was piece-work, and artisan, craft-type work, plus an agricultural proletariat in the banana-growing regions that was heavily over-exploited by the United Fruit Company, which possessed the largest landholding and had the largest number of agricultural labourers in the country.

Even in 1927, and despite the efforts made in the educational field, illiteracy was still a very serious problem, according to the Census of that year.[17] This was in spite of the fact, also, that the process of intermixing between the indigenous populations that had survived the Spanish conquest and the *conquistadores* and their descendants had been the most complete in the whole of Central America.[18] The limited population and the general high level of integration, on the other hand, also meant a peasant labour force that was scarce in numbers and racially largely homogeneous, which did not permit the kind of servile relationships existing in the rest of the isthmus.

The class differences that developed within the dominant coffee-growing bourgeoisie led at the end of the last century to it splitting into a number of different groups, some of liberal-reformist tendencies, and others conservative.

THE GROWTH OF POPULAR MOVEMENTS: STRIKES AND WORKERS' UNIONS AT THE BEGINNING OF THE CENTURY

It was also at this time that popular movements began to develop with greater energy and clarity.[19] In 1896 the 'Bakery Artisans' Mutual Society'[20] was established, though not in the true sense of being a labour organization, as employers also took part in it. In 1900 it was disbanded, being replaced by a 'Mutual Aid Society',[21] still of bakery workers. In 1905 the 'Federation of Artisans, Bakers, Building Workers and Carpenters'[22] was formed, and in 1908 the 'Typographers' Mutual Society',[23] whose activities were practically limited to the city of San José. A few years later, in 1913, the General Confederation of Labour (CGT)[24] was founded, with the participation of the Spanish immigrant Juan Vera. It was during this period that a number of Spanish immigrants arrived in the country who were sympathetic to or influenced by anarchism. They worked mainly in the bakery trades, and would play a very important role in the general strike that took place in 1921, as a consequence of the crisis produced by the First World War.

Due to the uncertainty caused by the war, there had been a series of fluctuations in the exchange rate of the Costa Rican colón against the dollar, and the coffee growers, who had been able to sell their harvests at very high prices, held back outside the country the foreign exchange produced by sales of coffee, provoking a fall in imports and a major fiscal crisis, as duties charged on imports formed the government's largest source of income.[25] The government had to take a number of emergency measures, among them the reduction of the salaries of public employees, which caused a great deal of discontent among the lower middle class, and particularly teachers. During this period several associations and unions were formed by different trades and semi-proletarian groups, such as the 'Society of Cabinet-makers and Carpenters',[26] the 'United Mechanics',[27] the '28th November Workers' Club'[28] and the 'General Union of Cabmen'.[29] With the devaluation of the colón, which fell to 4.50 to the dollar, and the decision by the coffee growers to keep their capital abroad also came an appreciable reduction in wages and an increase in rents, which rose to two or three times their former levels. As a result the agitation among the various trade organizations continued to increase.

This crisis culminated in the general strike of March 1921, through which a significant increase in wages of from 35 to 50 per cent was achieved throughout the country, together with the restriction of the working day to eight hours. It is of interest to note that during this strike there was the first attack of a terrorist nature in labour disputes in Costa Rica, a reflection of the Spanish anarchist influence in the movement.[30]

A major role was played by the Reformist movement, under the leadership of General Jorge Volio, a Catholic priest who had acquired the rank of 'General' fighting against United States forces in Nicaragua in 1912 and who left the Church in 1915. The Reformists came to prominence in 1923, instigating social agitation by means of a mixture of messages that included Christian, socialist and other elements. Thus, it was also at this time that the first law on accidents at work was introduced, thanks to the pressure exercised by the Reformist movement.[31]

The Costa Rican Workers' Federation[32] was founded on 9 April 1923 and this established relations, at least officially, with the Central American Workers' Confederation (COCA)[33] that was in operation in El Salvador. This effort towards greater organization was directly connected, moreover, both with the work of Aniceto Montero, who had founded a 'Socialist Centre'[34] which he hoped to develop into a party with a clear ideological position, and with the foundation of the Reformist Party. For its part, however, the General Confederation of Labour founded in 1913 had for some time not played any major part in the working life of the country, and it would not be until 1927 that this organization would acquire a more significant role.[35]

In 1925, a group of professionals and teachers who defined themselves as anti-imperialists decided to join together and found the 'Civic League'[36] with the object of combating the penetration into the country of foreign capital, principally represented by Electric Bond & Share, which held a monopoly over electricity supply, the Northern Railway Company, which controlled rail transport, and, above all, the United Fruit Company. The latter had operated in Costa Rica since the previous century and had taken on the characteristics of a State within a State, as the law that prevailed in its extensive holdings was that of the company rather than that of the country.[37]

In Costa Rica at that time, an increasing expansion in various sectors of artisan workers, in garment making, shoemaking, food production, building trades, cabinet-making and so on, and in the agricultural proletariat of the banana-growing regions, went together with a process of growing urbanization, a consequence of the effects of the world crisis of capitalism that followed the First World War. To this were added the social impact of the Russian Revolution, and the penetration into the country, in an often confused amalgam, of different currents of socialism and communism, via the Reformist movement, or Aniceto Montero. All these elements gave further impetus to this growing development and greater cohesion of different groups of wage earners, and to the consolidation of the social force represented by artisan workers.

JORGE VIVÓ AND THE FIRST CONTACTS WITH THE INTERNATIONAL: COMMUNISTS WITHOUT A PARTY

At some time around the year 1923 a group of artisan workers who had been active in the Reformist Party began to receive examples of the socialist, communist and anarchist press published in Spain, Argentina and other countries.[38] In 1926-7 the Cuban Communist Jorge A. Vivó arrived in the country, having been expelled from his own country by the Cuban Dictator Gerardo Machado. Vivó stayed in Costa Rica for some considerable time, and joined up with a group of craft workers to whom he gave classes in Marxism and labour organization, and with whom he organized Communist groups in Cartago, Limón, San José and Heredia. He also organized a workers' association that operated from a building in the Paso de la Vaca, in the centre of San José. He left the country in around 1930, called back by the International to take up a post in the Caribbean Bureau of International Red Aid.

In 1927 his presence was noted in San José, as he gave a talk on political economy[39] in the Popular University, an institution organized by anti-imperialist law students that included among its speakers several figures of substantial intellectual prestige within the country, such as Omar Dengo, Joaquín García Monge and Carlos Luis Sáenz. The committee of the Popular University included some workers' representatives, Gonzalo Montero Berry, a carpenter, and Lido Bonilla.[40] This 'University', which met in the Law Faculty of the official University, ceased to function a short time later, and was not reopened until May 1929, when it was re-established by the same group of students who shortly afterwards founded the Communist Party of Costa Rica. The role of the University was then stated to be that of a 'body charged with securing a greater level of education for the workers'. The General Secretary of the Popular University in this second period of operation was Manuel Mora Valverde, who would also be, from its foundation, the General Secretary of the Communist Party.

The Popular University in Costa Rica, in contrast to its equivalent in El Salvador, which was to a great extent an organization for peasant education that directly addressed the masses of the agricultural working class, was directed fundamentally towards urban artisan workers, who were the real social base of the Communist Party. In Costa Rica the Popular University received essential support from the association of cabinet-makers and carpenters, alongside petit-bourgeois intellectual elements attracted by revolutionary ideas. Following the foundation of the Communist Party, the University became one of its principal instruments for the popularizing of its ideas, as we shall see.

In December 1927 a small group of craft workers and intellectuals issued a manifesto to the people of Costa Rica which claimed to speak in the name of the Communist Party. The document concluded with the statement that 'The Communist Party of Costa Rica will become part of the Communist International, which is the association made up of all the Communist Parties of the entire world.' They also launched the slogan of proletarian dictatorship.[41] Among the participants in the meetings of this group were the already-mentioned Gonzalo Montero Berry, Carlos Marín Obando, and several foreigners, Latin Americans who had been driven into exile in Costa Rica by the dictatorial government of their respective homelands.

In 1929 the 'Popular Party'[42] was constituted in the Province of Limón, by members of the local group initiated by Vivó. This party, of communist orientation, published a newspaper titled *Lucha*, and succeeded in winning the election to the municipal council of Limón of Gilberto Berrocal, a Colombian, naturalized Costa Rican, who would later, in the 1930s, take an active part in the work of the Communist Party.[43] In this same year,1929, the Limón group also established relations with the group of law students who had reopened the Popular University, and who were linked to an organization called ARCO, the 'Workers' Cultural Resistance Association',[44] made up among others of Manuel Mora, Jaime Cerdas, Luis Carballo and Ricardo Coto Conde.[45]

In 1929 the communist group in Limón, self-titled the 'Limón Directorate of the Communist Party', which through Vivó had had contacts with many of the groups and figures within Latin American communism, received a message from the Communist Party of Uruguay in which they were informed of the desire of the Red International of Labour Unions that May Day should be celebrated in Costa Rica that year, and asked to inform Moscow afterwards of the results of the event. The group replied, however, that they did not possess the resources needed for such a task. They also received an invitation to send a delegate to the Latin American Labour Congress in Montevideo, also in May of that year, but, faced with the impossibility of sending anyone, both the Limón group, who in their international communications called themselves the 'Union Reorganization Group',[46] and the ARCO group in San José delegated their place to the Salvadorean representatives, as was indicated in the pamphlet published on the occasion of the Congress by the Latin American Union Confederation.[47]

On 2 January 1930, the communists of Limón papered the walls and public places of the town with a poster which reproduced a call from the Latin American Union Confederation, addressed to all the workers of the continent, for them to observe that date as the 'Continental Day for the Unemployed'.[48] One of the group, Joaquín Calvo, was arrested and sent to the capital, but pressure by worker's groups rapidly secured his release.[49]

A number of foreigners took part in the meetings of the Limón group, among them José Lavin, a Spaniard, who instructed them in Marxism, and the Guatemalan José Portilla, another leading communist in exile. They received Communist publications from a variety of countries, including the newspaper of the United States Communist Party.

The San José group centred on ARCO published from 1930 a newspaper, *Revolución*, which carried, mixed together, articles publicizing the achievements of Soviet Russia, and others arguing that what was needed in Costa Rica was a social-democratic party, that would establish a genuine democracy in the country. In 1930 they were again invited to a labour conference in Montevideo, for which they named Fausto Peraza as their delegate. From 1930 onwards the students of ARCO were in close contact with a number of labour and trade organizations, among them the General Union of Workers,[50] and organized a number of joint meeting and rallies. On 27 May 1930 a meeting was held under the auspices of the Society of Workers and Cabinetmakers[51] in support of a Law for a Moratorium on Rents and Domestic Tenancies, to alleviate in some way the miserable poverty of the working classes, and to initiate the organization of those workers who had become unemployed as a consequence of the world economic crisis. The meeting was chaired by Montero Berry and Fausto Peraza. Afterwards there was a confrontation with the police, who attacked the crowd as they were leaving the hall, and several of the leading figures were arrested.[52]

In the English-language section of the newspaper *La Tribuna* this meeting and the subsequent clash with the police were reported as 'the first communist disturbance seen in San José'. It was said that 58 communists had been detained and were being held incommunicado, and that the Chief of Police had suffered a minor injury due to a stone thrown by one of the workers. There were also several injured among the unemployed.[53]

The following day, the workers of the city's public works department declared themselves on strike. Their first meeting was attended by Jaime Cerdas Mora and Gonzalo Montero Berry, who offered them the use of the building of the San José Communist group (since they now considered themselves to be a Party) for the holding of this and subsequent meetings.

Similar clashes occurred throughout 1930 between the unemployed and the authorities.

On 7 November, the General Union of Workers, under the direct influence of the Communist group, held a public meeting to celebrate the thirteenth anniversary of the Russian Revolution. In the declaration issued on the day, they called on workers to struggle 'against the bourgeoisie and its hangman state', for a minimum legal wage, for assistance for the unemployed, and for the freedom of those imprisoned.[54] Manuel Mora and Jaime Cerdas spoke at the rally. Previously, on 5 August, speculation had appeared in the press about a possible affiliation of the General Union of Workers (UGT) to the Red International of Labour Unions, a development that does not seem ultimately to have come to anything in reality, as no record of it can be found in the documents or publications of the latter organization.[55]

The world economic crisis was having a far-reaching effect on the economy of the country. Coffee was at that time, still more than before, the only major export product, as banana exports had entered into something of a decline, and from 11 million bunches in 1913 had gone down to 7 million by 1928.[56] International coffee prices went down as a result of the crisis, so that, while in 1929 the coffee growers had received 10 million dollars for a harvest of 19.5 million kilos, in 1933 they obtained only 6 million dollars for 28 million kilos of coffee.[58] As a corollary, there was a sharp fall in imports. Imports of flour, for example, were reduced from 12 million colones in 1929 to 7 million in 1935, and already in 1932 the government ordered the incorporation into bread of 10 per cent of yucca flour, in order to make it cheaper for the urban workers who were its main consumers, since in the countryside maize tortillas and plantains were more commonly eaten in place of bread.

There was also, naturally, an increase in unemployment, which was particularly heavy in agriculture, but which affected every sector of the population, from the urban lower middle class downwards.[59] This last factor was the main immediate stimulus for the principal popular movements of the first years of the 1930s, and provided the spur for the final consolidation of the group that founded the Communist Party, by then, at last, as a permanent organization, on 16 June 1931.

8 The Foundation of the Communist Party and its Links with the International

THE FIRST STEPS OF THE SPECTRE

The first half of 1931 saw the development, one after the other, of a continual series of popular movements of different kinds. They were headed by the communist group, whose leadership won increasing prestige among the mass of workers.

On 11 February 1931, the newspapers published an abundance of commentaries on an ultimatum that had been sent to the President of the Republic by a group of workers, conceding him a limit of eight days in which to initiate some kind of plan to improve the terrible situation of the unemployed. The statement was signed by four carpenters, Miguel Poveda, Máximo Bermúdez, Alfredo Sosa and Gonzalo Montero Berry. The government considered the document to be of an openly subversive nature and ordered the arrest of the signatories, as well as of the law student Jaime Cerdas, who had made declarations in favour of the ultimatum.[1] The arrest of this group, all of them communist leaders, led to renewed meetings of the unemployed and further helped to create an inflamed atmosphere among the workers.

The government, meanwhile, had begun to undertake a certain number of projects that sought to pacify the mood of the unemployed and reduce the pressure of social tensions. However, the number of new jobs that were created was not remotely sufficient to relieve the destructive effects of the crisis to any significant extent.[2]

In that same month, the authorities also announced that they had expelled from the country, accused of being agents of the International, a number of foreigners, Cubans, Mexicans and Argentinians, who had been staying in Costa Rica as guests of several of the local communist leaders. They had also given talks, to substantial audiences, in San José.[3]

In the following months, as the effects of the crisis made themselves felt with ever greater severity, social agitation increased accordingly, and as a result the members of the communist group decided officially to constitute themselves into a Party, which they did so formally on 16 June 1931. On the first page of the Minute Book that records the foundation of the Party is the following sentence, 'Capitalism itself begets its own gravediggers', followed by the signatures of the members of the first Executive Committee, Manuel Mora, Jaime Cerdas, Efraín Jiménez, Luis Carballo and Gonzalo Montero Berry, three law students, a shoemaker and a carpenter.[4] The symbol of the new party was a red flag with a purple border and, in the centre, on a yellow background, the hammer and sickle.

The newly created Communist Party immediately threw itself into the work of establishing class-based labour unions, on the basis of the trade associations in which it had influence. The first to be constituted was the Cabinetmakers' Union,[5] using the Society of Workers and Cabinetmakers, referred to in the previous chapter, as a starting point. However, the difficulties they encountered in this task, the aim of which was to organize sections of the petit-bourgeoisie that had been proletarianized by the effects of the world crisis, led them to draw back and agree on a series of steps which they felt would need to be undertaken first before further progress in this direction. These steps were intended, as they saw it, first to educate these social groups in a class sense, as in the opinion of the Party such sectors had still not acquired sufficient awareness of their passage from the petit-bourgeoisie to the proletariat.[6]

With the aim of broadening their influence among these social groups they decided once again to reopen the Popular University, which had fallen into another period of inactivity, and use it for the teaching of such courses as General History, Political Economy, and the History of Imperialist Penetration in Latin America.[7] On 6 October of that year the 'Lenin Library'[8] was created within the Popular University, with the cooperation of the Communist Party, which donated 500 volumes of revolutionary content, both books and magazines.[9] The majority of these had been received via the League against Imperialism, relations with which were limited to the exchange of propaganda. A Costa Rican section of the League did function in 1933, but its activities were mostly directed towards the publication of manifestos and similar propaganda. The real peak of anti-imperialist agitation in Costa Rica had been in the 1920s, and had been led by the Civic League, to which we have referred, and the *aprista* groups.

Moreover, when the Communist Party did succeed in finally establishing itself as such, after 1931, it did not have sufficient cadres to be able to maintain a variety of organizations, and carried on its work among the population directly, as a legal party, not via the League or International Red Aid. In addition, one should stress again that the conditions of relative liberal tolerance that existed in the country did not make it a vital matter for the Party to conduct its activities through front organizations. Instead, from the beginning, as we shall see, the Communist Party felt able to contemplate open participation in elections, as a class party.

The banana workers' strike of 1934, for example, a campaign that combined an anti-imperialist element as a struggle against an American consortium with an equally strong social aspect in being resistant to the most powerful single employer in the country, was led openly, from the front, by the Party.[10] For their part, both the Caribbean Bureau and the League against Imperialism limited themselves to occasionally sending propaganda, and never took any interest in the CPCR. Their attention was concentrated at that time on Nicaragua and El Salvador.

In 1933 Manuel Mora gave a letter to Emilio Valverde, a young intellectual who was then a militant of the CPCR and was due to travel to New York, for him to deliver to Ricardo Martínez, the leading Venzuelan Communist, at the offices of the League against Imperialism. Martínez had at that point been assigned to the New York central office of the League by the International. Valverde carried out his mission, but did not receive any reply.[11]

The contacts with Latin American exiles connected with the League who passed through the country were maintained solely by the General Secretary, Mora, in a direct and personal manner. Not even the rest of the Politburo were fully aware of these contacts, except when capital could be made out of such visits for propaganda purposes. Exceptionally, when Pedro Saad, Secretary of the Communist Party of Ecuador visited Costa Rica, and took part in the meetings of the Central Committee of the Party, his presence was reported.[12]

At the same time as they were founding the Party, the Costa Rican Communists also set about the publication of a weekly newspaper, *Trabajo*, the first issue of which appeared on 14 July 1931. In the first edition the existence of the new organization was made public and it was stated that, although *Trabajo* was a continuation of the earlier *Revolución*, published by ARCO, it was significantly different from it. This was, it said, because *Revolución*, 'for tactical reasons', had not had a clearly defined ideological line, whereas the new publication would be the official organ of the party of the workers. The objectives that were proposed for *Trabajo* were to disseminate Communist ideas in the country and to counteract the influence of the bourgeois press, which was attacking the Communists daily.[13] The Communist Party of Costa Rica set out to achieve this aim, to spread knowledge of and gain support for Communist ideology, by identifying itself with the most radical possible ideas and slogans of social transformation.

REVOLUTIONARY THEORY AND ELECTORAL LEGALITY: THE DEMOCRATIC TEMPTATION

With regard to the nature of the revolution, they did not even consider the creation of a popular-democratic dictatorship of the workers and peasants, but instead moved directly to pushing the slogans of proletarian dictatorship. These slogans were taken in a literal manner from French-language publications of the Communist International, as can be deduced from the peculiar idioms that appeared as the result of an excessively literal translation. An article of October 1931, for example, went as follows:

> Our 'words of order' (*palabras de orden*) are the following: revolutionary assault of political power, annihilation of the bourgeoisie as a dominant class, absolute control of the administration and economy of the country by a workers' and peasant government. We will carry out this plan of action without demagoguery, but with implacable energy ... As revolutionary Marxists, we have an intransigent conviction that great social transformations cannot be entrusted solely to the laws of evolution, that violence and revolution are indispensable when one wishes to demolish an oppressive and harmful order of things down to its foundations.[14]

One can see that the term *palabras de orden* is a literal translation of the French *mot d'ordre* ('watchword'), as it does not have any real meaning in Spanish, in which the more normal equivalents would have been *lemas* or *consignas* ('mottos' or 'slogans'). At the same time, they also declared themselves to be in favour of an insurrectionary revolutionary policy that sought the complete overthrow of the bourgeoisie and the absolute control of State power by the workers, in alliance with the peasantry. The petit-bourgeoisie were not, therefore, given any specific political role in their declarations. The insurrectionary nature of their ideas is confirmed by an article that appeared in February 1933, in which, after a declaration that their revolution would be permanent, though in the sense of involving constant activity, we come to the following revealing statement: 'The armed coup (*cuartelazo*) will be our final stage, and we will reach that point in a logical and scientific way, without ever resorting to opportunistic and nonsensical methods.'[15] One should recall here the insistence the International had laid, in dealing with Latin America, on identifying this kind of political approach with the futile conceptions of the petit-bourgeoisie.

In December 1933 the Party declared, basing themselves on texts from Lenin, that they would work within the country's parliament as long as they were not strong enough to dissolve it. But only in November of that same year they had stated that the redemption of the workers would not be won through the parliamentary path, but through that of revolution.[16] However, in spite of the fact that their immediate slogan was indeed 'the organization of the proletariat as a class and the destruction of bourgeois supremacy and conquest of political power for the proletariat',[17] the political structure of the country effectively obliged the Communist Party to participate in the electoral process, and, by doing so, placed it little by little within the channels of participation that ensured its incorporation into the national political system.

In Costa Rica, in contrast to El Salvador, the economic crisis did not lead the Communist Party to achieve great influence among the agricultural proletariat. Instead, its radius of action was limited rather more to the provincial capitals, where it obtained extensive influence among the broad mass of the urban lower middle class. The democratic legality that existed in the country allowed it to reach these groups without great difficulty.

They first attempted to register themselves for election as the 'Communist Party of Costa Rica', but the government, the executive power, which was the authority legally responsible under the Constitution for considering such applications, refused to accept this, a decision which was ratified by the Congress in a resolution of 8 October 1931.[18] Faced with this situation, the Party decided to set up the 'Worker and Peasant Bloc',[19] which they themselves called a 'class party', for the municipal elections which were approaching. The campaign platform of the Bloc was a series of social measures designed to improve the situation of working people, with primary importance being given to solving the problems of the unemployed. An effort was also made to put forward candidates for the municipal councils who were exclusively workers from the city and the countryside.[20] Nevertheless, their candidates were for the most part, initially, from artisan, craft backgrounds. The Bloc won great popular support, and was able to secure two seats in the Municipality of San José, which were occupied by Adolfo Braña, a Spanish immigrant and a mechanic by trade, and Guillermo Fernández, a painter.

The Communist councillors immediately set about obtaining funds to set up public works with which to give work to a significant number of the unemployed. They rapidly secured 100 000 colones for this purpose, which further increased the popularity of the Party and its influence among urban workers. They also decided to regulate the municipal finances, beginning by pressing shop owners and traders to renew and pay for trading licenses that had expired, as they were legally required to do. Within a short time the receipts of the municipal authority rose from one million to five million colones, which significantly increased the possibilities of improving services for the poorer classes of the capital.[21]

Similarly, they also sought to encourage a reduction in the bureaucratic apparatus of the capitalist Municipality. The Communists' newspaper *Trabajo*, while giving ample coverage in its pages to the work of the Communist councillors, justified the electoral participation of the Party as a decision that had only been taken in order to be consistent with the tactics of the international struggle. They explained that they had to draw a parenthesis in their work of revolutionary indoctrination of the masses in order to dispute the municipal candidacies with the bourgeoisie.[22]

While they were making every effort to build up the legal organization of the Party, however, they were still issuing statements in which they declared themselves in favour of revolutionary violence, as a weapon of the workers with which to throw off the yoke of exploitation; condemned international wars between bourgeoisies; declared the aim of their struggle to be 'all power for the workers', and emphatically refused to collaborate with bourgeois governments, as, they said, only a workers' government could provide a solution to cyclical crises, by means of a rationalization of the economy.[23]

May 1933 saw the celebration in San José of the Second Congress of the Central American Students' Confederation (CIADE).[24] The representatives of the Communist Party sought to take part in the Congress, according to their statement in *Trabajo*, not only because they considered it a duty for all communists, but also for another reason 'of a concrete political nature'. 'We refer,' they continued, 'to the duty we have, as a disciplined organization, to carry out the directive circulated to the Communist Parties by the Communist International, that they should rectify their attitude towards students.'[25]

The young Communist Party thus sought to align its activities with the general outlines of policy that were conveyed in the propaganda of the Communist International. However, their attitude, which left ample scope for local interpretation, should not be understood as signifying organizational links like those that were established where the International really did develop an effective presence. The declarations, whether direct or indirect, made by the Party's delegates and sympathizers in the Congress all followed the most strict sectarian line of trying to 'communize' the students' movement and denouncing all those seen as potential competitors. The speech made by the Mexican labour leader Vicente Lombardo Toledano, who defined himself as a non-communist Marxist socialist, was described in the following terms: 'His voice wanted to break down in sobs. A perfect play-actor, he knows how to give an emotive and pathetic tinge to the modulations of his throat and the trembling of his hand with every gesture.' Lombardo's support for a motion put to the Congress in defence of Sandino, meanwhile, they explained by saying, 'That's logical. Lombardo sees in Sandino his own double, with the difference that the ex-anti-imperialist of Nicaragua did fight against imperialist intervention for some years, while the Mexican charlatan has always been at its service.'[26]

The Costa Rican Communists notably followed the line of the International both with regard to El Salvador, though in this case more by omission since they made no comment on the grave events that had occurred in that country the previous year, and to Nicaragua. Their summary of the Congress read:

There were two Sandinista agents at the Congress: a student, Miranda, who had come specially from Managua, and who restricted himself to making atrocious speeches, without taking breath, with his tongue sticking to the roof of this mouth, in defence of Sacasa and the 'hero' of Las Segovias; and some sort of Managua municipal building contractor, Salinas de Aguilar, a man crushed beneath the burden of an overwhelming state of mental cretinism, who did not open his mouth in any of the discussions, limiting himself to waiting patiently for the delegates to discuss a motion of sympathy with the traitor of Las Segovias. Against this poor Señor Salinas was our faction. They loudly defeated him when it came upon him to defend his 'hero'. They left him looking ridiculous at every opportunity. The motion on the vote of thanks to Sandino was passed. But it had been morally defeated.[27]

The League against Imperialism of the United States sent the Communist militant Dora Zucker, a specialist in the organization of black workers, to the Congress in representation of the National Student League,[28] which, *Trabajo* reported, had been in existence for a little over fourteen months, and had, 'with its official newspaper, the *Student Review*, organized demonstrations outside the Cuban legation in New York, in protest at the crimes of Gerardo Machado, and organized a Student Congress against war in Chicago, which was attended by Mexican and Cuban delegates'.[29] For the official organ of the Communist Party of Costa Rica, Zucker was 'a militant incapable of empty posturing', who directed her attacks particularly against four of the other delegations: those from Mexico, El Salvador, Nicaragua and Puerto Rico. The latter had objected to her presence, as an American, at the Congress, to which she responded by accusing them of being confused and, given their nationalist position, a potential instrument of fascist manipulation. She accused the other three delegations of being opportunists, without, like the Costa Rican Communists, making the least reference to the Salvadorean massacres of the year before, although with regard to the Nicaraguans she did specify 'their position as cronies and accomplices of the tandem of betrayal, Sacasa–Sandino'.[30]

In all, therefore, a simple restatement was made of the essential features of the policies adopted by the Comintern in Central America. In view of this it is not surprising that Zucker should have made express contact with the Communist Party, which provided her with a venue for her to give a talk on imperialism, world affairs and the defence of the Soviet Union. Following that it assisted her to travel to the Province of Limón, accompanied by the Party leaders Jaime Cerdas, Adolfo Braña and the black tailor Harold Nicholas, in order for her to make contact with some black union activists in the Province.[31]

However, a series of social and political events would very shortly sever any possibility that this contact might have been developed further, thus lessening the organizational links with the Communist International via the League against Imperialism. In effect, immediately after their return from Limón, on 23 May 1933, there was a heavy wave of police repression, in which Braña was arrested and expelled from the country.

This had occurred in the aftermath of a demonstration of the unemployed organized by the Party's Unemployed Committee in San José the previous day,[32] which had ended in a violent confrontation between police and workers, leaving four police officers wounded and one dead. Among the demonstrators, five men had been seriously injured with bullet wounds.[33] The result of this bloody encounter was a hardening in the attitude of the government towards the Communist Party. The President of the Republic declared that his government had given the widest possible freedom to Communism as long as it operated on the level of ideological struggle, but that they could not permit it to resort to violence.[34] This brought forth the retort from one of the members of the Party's Central Committee, Luis Carballo, that they were prepared to take advantage of the revolutionary situation that presented itself, as they had learnt from the experience of the 22nd that one had to answer the violence of the bourgeoisie with revolutionary violence, and that the bullets of the government had to be answered with Communist bullets. These statements, made in a public meeting in the Party's main meeting hall, were heard by some fifty policemen who were present and ready to intervene at the slightest sign of disorder, but the incident did not develop further. The reaction of the government to this meeting and its atmosphere of violence, however, was to deport the Spaniard Braña and confiscate the archives and library of the Communist Party, in addition to ordering a close watch to be maintained over its leaders.[35]

Nevertheless, none of this prevented the Worker and Peasant Bloc from putting forward its candidates for the elections to the Chamber of Deputies in 1934 and obtaining two seats, one for Mora, the General Secretary, and the other for Efraín Jiménez, a shoemaker and also a member of the Central Committee. The nomination of Manuel Mora was imposed upon him by the rest of the Party. He had not wished to accept, expressing a view that most Party members considered 'neo-workerist' and petit-bourgeois. Mora's attitude was echoed within the Party by the Venezuelan Rómulo Betancourt – who was then exiled in Costa Rica and had become part of the leadership of the CPCR – by the writer Carmen Lyra and by the teacher Arnoldo Ferreto, all of whom argued for the list of candidates to be composed purely of workers and peasants. It is interesting to note that in his speech refusing to accept the nomination, Mora also declared that it should be 'workers of the workshops and the fields' who should make up the candidature.[36]

However, the Party's influence among peasants was still very limited, in spite of the fact that the agrarian sector had been the most affected by the crisis, with 75 per cent of the unemployed coming from among agricultural workers.[37] It would not be until after the strike of 1934 had begun that a movement took shape among poor peasants on the Atlantic Coast, who supported the strike by providing the strikers with food produced on their own small plots. Peasant groupings were also developing in the Province of Heredia, under the leadership of a basketweaver named Herminio Alfaro. He came to be a leading figure in the Communist Party, before being prematurely assassinated by supporters of the government in 1935, when the Presidency was no longer held by the Liberal Ricardo Jiménez but by León Cortés, a lawyer of more conservative and authoritarian tendencies.[38]

Although its political practice was moving ever closer to being one of promoting necessary adjustments to make the painful situation of the working people of the country more bearable, as a political concept the Bloc continued to be understood as being the communist party, the party of the working class, of the proletariat, and of the bloc of the two classes, the workers and peasants. This meant – though for its main organizers in Costa Rica it was all the same – that the nature of the Party was in effect that of a worker–peasant one, not to say petit-bourgeois and artisan, which was precisely what the statement and resolutions of the International had repeatedly warned against.

It was during this same period, in 1934, that the existence of the Bloc as a class party was justified in the following terms: 'in the face of these pirate banners and the programme of hunger, fascism and war of imperialism, the proletariat is struggling fervently for its class goal: a single worker and peasant government capable of ensuring peace for all the peoples and bread for every mouth'.[39] This struggle was not at that time conceived as being purely parliamentary, even though in practice the movement was becoming steadily more assimilated into the existing political system. In May 1935 *Trabajo* declared that the battle would be to the death, and that the fate of Costa Rica would be decided in the streets: either fascism would succeed in installing its ferocious reactionary dictatorship, which would smother every idea of freedom and culture, or Communism would establish its workers and peasant government.[40]

July 1934 saw the publication of the first edition of a new newspaper, *La Voz Sindical*, the appearance of which signified a consolidation of the influence of the Party in the labour movement, represented by the strengthening of several unions and the subsequent creation of the first union confederation in Costa Rica directly linked to the Party, the Workers' Union Confederation.[41] 'The birth of the Confederation,' it was said in the newspaper, 'signifies the point of departure for a vast crusade of organization and preparation of the working masses of the country for the great class confrontations, for the great struggles, for the great strikes' that were approaching at that time of crisis for world capitalism, and which would be transformed 'into veritable combats against the bourgeoisie and its servant state, and against imperialism'.[42] The newspaper itself was considered as being firmly controlled by the Party.[43]

The struggle to achieve the demands of workers was frequently accompanied by declarations to the effect that such struggles would ultimately be absurd if there were not also a restructuring of the entire productive apparatus of the country.[44] However, their political actions were oriented more and more towards the consecution of those same limited demands. In the circumstances, Communists put forward two programmes: one a general and maximum programme, going as far as the abolition of private property, which was common to all the Parties that were members of the Communist International, and another that was minimum or national. These minimum programmes were established by the Communist Parties of each country taking into account the particular correlation of forces, nationally and internationally, in each case, the level of economic development, the number of workers, their level of militancy and organization, the development of class consciousness among the mass of workers and peasants, and so on. In this way it was determined which immediate and attainable reforms would be undertaken when in power, always assuming that the Party concerned would have the command of the State in its hands before capitalism as a whole had been destroyed by the Communist Parties of the other countries: in other words, in the circumstances of governing a country in which the State would still be an instrument of the bourgeoisie. It was taken as given that 'in drawing up a minimum programme, the Communist Parties did not set for themselves an insuperable limit, some kind of fixed frontier [that would be] like a prison wall'.[45]

However, in Costa Rica, alongside the declaration of the need to build up the Communist Party as the indispensable vehicle for the emancipation of the country's working class, the minimum programme of the Party (which did also, this time, reproduce some of the slogans launched by the International) included as point 24, 'Constant and determined cooperation in the work being undertaken for the formation of a great Soviet Socialist Republic on the American continent.'[46] This Soviet Republic and the corresponding worker–peasant government would have to exercise a dictatorship. Moreover, this dictatorship would be directly proletarian. 'It is necessary,' the Party said, 'for the dictatorship of the workers' government to be very strong. Dictatorship signifies a government that is particularly severe, and great determination in the repression of its enemies. It is natural that in such a state of affairs not all men should be able to enjoy the different freedoms . . . The dictatorship of the proletariat cannot be reconciled with the freedom of the bourgeoisie.'[47]

It is clear from this that, for all the supposedly 'minimum' nature of the programme, what was being put forward was a radicalism that was total and absolute. At the same time, this radicalism nevertheless also clearly demonstrated that the Party had still not even remotely digested the many discussions and theoretical and programmatic elaborations that the International had accumulated in its already extensive history.

Moreover, alongside this radicalism, which declared itself in favour of the affiliation of the Party to the International, proletarian and peasant dictatorship, the defence of the Soviet Union, the criticism of bourgeois democracy, and so forth, a pragmatic and more realistic tendency, prepared to use the establishment and adapt itself to it, was growing. The programme of proletarian and peasant revolution slid towards being a progamme of political and social reforms. This was an additional indication of a weak and non-organizational relationship with the Communist International, which if it had had a real presence would have at least attempted through its publication to give a clearer direction to the disorientated radicalism of the young CPCR, making the latter align itself with, at the very least, the most extreme of the positions adopted by the Comintern with regard to the colonial, semi-colonial and dependent world, and Latin America in particular, especially after the VI Congress of the International in 1928.

THE CARIBBEAN BUREAU AND COSTA RICAN COMMUNISM: AN ABANDONMENT THAT LED TO SALVATION

During this first period, therefore, for the CPCR the matter in hand was not the realization of the bourgeois-democratic revolution, but the virtually direct construction of socialism. It was not a democratic dictatorship of the workers and peasants (a concept that had divided Trotsky, Stalin, Bukharin and Zinoviev with regard to China) but a proletarian dictatorship that had to be established in Costa Rica. This was, again, a reflection of a, to say the least, loose political and ideological relationship with the International and its various bodies charged with working in Central America.

The most important piece of evidence that has remained regarding financial aid from the International and the political links between it and the Communist Party in Costa Rica is a document from 1936, consisting of a letter written by the Cuban Blas Roca, a member of the Executive Committee of the Communist International and General Secretary of the Cuban Party. This letter was stolen by an individual named Palacios, who was then living in Mora's house, and passed on to the Communist Party's opponents for publication. In it, it is clear that Roca made detailed political recommendations on the behaviour that in his judgement should be adopted by the Communists in the forthcoming elections. The position of the Communist Party of Costa Rica was antithetical to that put forward by Roca, who cited as a source of authority conversations that he had had, together with Rodolfo Guzmán, a member of the Party who was studying labour organization in Russia, with representatives of the International in Moscow. Nevertheless, the Costa Rican Party remained firm in this position and, though it suffered a serious electoral defeat, soon managed to recover from it and continue its activities as normal. An amount of money that is mentioned in the letter was evidently intended as a contribution to financing the electoral campaign.[48]

Costa Rica formed part of the Caribbean Bureau of the International, or more accurately came under its jurisdiction. In a report on the history of the Costa Rican Party written for the library of the Institute of Social Sciences in Moscow in 1965 severe criticisms are made of the interventions of this Bureau in regional affairs, the influence of which was mainly felt in Costa Rica after 1935, and principally through the intermediary of the Communist Party of Cuba.[49]

It has been stated, in the course of a study of the Venezuelan Section of the Communist International, by Manuel Caballero, that 'the Caribbean Bureau apparently originated in a decision of the VI Congress of the Communist International, in 1928', a view supported by the statements made in his book *Veinte Años de Política 1928–1948*, published in Madrid in 1968 (Editorial Mediterráneo, p. 57), by Bautista Fuenmayor, an active participant in Venezuelan politics at that time.[50] According to Caballero's account, the Caribbean Bureau in particular was a further development of a proposal made by Ricardo Martínez in the First Latin American Communist Conference, held in Buenos Aires in 1929, in which he put forward the idea of creating a Latin American Sub-Secretariat based in Mexico, together with two of what today would be called 'schools for cadres', one in Argentina and the other in New York. This is the first reference we have to the Caribbean Bureau. In April 1938, Caballero writes, *El Martillo*, official newspaper of the Venezuelan Section of the Communist International, 'declared that "the Caribbean Bureau does not exist" '. Between these two dates, the Caribbean Bureau did exist and function. It was made up of Alexander Biterlman, Earl Browder, a representative of the Communist Youth International and Ricardo A. Martínez. Martínez later left the Bureau to go to Montevideo to join the Secretariat of the Latin American Union Conference,[51] the formation of which had been decided by the IV Congress of the Red International of Labour Unions (the *Profintern*).[52]

However, in our view the idea of creating regional organizational entities or 'bureaus' does not seem to have originated with Ricardo Martínez, but rather to have come from Vitorio Codovila, the veteran leader of Argentinian Communism, of Italian origin, and a senior leader of the South American Bureau of the International and representative of the International in Spain during the Civil War. 'The great weakness in the anti-imperialist struggle,' Codovila said, 'is the rivalry among the different bosses (*caudillos*). I would suggest a division of Latin America into sectors. One sector for the Caribbean; another for the Bolivarian countries, the third made up of Argentina, Chile, Uruguay and Paraguay, and lastly, a fourth, that of Brazil.'[53]

All the documents and reports that are available on the organizational relationships and functions of the different Communist leaders tend to support the belief that it was from Codovila and not Martínez (or rather, perhaps, through the latter as a subordinate to the former) from whom first came the idea of such an organizational and functional division within the Communist International.

Moreover, the description of the Caribbean Bureau given by Caballero omits to mention, in addition, the significant role played in the structuring and operations of the Bureau by the Cubans, as well as by those of the Venezuelans themselves, like Aponte and Gustavo Machado, who operated in direct contact with it. The Mexicans did also wish to assume a more prominent role, but did not succeed in doing so, due to the chronic deficiencies and weakneses, which would prove to be incurable, of the Mexican Communist Party.

In this situation, the development of the international relations of the Costa Rican Party, after 1936, was mainly oriented in two principal directions: towards Cuba, where several of its members were sent for different reasons,[54] and towards Mexico. The latter contact was due to the activities of the Latin American Workers' Confederation,[55] led by Vicente Lombardo Toledano, though this relationship really developed some years later, and in spite of the taunts that the Party had thrown against Lombardo in 1933 on the occasion of the dispute over Sandino and the Student Congress of the CIADE.

The most important direct contact with the International, which proves there was at least a very basic level of liaison with it, was the journey undertaken by the previously mentioned Rodolfo Guzmán, a shoemaker and leading militant of the Party, who in 1933 travelled to the Soviet Union to study at the School of Labour Organization in Moscow. The initial contact to permit a member of the Party to study in Russia had been made directly from Costa Rica by Rómulo Betancourt, then a militant of the Party and an important figure in its leadership, via Apolonio Palazio. Palazio, believed to be Colombian, had been a prominent figure in the Central American labour movement since 1932, when the Central American Workers' Confederation (COCA), in which he held the post of Secretary for External Relations, had made its base in Costa Rica. He later edited the magazine *Revista Obrera* in Nicaragua.[56]

According to Guzmán's own account and other reports, he first made direct contact with agents of the Comintern, in order to continue his journey, in Paris, where he had arrived supplied only with an address in the rue Faydeau. Moreover, this was only one limited contact, and did not suppose any kind of continuity. On his return from the USSR Guzmán did not maintain any particular links either with the School or with any of his former classmates.[57]

The Communist Party declared itself to be a Section of the Communist International in the manifesto published on 1 May 1934. However, the International would not in fact begin formally to study its application to become a full member until 1935, when the matter was passed over to a Special Commission appointed by the Congress of that year, for them to take a final decision once the Congress was over.

In this 1934 manifesto the slogans used were 'Forward the agrarian and anti-imperialist revolution in Latin America' and 'Long live the International Proletarian Revolution'. Nevertheless, apart from points of an internationalist nature that were directly linked to the defence of the Soviet Union and the imminence of fascist aggression, the main substance of the document was directed towards stating the Party's immediate policy of support for popular demands, calling on workers, peasants, small workshop-owners, small traders, lecturers, professionals, poor students and school teachers to struggle against fascism and support of democracy, and take part in mass actions to do so.[58]

At that time the Party, together with others in Latin America, was still classified by the International simply as a sympathizer. Their status as full members of the Communist International, as has been mentioned, would not be discussed until the VII Congress, in which the organization was formally informed of the application and the Executive Committee was charged, as a Special Commission, with taking the required decision.[59]

In the meantime, as has been indicated, the strongest influence exercised by the international Communist movement over the Costa Rican Party was that which came via the Cuban Party. The attempts that had initially been made to establish the United States Communist Party in the role of mentor for the young Latin American communist movement had not produced positive results. Though the relevant offices continued to operate from New York, the fact was that Cuba, as the base for one of the best organized and best financed Communist Parties in the continent, was steadily acquiring the status of a centre of gravity, towards which the Communist Party of Costa Rica would incline. However, the solidity of such links should not be exaggerated. The letter from Blas Roca previously mentioned, for example, which contained specific political recommendations regarding the elections due to take place in Costa Rica, was accompanied by the sending of a certain amount of money. However, far from proving that a directly dependent relationship existed between the Party and the centre of the Comintern in the Caribbean, this incident in fact demonstrates precisely the opposite: a relative independence, that would enable the Costa Rican Party to remain within the rules of the national political process, which guaranteed it its legality and its ability to function openly. Relations between the centre and the periphery were never this loose in nature – or so comprehending of local peculiarities – within the International wherever it was truly able to exercise its will. The vertical nature of the authority structure of the Comintern would never have permitted it.

This being the case, the debt owed by the Communist Party of Costa Rica to the International can really be isolated to two specific, separate stages in its ideological development: in the background to its formation, and in the development of the popular front policy after 1936.

In the first period, the international movement simply created the minimum conditions necessary in terms of propaganda, culture and ideology for the development of a party like the CPCR, though paradoxically the APRA and other nationalist tendencies from among the petit-bourgeois intelligentsia, as well as the social and political movement inspired by the Reformist Party, had contributed to no lesser extent to creating these same conditions. With respect to the second stage, that of the popular front, the policy adopted internationally merely constituted a reaffirmation of a political orientation that had already been gaining influence for some time within the Costa Rican Party: that which favoured cross-class participation, in that elements from the most varied social sectors were invited to unite with the popular movement, and a policy of reforms that would impede the advance of fascism. The latter by extension also justified the defence of democratic institutions that were threatened by reactionary forces, together with their preservation by means of essential modifications in the social and economic structure of the country, which would in turn permit the strengthening and further development of the bourgeois-democratic system. As for the State, it would be required to play an anti-imperialist role, support small producers, and facilitate the development of industry and social and economic activity that could retrieve the natural wealth of the country from the hands of Yankee-imperialist capital.

The slogans, strategy and tactics drawn up by the International for Latin America in general, and Central America in particular, found echo in Costa Rica only in the various manifestos and proclamations, except for one issue: an unswerving solidarity with the defence of the Soviet Union. In November 1936, the General Secretary of the Communist Party, Manuel Mora, then a Deputy in the national Congress, made a speech oposing a law for the control of the circulation of literature classified as extremist through the post. In it, referring to the question of whether there was harmony or struggle between the classes, he said:

> I reply to the honourable Deputy that this harmony cannot exist as long as the ruling class has its grip on the people's throat . . . Nevertheless, honourable Deputies, I, as a representative of the Communist Party, offer you my hand this afternoon and declare to

you: that if you are moved by goodwill and good faith, if you are prepared to respect democracy and do justice to the people, we will not have any objection to collaborating with you, dispensing with doctrinaire sectarianisms and political intransigence. Let us form one front to struggle for democracy and the well-being of the people.

Given this situation, it is possible to argue that the strategy and tactics that were predominant among Costa Rican Communists, after the verbal excesses of the first few years, had nothing at all to do with the strategy and tactics of the International. It was of influence previously, in the preparation and fertilization of the political and ideological terrain. It had influence later, with the policy of the Popular Front. However, this policy had, as we have seen, also originated in Costa Rica within the Communist Party itself, due to the particular character of its leaders, the existing social situation, the political and cultural traditions of the country and the flexibility of the political system, which was able to assimilate the young Party and convert it into a contributory element in its own subsequent modernization.[61] To all of which was added another, by no means insignificant, political peculiarity, of great significance and consequences, that there did not exist in the country, as a potential partner in any eventual alliance, any kind of Socialist Party.

The national political system in Costa Rica, as we have noted, differed with other such systems in Central America in that it demanded the participation of social sectors other than the military or the holders of economic power in the formation of the State authorities. In a social context of scarcities of land, capital and labour, as indicated in Chapter 7 of this book,[62] the Costa Rican political system became flexible, permitted varied sections of the population to formulate their own demands, and found itself obliged, as a matter of essential importance in the determination of which grouping would exercise political power, to attempt to offer responses to them. When the Communist Party made its appearance, with an ambivalent policy of social revolution and well-justified reforms, the favourable response shown to the latter, and the absence of any far-reaching conflicts that might have given encouragement to revolutionary feelings and obstructed the functioning of the system, effectively rewarded, one might say, the reformist conduct of the Party, revealed its demands to be workable and constructive, and ultimately led to its assimilation.[63]

Perhaps what best symbolized this was the 1 May Parade held to celebrate the social reform and system of social assistance that was initiated in 1942, which was attended by the President of the Republic, Dr Rafael Angel Calderón Guardia, the Bishop of San José and head of the Catholic Church in Costa Rica, Monsignor Víctor M. Sanabria, and the general Secretary of the Communist Party, Manuel Mora. Though this took place against the backdrop of the Second World War and the alliance against the Axis, there were also more profound internal reasons that would justify and explain such an event – one of which, and perhaps not the least in importance, being the previously mentioned fact that the Communist Party of Costa Rica had not, in contrast with the Communists of El Salvador, had real organizational links with the Comintern. This, more than serving to avoid a revolutionary fever prevented, as shown from the history of the Communist International in Central America, a catastrophe similar to those which engulfed the peoples of Nicaragua and El Salvador.

We have seen that what existed in Costa Rica, more than autonomy, was independence with respect to the International. The organization abandoned the region, to turn all its attention to Europe. However, this abandonment would prove to be a means of salvation.

9 A Euro-Communism in the Central America of the 1930s

TICO-COMMUNISM: A COSTA RICAN INNOVATION[1]

Relations between the Costa Rican Communist Party and the International were not, then, of a sufficiently institutional nature to permit any real control over or direction of the Party's political activities within the country.

A case in point is what was, as has been mentioned, the most important event in the development of the labour movement during the period we have been examining, the banana workers' strike of 1934. This was led by Carlos Luis Fallas, then a banana worker and later a writer, and Jaime Cerdas Mora, a law student. Both were members of the leadership of the Communist Party. The participation of the General Secretary, Manuel Mora, was oriented more towards the field of propaganda and the parliamentary activity connected with the conflict.

However, this dispute, even though it led to much speculation in the country on the possible involvement of foreign communist agitators, was not on the other hand supported by any real intervention by the International. This was reflected, moreover, in the virtually non-existent international impact given to the conflict, of which there was scarcely a mention in the preparatory material for the VII Congress of the Comintern, during which, as we have seen, the CPCR's request for full membership was formally put forward. The same can be said with regard to the various front organizations, such as the RILU.

The socio-political characteristics of the country, those of a bourgeois liberal democracy, with strong constitutional and legalistic traditions, did not fail to have an effect on the principal leaders of the fledgling Communist Party. Its most important figures were lawyers, or at least law students, firmly attached to the political idiosyncrasies of a country, without irreparable conflicts, with a respect for opposing political ideas, and so on. Their style made it easier for the political system to meet the first forays of the Party with a high degree of skill and political flexibility. Thus, for example, when the Communist municipal councillors secured, as a great popular victory, the closure of the principal retailers of San José, who had not paid their local taxes and charges, the response given to the furious shopowners by the Liberal President of the time, Ricardo Jiménez, was that the law in this case was on the side of the Communists, and that therefore they would have to pay what they owed in order to reopen their businesses.

With its individual demands limited ever more frequently to questions related to specific abuses by employers and major capitalists, it can be said that the political objectives pursued by the Party and the direction of the pressures it exerted in practical terms became gradually transmuted into those of modernizing and improving, indirectly, by means of a series of reforms, both Costa Rican society and the State. As a result, once it had left behind the period of ultra-radicalism that had talked about dictatorship of the proletariat, the overthrow of capitalism, and so forth, the Communist Party of Costa Rica carried on its activities in a manner that was in effect essentially reformist and cross-class based.[2]

From the point of view of the social composition of its supporters, whether at the level of leadership or at the base of the Party, the predominance of the petit bourgeoisie, of great numerical importance in the country, was virtually absolute, in spite of the claims made to be the Party of the working class.[3] As for its objectives, they became for the most part limited in scope to the towns and cities, in which the Party sought first of all to alter labour relations to make them more favourable to the worker. The small peasants, together with the agricultural labourers, remained tied by the bonds of paternalism to the conservative sectors of the country. The mass of labourers, controlled, as Samuel Stone has shown in his work,[4] by this system, remained firmly behind the traditional elite, to the extreme of allowing themselves to be sacrificed in the Social Reforms of 1942, in which they were specifically excluded from the protection provided for other workers against accidents at work.[5]

The presence of American, and to a lesser extent European, capital had given rise to a plantation proletariat fully subject to capitalist relations in some of the rural areas, in addition to a substantial number of trade and service personnel in these same districts. These groups could have played a very important role in a country like Costa Rica, in which the lack of an industrial working class meant that the social and political weight of an agricultural working class was greatly increased.

However, the predominant orientation among the workers in this sector was above all towards action over specific labour demands as such, without broader elaborations or wider organization.

Hence, in spite of the small remaining residue of the earlier verbal extremism (which, according to the General Secretary, Mora, had been due more than anything to the excitable petit-bourgeois radicalism of Rómulo Betancourt) the Communist Party followed relatively short-term goals that specifically took into consideration the social and political limitations presented by the social realities of the country. It is characteristic that constant insistence was made in the statements of Manuel Mora, then a Deputy as well as Party General Secretary, on the need to strengthen the participation of the State in the social and economic life of the country, in order to counteract the influence of imperialism and great foreign capital. During more acute periods of crisis, his prescriptions appeared primarily oriented towards the presentation of political and economic programmes that would, without prejudicing workers' interests, make it possible to avoid the crisis becoming converted into a revolutionary confrontation.[6] It was the Communists who, on repeated occasions, proposed a series of measures typical of economic policies of the Keynesian kind: the development of public works projects to provide work and combat unemployment, for example.[7]

One feature that is particularly striking is the near total absence of any systematic policy or programme of political action aimed at breaking down the traditional social and political dominance of the coffee-growing and exporting class in the countryside. This was a reflection both of the social situation in the country as a whole, with its abundance of small producers and absence of acute agrarian conflicts, and of the composition of the Party itself, which as we have said recruited its members mainly in and around the towns. It should be recalled that in 1936 the Central Committee declared with regard to large-scale rural property that they did not consider 'that its suppression is required at the present time. But we do believe that it can be restricted and regulated for the benefit of the people.'[8]

In the face of the so-called imperialist avalanche, the Communist Party did not put forward any of the fundamental policy concepts that had been approved by the International: the carrying out of a bourgeois-democratic revolution, led by the proletariat, by means of the creation of soviets that would permit the establishment of a revolutionary-democratic dictatorship of the workers and peasants, as a transitional stage towards socialism.[9] Instead, what was proposed by the CPCR was, firstly, in its initial period, the simple dictatorship of the proletariat; and then, once it had overcome its extremism, the strengthening of the State, and the need to defend and unite the Costa Rican people, without excluding elements from the coffee-growing bourgeoisie, and conserving the existing democracy, in order to put into effect a policy of anti-imperialism.[10]

This concept of democracy, as a 'pure' political form that should be preserved and protected in the midst of all the processes of social transformation, was a constant motif in the statement and resolutions of the Communist Party.[11] The General Secretary said in the Congress of Deputies in the late 1930s:

I declare that if I believed that in order to put into effect the postulates of the doctrine that I maintain it were necessary to destroy the liberty and all the qualities of the human personality, I would be the first adversary of socialism. It is for this reason that I will struggle with all my strength to defend Costa Rican democracy, without this being in contradiction with either my ideas or my temperament. And I return to my subject: the new regime in the Soviet Union has now been consolidated. If the leaders of that country were to persist, at this stage, in maintaining a dictatorship – for the pleasure of maintaining it – we, the socialists, at least I speak for myself, would call them to account and call them traitors. That aside, I declare yet again that we Costa Rican Communists, are Costa Ricans, who act in accordance with our own realities, and that we do not receive nor will receive orders from agents from outside the country[12].

What one could see here, of course, was a deliberately confused mixture of a Marxist–proletarian conception and the concept of a bourgeois liberal democracy. Nevertheless, for all this confusion the Communists throughout this first period were still able effectively to set about their major tasks of the strengthening of the State, the improvement of living conditions for workers, and so on, while simultaneously putting forward as a condition for and also an additional objective of this process the preservation of that bourgeois democracy that was identified with the essence of Costa Rican nationhood. In 1939 Manuel Mora said:

Neither a complete communist revolution can be on the agenda in our country, since Costa Rica is an economically backward environment, nor can violent revolution be on the agenda, as long as we enjoy democratic institutions that guarantee us the right to think, speak, assemble, organize ourselves and propose and obtain the demands of the Costa Rican people. On the countrary, our Party, in Costa Rica, has to make every effort to defend democratic institutions.[13]

This created for the Costa Rican Party, and above all its leaders, the aura, even among major holders of capital in the country and the leaders of other political parties, of being different from other Communist Parties and their leaders.[14]

DEMOCRATIC POLITICAL SYSTEM AND NATIONAL COMMUNIST PARTY: A MUTUAL USEFULNESS

In consequence the Communist Party had to renounce in fact, and also, after the first few years, even in word, any kind of revolutionary perspective that was not conceived within the framework of existing institutions. Was it indispensable, Mora asked:

> to appeal to arms and stain our soil with blood? It is not indispensable in Costa Rica in present circumstances, and if we are able to ensure that our actions are the correct ones for the situation it is very possible that it will not come to be so in the future . . . revolution is not solely and necessarily the armed action of the people, but also the transformation of systems and institutions that are outdated and obstructive of general welfare.[15]

From this stemmed the Party's predominantly legalistic, electoral and parliamentary character;[16] similarly its policy of alliances, with their essentially reformist objectives oriented not towards putting the apparatus of the State in crisis but to making it into a functional instrument, in union with other classes, in order to 'place it at the service of the labouring classes (*clase trabajadora*) and the country'.[17] The introduction of the term *clase trabajadora,* made by the General Secretary of the Party in substitution of the inapplicable *clase obrera,* is in itself indicative of the conflict in which a Communist Party like that of Costa Rica found itself, in a country with well-rooted liberal-bourgeois traditions, legalized without an industrial working class to sustain it, and made up of elements whose origins were essentially among intellectuals and small-scale craft workers.[18]

In the case of the CPCR, in fact, its Communist identity, its class character and its revolutionary political significance came not so much from its own activities, which, as has been said, far from destroying the established system tended to modernize it, playing a role that was largely functional for this same system, as from its declared identification with the politics and the international symbol represented by the Soviet Union and its Communist Party. The permanent, open and systematic defence of the USSR, very often in a manner that was in contradiction with the political realities that were actually developing within the Soviet state, was the principal element of definition of the CPCR.[19]

Their labour activities, like their political campaigns, were in practice limited to action over simple economic demands, as regards the union organizations, and to the proposition of reforms, with regard to the State and society as a whole.[20] Socially, the Party, during these first years in which it went through periods of a sectarianism typical of a petit-bourgeoisie radicalized by crisis, was not any kind of class party. Its proclamation of itself as such did not go beyond being a simple declaration of intentions. The reality was different: it was an organization with a broad popular base, built mainly upon petit-bourgeois elements of intellectual and artisan origin, which played a role that was radical-democratic, without at any time going outside existing institutional and juridical structures, except in incidental areas such as strike movements which, due to the deficient and class-based legislation then in operation, had still not been given any recognition in law.

The names employed by the Party in its participation in elections are highly illustrative in this regard; firstly, the Worker and Peasant Bloc, and then, later, the Popular Vanguard (Vanguardia Popular). At all times, though, it remained a radical-democratic, petit-bourgeois organization, that only became proletarianized to some degree through the contacts it had with the agricultural working class of the banana-growing areas, and with the shoemakers' unions. This latter contact did for a time signify the participation of factory workers of a kind, as many shoemakers were then working in large workshops, with a significant level of concentration of labour and a crude system of division of labour. However, these factories were later broken up, following the authorization of piece-work in the trade, and replaced once again by the backward and fragmented system of individual craft working, subject to the acutely exploitative disciplines of domestic piece-work.

One aspect of this situation was that the detailed statements of the Communist leadership to the effect that their objectives could be summed up by saying that they wanted a *comunismo a la tica*, some kind of *tico-comunismo*,[21] despite going against everything that had been approved and agreed in the International, had no negative effect on relations with the central Communist organization nor did they lead to any specific condemnation of the Party. It played well the role of untiring defender of the Soviet Union. The Party (particularly Mora, its most influential leader) was a propagandist for Marxism that was manipulated from a nationalist point of view. Central concepts such as democracy, the class organization of the Party, the revolutionary utilization of Parliament and so on were given new meanings. When these features became most clearly visible, it was at a time when the whole of the International had thrown itself behind the policy of the Popular Front, so there was no apparent contradiction.

The latter policy would be one of the major considerations that influenced the declarations made by Mora in 1945, to the effect that in existing conditions 'the class struggle had been replaced by class collaboration'.[22] In saying this, he not only reflected the opinion of Earl Browder, leader of the Communist Party of the USA, which had been publicized via the Party in Cuba, but also a policy of his own organization, which had been steadily gaining in influence thanks to the openness and vigour of the country's political system, and its guarantee of the right of legal participation for the Communist Party.[23]

ABSENCE OF THE INTERNATIONAL AND SUCCESSES OF THE COSTA RICAN COMMUNIST PARTY

In these circumstances, the CPCR was able to weather the most acute moments of the crisis that in the rest of Central America led not only to the prohibition of the various Communist Parties, but also to the physical liquidation of their cadres and militants. The policies followed by the Party thus showed themselves to have evolved in a manner that corresponded to the social and political situation in the country.

These events profoundly affected the future of the Left in Central America, because, once the Communist Parties that were directly linked to the USSR had been destroyed or their subsequent growth limited to a virtually vegetative level, and their existence restricted to little more than a name on the occasional manifesto or document (with the one exception of the Guatemalan Party of Labour,[24] which was able to quickly take advantage of the opportunity created in the country by the fall of the regime of Jorge Ubico), the only Party of this kind that was left with vitality and organization, even in spite of the repression suffered after defeat in the Civil War of 1948, was that of Costa Rica. In the rest of Central America, one would have to wait for the impulse given by the Cuban Revolution and the development of a variety of guerrilla and Castroist movements throughout the region for the Communist movement, now in its Cuban version, to be reconstituted and play a significant role. As a result of this, Castroism acquired under its protective wing a series of political movements in Central America that were 'its own', as one might say, which rapidly gained a position of hegemony among the left of their respective countries; while in Costa Rica this hegemony has always been, and continues to be, held by the Communist Party (under the name Vanguardia Popular).

The differences between the tactics employed by Cubans and Soviets in the region, which varied according to their different perspectives and needs and, above all, their respective interests as national states, are of no small importance for the explanation of these and subsequent differences between the various popular movements themselves. On the contrary, they would be determining factors in many of the tactical choices and strategic orientations of the different political organizations that the regional crisis would bring to the fore in these countries, with regard not just to their political and ideological discourse but also to their very basis of political support.

Returning to the Costa Rican Party, after proclaiming, therefore, its initial objective as being the achievement of the dictatorship of the proletariat, social realities obliged it to modify this goal to one of a democratic State that would recover the natural riches of the country from the control of imperialism, follow an independent foreign policy and constitute a central axis and focus of union for all the anti-imperialist forces in the nation, while simultaneously preserving the existing liberal democracy. The change of its name from Communist Party to Popular Vanguard Party (Partido Vanguardia Popular) was not simply the result of a tactical manoeuvre, but reflected substantive issues in terms of moral, social and political attitudes within the movement, and in its specific programme.[25]

It sought to modify the established social system by means of structural reforms that did not in any way seek to destroy the superior position of the traditional ruling classes, but rather to redefine their relations with the other classes in society. Its fundamental conflict with this system did not, therefore, arise out of its actual political activity, which was more likely in the long run to be useful to it. It arose, as we have indicated, from the Party's ideal identification with the aims, policies and international image of the Soviet Union, which by this time, following its failures in Nicaragua and El Salvador, had ceased to take an interest in the region, and did not have organizational links with the Costa Rican Party.

The result of this was that the latter became a mass movement that was democratic and pugnacious, and which existed in relative isolation from the Communist International. As has been mentioned, it was not that no links existed; the contacts with Ricardo Martínez in New York, the sending of Rodolfo Guzmán to the union school in Moscow, and so on, demonstrate the contrary. It was only that the isolation of the country, its small size and the flexibility of its political system, which, uniquely in Central America, conceded legality to the Communist Party, permitted the Party's leaders to follow a course that in practice, and ultimately, though with a certain delay, also in language, renounced a revolutionary policy that did not correspond to the conditions existing in the country and sought in the light of concrete practice, of their empirical experience, responses to the urgent social and political needs of Costa Rica.

The fact that it was precisely in Costa Rica where the Communist movement managed to make most progress – albeit along a path that encouraged reformism and put off the prospect of revolution in favour of gradual change and the consolidation of bourgeois-democratic freedoms, while in the rest of Central America, and particularly in Nicaragua and El Salvador, both the political leadership and the other democratic elements were decimated in waves of repression – clearly suggests one initial judgement on the role of the International in the region. Everything seems to support the belief that it was in fact this weakness of the ties with the Comintern and the absence of any real political will to attempt to put into effect within the country the resolutions that were received from abroad – resolutions that not only sounded unworkable but were ultimately incomprehensible, given the prevailing conditions – that made it possible to conserve in Costa Rica a number of popular gains, create independent democratic organizations and move forward in the direction of social progress, even if this was at the expense of the socialist and communist perspective that, though present in the subjective ideas of the Party's members, was always remote from its actual political practice. This practice was itself, in turn, only feasible due to the absence of real organizational links, and effective political controls, between the Communist International and the CPCR.

It was also not possible to formalize diplomatic ties between Costa Rica and Moscow. Although it was argued by the Communist Party that the government had 'tacitly recognized the Soviet Union', the tragic death of Oumansky, the first Soviet Ambassador, prevented the development of this relationship.[27]

Many years later Manuel Mora, General Secretary of the communist Popular Vanguard Party, himself acknowledged this lack of contact between the Communist International and the Communist movement in Costa Rica. In a statement made in 1978 he said, 'When the Second World War broke out, we were also guided by our principles. The propaganda financed by world imperialism did not succeed in deceiving us. We maintained our faith in the Soviet Union and in its Communist Party, and we were not mistaken. *At that time we did not have any relations with the Soviet Party. We came to establish such relations in 1955, twenty-four years after our foundation.*'[28]

Conclusion

For the International, the real centre of interest in Central America was in Nicaragua, in Augusto César Sandino's struggle against American intervention. This campaign was given support via the League against Imperialism.

The Comintern had four objectives in Nicaragua: (a) to support the nationalist struggle against Yankee intervention; (b) to convert it from a nationalist campaign into a struggle for social emancipation; (c) to intensify the tensions that existed between the United States and Britain over the control of Latin America; and (d) to use it as the basis for a massive worldwide campaign of anti-imperialist propaganda, in order to mobilize public opinion and in particular that of the petit-bourgeois democratic intelligentsia, against US interventionism in the Caribbean.

We have shown that, in effect, there were partial successes achieved in the first of these objectives, thanks, above all, to the small-nation nationalism of the Nicaraguan people; resounding failures in the second and the third; and quite a substantial degree of success, though without any permanent organizational consequences, in the fourth.

The tactics employed consisted of attempting to secure the ideological conversion of the leader in order to control the movement. It was for this reason that there was neither a Communist Party in Nicaragua nor any other surviving organization with the potential to continue Sandino's struggle, after the General had unjustly and slanderously been declared a traitor who had let himself be bought by American imperialism.

This essentially leader-centred, *caudillista* approach demonstrated an objective disregard for internal phenomena within the country and for the specifically Nicaraguan prospects and potential of Sandino's movement, and, concomitantly, an overestimation of its international significance. Sandino thus became for good or ill an isolated leader figure, a *caudillo*, not just for his own people but also for the Communist International. The latter, for its part, was unable to implement any kind of recognizable policy through its influence with him. The problems in constructing a Party within Nicaragua were not even considered, nor were any lessons drawn from the guerrilla experience in Las Segovias that could have been useful and of value for the Latin American communist movement as a whole. Nicaragua was nothing more than a profitable propaganda episode to be used in a skilful and unscrupulous manner, and which remained only a mark in the collective memory of the country that survived in spite of all the efforts made to denigrate the guerrilla leader's achievements.

A politico-military conception of the problem was also lacking, one suitable both for application in the reality of Nicaragua at that time, and for later development and enrichment with other examples from practical experience. The United States forces, on the other hand, for their part certainly did apply in China some military tactics that they had previously tried out with success in Nicaragua.[1] The problem of the relationship between the Party organization and the guerrilla forces fighting in the countryside was equally left unconsidered. These political errors and ambivalent theoretical attitudes were reflected too in the disparities and tensions in Sandino's entourage, provoked by the APRA and the Comintern, symbolized by Pavletich and Martí. Whatever may have been the expectations of the International, ambiguities of language – such as the use of 'proletariat' and 'united front' in *Sandinista* manifestos – are deceptive, as it is clear from all of Sandino's conduct that his movement was one of national liberation, with a broad democratic and popular base, and a product of the traditional Latin American attitude of self-assertion in the face of the expansionism of the United States. The Comintern gave its attention to external and propaganda questions, to its own formulas and pre-conceptions, but was incapable of responding to the realities of Nicaragua and the national aspirations of its people. These hopes and expectations deserved better than to be reduced to the status of a simple launching-pad for ill-founded theses as far removed from real conditions as those that the Communist International sought to apply in the region.

The tragedy of Sandino did not result solely from the actions of his enemies and adversaries. His betrayal and murder by Somoza, and the imperialist attitude of the United States in that particular period of history, reflected known interests and well-defined policies. The tragedy was also caused, however, by many of his friends and allies, who did not acknowledge Sandino's right to think first of all of the needs of his own people. His links with the Mexican President Plutarco Elías Calles were, for example, one element in this double tragedy. For, necessarily obliged to maintain a close relationship with Mexico in order to sustain his arduous campaign, Sandino was then required to pay the consequences of any of Calles' policies. The latter's break with the USSR made him into an ally of Yankee imperialism in the eyes of the Comintern. Since Sandino was linked to Calles, the guerrilla leader was therefore then in turn considered to have sold out to imperialism, at second hand. In reality, the viewpoint of the International was very simple: whatever was not linked in with the immediate needs and convenience of the USSR, understood in the most simple and direct manner possible, automatically became reactionary and pro-imperialist. Against such forces, any and all means were valid, including the labelling as a traitor of the erstwhile hero of Las Segovias.

In contrast to the situation in Nicaragua, in El Salvador the International operated mainly as an intermediary for International Red Aid, and under the slogan of 'class against class'.

During the same period, Chen Kuo Tao and Wang Ming's adventurism flourished in China, as a reaction against the supposed rightist deviations of the old leadership of the Communist Party in that country. In Central America, the rightist error would have been the support given to Sandino, and leaving the effective direction of the movement in the hands of leaders from the radicalized nationalist petit-bourgeoisie. The leftist reaction would be the insurrection in El Salvador. An appropriate analogy, of the type so dear to the International, arises here spontaneously: after the betrayal by Chiang Kai Shek, the Canton Commune; after that by Sandino, the Salvadorean rising of 1932.

The attitude shown towards the struggles and tragedies of both of these Central American peoples by the International and its leaders was not just irresponsible, but contemptuous. They declared the Nicaraguan fighters to be traitors, and labelled the Salvadoreans as *macheteros* or 'machete gangs'.[2] The Comintern also dissociated itself entirely and denied having any contact with the revolutionaries, while opportunistically condemning them to oblivion.

The actions of the Communist International in Central America demonstrate the manner in which a Eurocentric model was imposed over and above experience, dogma over reality, and texts before real life. In spite of Comintern's sectarianism, political processes struggled to make their way forward. However, the conglomeration of texts and dogmas, given priority over actual events, still continued to lead the living, real and spontaneous movement of the masses into a blank wall time and again.

It is for this reason that the third example we have analyzed, that of Costa Rica, where the International was virtually conspicuous by its absence and where substantial and permanent gains actually were made, is so valuable and so highly significant.

As we have seen, in Nicaragua the *Sandinista* movement was clearly one of national liberation, against US intervention and its puppet governments, while in El Salvador the local movement was one with deep social roots that were predominantly agrarian, albeit that it also contained important urban components, and used proletarian slogans. In Costa Rica, on the other hand, one saw the only example of a legalized Communist Party that operated effectively in a relatively developed bourgeois liberal democracy.

The open nature of the Costa Rican political system facilitated the incorporation into the political structure of the newly-formed Communist Party. This organization even acted as a functional element for strengthening the democratic institutions of the country. The absence of organizational links with the Comintern allowed its leaders to diagnose freely the different factors that made up their own national realities, and to attempt indigenous responses to them that were open to being corrected and developed in the light of the concrete evidence of their results.

As Rómulo Betancourt, the future President of Venezuela who in the 1930s was among the leaders of the Costa Rican Communist Party, observed:

The so-called Caribbean Bureau of the International is the most perfect example of ineptitude and verbose petulance that one can imagine. As of today, after almost a year of contacts with the group here, they have still not managed to agree terms with it . . . Because, what they call 'accepting the line of the International' is to take in, without the benefit of an inventory, all the abstract clichés a hundred and more kilometres removed from reality that are put together among the little cliques of New York. And, while they carry on without sorting out the most vital points at issue, they continue unbending in sending out the same set of directives by every mail . . . All this gives the impression of a suffocating bureaucratism, of a disregard for fundamental questions in favour of an excessive attention to everything that is mechanical, formalistic, to the politics of duplicated circulars.[3]

This description of the Bureau by Betancourt was combined with a recognition of the strong position of the Costa Rican party in its own environment, while at the same time criticizing the Party itself for its 'democratic illusions' and for 'a certain tendency, which has even infected some of its leaders, to establish themselves and settle down in legality'.[4] However, the complete disjunction between the slogans of the International and the practical realities of this environment could only reinforce the national identity of the Costa Rican Communist movement and further encourage it to operate independently and strengthen its autonomy through the broad overall successes that it accumulated in its favour on the basis of its realistic policies.

The milieu in which the Communist Party of Costa Rica was required to operate was of course substantially different from the classical Central American environment that had to be dealt with by the movements in Nicaragua and El Salvador. However, it was the weakness of its organizational links with the International that enabled the small Party to avoid the sectarian adventurism that was seen to be fatal in the other two countries.

Failure firstly in Nicaragua and then in El Salvador coincided with a fascist offensive in Europe and the growing threat of a war against the USSR. Since the real political significance of the region was lost on Stalin and the Soviet Party, the Comintern virtually abandoned it, precisely at the point when the young CPCR was emerging with some strength. This was clearly a factor of decisive importance in enabling the Party to adjust itself to reality, disregard the 'ukases of the International', as Betancourt called them,[5] and approach the problems of social change in Costa Rica creatively. This saved the Party from the situation pointed to by Carlos Rafael Rodríguez when, in drawing up a pessimistic balance of the experiences of those years, he wrote, 'while we were dependent on reports drawn up thousands of miles away, and without any real contact with our continent, frustrated efforts only repeated themselves'.[6] It also made it possible for the General Secretary of the Party to proclaim as their task, in 1939, the establishment of a *'comunismo a la tica'*.

A final balance of the record of the International in the region must therefore be highly negative. It failed to comprehend the real social and political structure of Latin American societies. It was not able to identify the motive forces that were bringing about change in Central America, nor to define the social elements that could have sustained genuinely revolutionary policies in the region. It failed in its analysis of social classes and, consequently, in the fundamental question of the Party. It was unable to resolve the problems created by an approach to military questions that bound together an operative and effective military structure with Party organization, and was mistaken in its conception of the very nature of the Latin American revolution. Moreover, these are all errors that could be perceived through the internal logic of its own Marxist-Leninist categories.

One should acknowledge, however, that the Comintern did in some way intuitively come close to the realities of Nicaragua and El Salvador, when it differentiated between the organizations through which it should channel its operations: the League against Imperialism in the first case, and International Red Aid in the second. This to some extent signified a recognition of the nature of the problem in Nicaragua as being one of national liberation, and of the predominantly social-revolutionary character of the situation in El Salvador. However, this was only one moment of inspiration, which did nothing to avoid the dramatic consequences of an essentially mistaken policy. With this policy the International put forward, from Moscow, illusory objectives alien to reality, and launched upon a hopeless struggle men who only sought the independence of their homeland, or a social emancipation that the depth of existing injustice had for them made an urgent necessity. In Central America, the Central Americans provided the dead, who in the annals of the International were then denied the least recognition for their sacrifice. For them there were neither flowers nor tributes, as their Mexica and Toltec forebears might have desired. There was only an effacement from memory and a consignment to oblivion, the product of the purest and most disdainful opportunism.

Notes and References

Introduction

1. Letter by Marx to Siegfried Meyer and August Vogt, 9 April 1870. In Karl Marx and Friedrich Engels, *On Colonialism* (New York, International Publishers, 1972) p. 335.
2. Karl Marx, *Capital* (London, Penguin, 1976) Preface to 1st edn, p. 92.
3. See Karl Marx, and Friedrich Engels, *Selected Works* (Moscow, Progress, 1968) particularly the *Communist Manifesto*.
4. In V.I. Lenin, *Selected Works* (Moscow, Progress, 1968) pp. 50–148.
5. See 'Lecture on the 1905 Revolution', in V.I. Lenin, *The Beginning of the Revolution in Russia* (Moscow, Progress, 1956) pp. 57–75.
6. *Pravda*, 5 May 1922. In V.I. Lenin, *Collected Works* (Moscow, Progress, 1966) vol. 33, p. 350.
7. In Jane Degras (ed.), *The Communist International 1919–1943. Documents* (London, Frank Cass, 1971) vol. I, 1919–22, p. 43. Emphasis by the author.
8. See M.N. Roy, *Memoirs,* sponsored by the Indian Renaissance Institute (Dehara Dun, Bombay, New Delhi, Calcutta, Allied Publishers, 1964) pp. 378–81. See also M.N. Roy, *Selected Works* (ed. Sibnarayn Ray) (New Delhi, Oxford University Press, 1987) vol. I, 1917–22; Alfred Rosmer, *Moscou sous Lenine* (Paris, Maspero, 1970) vol. I, p. 117 ff.; Pierre Andre, *Compte Rendu des débats d'aprés les journaux de Moscou* (Paris, Bibliothéque du Parti Socialist de l'Humanité, 1920); 'Russian Protocol', pp. 105–7 in Enrica Collotti and Chiara Robertazzi, *La Internacional Comunista y los Problemas Coloniales 1919–1935* (Paris–Geneva, Droz, 1973) p. 31 ff.; Second Congress of the Communist International, *Minutes*, Petrograd, 17 June/Moscow, 23 July–7 August 1920 (Petrograd, n.d.); Demetrio Boersner, *The Bolsheviks and the National and Colonial Question (1917–1928)* thesis 106, University of Geneva, Institut Universitaire des Hautes Etudes Internationaux, 1957.
9. Partido Socialista Popular.
10. Carlos Rafael Rodríguez, *Lenin y la Cuestión Colonial* (Chile, Editorial Prensa Latinoamericana S.A., 1973) pp. 91–2.
11. Roy, *Memoirs*, pp. 380–1.
12. Ibid, p. 379.
13. See 'Russian Protocol', pp. 110–12 in Collotti and Robertazzi, op. cit., p. 33; and Boersner, op. cit., p. 87. This same Fraina was sent to Mexico to organize and head the Comintern Bureau in Latin America, according to Roy in his *Memoirs* (p. 371).
14. Alianza Popular Revolucionaria Americana.
15. Eugene Varga, 'La situation économique mondiale au prémier trimestre 1926', La *Correspondance Internationale*, no. 48, 28 May 1926, p. 753;

180

see also *La Correspondance Internationale*, no. 17, 5 February 1927, p. 232 and no. 9, 19 January 1927; J.F. Penelon, 'Chile and Anglo-American Imperialism', *Communist International*, no. 23, 1926, pp. 70–80; article by L. Heller in *Communist International*, no. 9, 1 March 1927, pp. 424–31; 'A propos de l'insurrection en Bolivie', *La Correspondance Internationale*, no. 90, 31 August 1927, p. 1250; Eugene Varga, 'La situation économique mondiale', *La Correspondance Internationale*, no. 63, 10 June 1927, p. 848.

16. See 'VII Executive Elargi', La *Correspondance Internationale*, no. 140, 23 December 1926, p. 1788. On this subject see also 'Protocol of the VII Plenum of the Executive Committee of the Communist International', 22 November 1926, p. 221, quoted in Boersner, op. cit., p. 208; and articles by Manuilsky in *La Correspondance Internationale*, no. 142, 28 December 1926, p. 1834; and Dubrovsky in *La Correspondance Internationale*, no. 138, 20 December 1926, p. 1743.

17. This occurred, for example, in the case of students from Latin America, who were educated as Party cadres at the Communist University of the Toilers of the East. See *La Internacional Comunista. Ensayo histórico suscinto* (Moscow, Editorial Progreso, n.d.) p. 235.

18. See *La Correspondance Internationale*, no. 53, 7 June 1928, p. 623.

19. This was one of the most important documents on Latin America examined in the discussions of the International, see *La Correspondance Internationale*, no. spécial XXXVIII, no. 118, 9t October 1928, p. 1261 ff. For the report and contribution by Kuusinen, see *La Correspondance Internationale*, no. spécial XL, no. 122, 15 October 1928, pp. 1318–19. In his memoirs Humbert-Droz places the preparation of his report and the theses contained in it as having been after his visit to Latin America, when in reality they had been completed much earlier. He was in Latin America between February and August 1929; the report had been presented, as we have said, to the Sixth Congress on 16 August 1928: see Jules Humbert-Droz, *De Lénine á Staline* (Neuchatel, Editions de la Baconnière, 1971) pp. 9, 380, 381, note 1 ff.

20. *La Correspondance Internationale*, no. spécial XL, no. 122, 15 October 1928, pp. 1264–5.

21. Ibid, pp. 1265–6.

22. Ibid, p. 1267.

23. N. Bukharin, 'La situation Internationale et les taches de l'I.C.' La *Correspondance Internationale*, no. spécial XI, no. 72, 1 August 1928, p. 837. The Brazilian delegate González said in the 24th session, on 4 August, that 'the antagonism between American and English imperialism is becoming particularly acute in these countries and must lead to a war between them (the two powers)'. See *La Correspondance Internationale*, no. spécial XXXI, no. 106, 20 September 1928, p. 1132; also the intervention by Lovestone, of the USA, in the 19th session on 2 August, La *Correspondance Internationale*, no. spécial XXVII, no. 97, 2 September 1928, p. 1038.

24. See 34th session, 17 August, *La Correspondance Internationale*, no. spécial XLII, no. 125, 19 October 1928, pp. 1360–1. Paredes was a founder member of the Communist Party of Ecuador in 1926. A doctor

by profession, he also founded the Workers' Confederation of Ecuador (*Confederación de Trabajadores del Ecuador*, CTE) in 1944 and was the first President of the Ecuadorean Federation of Indians (*Federación Ecuatoriana de Indios*, FEI). A member of the Constituent Assembly in 1945, he was founder and editor of *Antorcha*, the first Communist Party newspaper in Ecuador, and also of the weekly *El Pueblo*, the newspaper of the Party Central Committee in the 1970s. Like Pedro Saad, he showed particular interest in Central American affairs. He died of a heart attack in Quito at the age of 81 on 13 September 1979.

25. See 34th session, 17 August, La *Correspondance Internationale* no. spécial XLII, no. 125, 19 October 1928, pp. 1365–7. Still clearer evidence of the confusion that existed on this key point was provided by the intervention of the Colombian delegate, Cárdenas, who in the 38th session on 20 August declared, 'I expect that the revolution in Latin America will be something intermediate between the socialist revolution and a petit-bourgeois revolution', *La Correspondance Internationale*, no. spécial XLVII, no. 139, 20 November 1928, p. 1575.

26. See 'El movimiento revolucionario Latinoamericano. Versiones de la Primera Conferencia Comunista Junio 1929', *Correspondencia Sudamericana*, Buenos Aires, n.d. On the Montevideo conference, see M. Ch., 'Conference des syndicats de l'Amérique Latine contre la guerre', *La Correspondance Internationale*, no. 37, 4 May 1929, p. 522 ff.; and 'Salut á la Confédération Syndicale d'Amérique Latine', in *Internationale Syndicale Rouge*, no. 101, June 1929, pp. 319–21, in which the participation is recorded of the General Confederation of Labour (*Confederación General del Trabajo*) of Costa Rica and the Regional Workers' Federation (*Federación Obrera Regional*) of Guatemala and El Salvador, as will be examined in more detail below.

27. Humbert-Droz's impressions on his journey can be found in his memoirs, *De Lénine á Staline*, pp. 9, 380–1, note 1 ff. He mistakenly places the date of the second conference in July, one month after it was actually held.

28. *La Correspondance Internationale*, no. 10, 1 February 1930, p. 100.

29. See second part of 'Draft thesis', *La Correspondance Internationale*, no. 11, 5 February 1930, p. 112.

30. See G. Sinai, 'A Cuba se constituent les soviets', La *Correspondance Internationale*, no. 98–99, 15 December 1933, p. 1207. See also the Manifesto of the Communist Party of Cuba ('only a government of worker and peasant soviets will liberate Cuba from the yoke of Yankee imperialism and its indigenous agents . . . Long live the anti-imperialist agrarian revolution!') *La Correspondance Internationale*, no. 70–71, 2 September 1933, p. 861; and J. Gómez, 'Les événements révolutionnaires á Cuba et les taches du P.C.', *La Correspondance Internationale*, no. 75–76, 11 September 1933, pp. 926–30, which insistis upon the creation of the democratic revolutionary dictatorship of the workers and peasants on the basis of soviets. This recommendation was generalized, and considered as much applicable in Spain as in China, in the Orient as in Latin America. See, for example, 'Pour le pouvoir des Soviets', *L'Internationale Communiste*, no. 22, 20 November 1934, p. 1463.

31. This conclusion is shared, albeit with certain differences with regard to causes, by Degras in *The Communist International*, vol. III, pp. v–vii, and similarly Fernando Claudín, *La Crisis del Movimiento Comunista. De la Komintern al Kominform* (Paris, Ruedo Ibérico, 1970) ch. I.

32. See M. Ch., 'La tactique de l'unité aux pays de l'Amérique Latine', in *L'Internationale Syndicale Rouge*, no. 8, 30 April 1932, p. 410; also 'Lettre ouverte á Haya de la Torre', *La Correspondance Internationale*, no. 44–45, 1 June 1935, pp. 659–61. For the negative reply by the APRA, see no. 95–96, 19 October 1935, p. 1399.

33. Claudín, op. cit., p. 130.

34. Rodríguez, op. cit., p. 109.

1 A Revolution in Incubation: Nicaragua in the 1920s

1. *Communist International*, no. 166-17, 1921.

2. *La Correspondance Internationale*, no. 216, 5 November 1922, p. 11; quoted in Enrica Colloti Pischel and Chiara Robertazzi, *La Internacional Comunista y los Problemas Coloniales, 1919–1935*, (Paris-Geneva, Droz, 1973) p. 127.

3. *Communist International*, no. 14, 1925, p. 9.

4. 'Résolution sur le traité de Versailles', *Les quatre premiers congrès mondiaux de l'International Communiste, 1919–1923* (Paris, François Maspero, 1972) p. 168.

5. Demetrio Boersner, *The Bolsheviks and the National and Colonial Question (1917–1928)*, thesis, University of Geneva, Institut Universitaire des Hautes Etudes Internationaux, 1957, p. 147.

6. Workers' Socialist Unification – Unificación Obrera Socialista. FRT – Federación Regional del Trabajo.

7. COCA – Confederación Obrera Centroamericana.

8. Workers' Federation etc. – Federación Obrera de la Defensa Legal del Trabajo.

9. Union Action Committee – Comité de Acción Sindical.

10. Society for Workers' Life Insurance – Sociedad de Seguros de Vida de Obreros.

11. 'Le mouvement ouvrier au Guatemala', *La Correspondance Internationale*, no. 89, 18 September 1929, p. 1216.

12. I. Pérez, 'Le Honduras sous le joug de l'impérialisme', *La Correspondance Internationale*, no. 100–101, 9 December 1933, p. 1250.

13. *Statistical Abstract of Latin America 1966* (Los Angeles, Latin American Center, University of California, 1967) pp. 48–9.

14. *Memorias del Recaudador General de Aduanas*, Managua, cited by Pedro Belli in 'Prolegómenos para una Historia Económica de Nicaragua de 1905 a 1966', *Revista del Pensamiento Centroamericano*, vol. XXX, Managua, January–March 1975, no. 146, p. 9.

15. Ibid, p. 12.

16. Ibid.

17. Edelberto Torres, *Interpretación del Desarrollo Social Centroamericano* (San José, EDUCA, 1971) p. 77; José A. Alonso, 'Elites gobernantes y

Familismo en Nicaragua', *Revista de Estudios Centroamericanos,* vol. 28, no. 296, pp. 339–40.

18. Belli, op. cit., p. 9.
19. Ibid.
20. Harold Norman Denny, *Dollars for Bullets (The Story of American Rule in Nicaragua)* (New York, The Dial Press, 1929) p. 49. The author, a correspondent for the *New York Times,* undertook research in Nicaragua in 1927–8.
21. Torres, op. cit., p. 71.
22. Ibid, p. 75.
23. See Chapter 2, page 00, in the present volume.
24. The first documentary record of American interest in the canal route through Nicaragua consists of the letter sent on 8 February 1825 to John Quincy Adams, Secretary of State under Monroe, by Antonio José Cañas, Ambassador of Central America in Washington, in which the latter declared that his principal mission was to promote 'The opening of a canal for the communication of the Pacific and Atlantic oceans in the province of Nicaragua'. See *Correspondencia de las Naciones Latinoamericanas,* selected and edited by William R. Mannings (Buenos Aires, Editorial La Facultad, 1931) vol. II, pp. 1041–2.
25. Diego Manuel Sequeira, *Emission et Amortissement des Emprunts Extérieurs de la République de Nicaragua pendant le Premier Quart du Siécle,* doctoral thesis, Paris, Librairie Générale de Droit et de Jurisprudence, 1931.
26. Raymond Leslie Buell, 'The Central Americas', *Foreign Policy Association,* Pamphlet No. 69, New York, December 1930, p. 13.
27. Ibid.
28. See Thomas F. Lee, *Latin-American Problems, Their Relation to our Investors' Billions* (New York, Brower, Warren 38; Putman, 1932) pp. 147–9.
29. Charles Wurm, 'The Intervention of the US in Nicaragua', *Communist International,* vol. 9, no. 4, January 1927, p. 12.
30. Sequeira, op. cit., p. 8.
31. Quoted in Gregorio Selser, *Sandino, General de Hombres Libres* (Buenos Aires, Editorial Triángulo, 1958) vol. I, pp. 43–4.
32. Dana Munro, *Intervention and Dollar Diplomacy in the Caribbean, 1900–1921* (Princeton, NJ, Princeton University Press, 1964) p. 162.
33. Sequeira, op. cit., pp. 36–7.
34. Raymond Leslie Buell, 'The United States and Central American Stability', *Foreign Policy Reports,* vol. VII, no. 9, 8 July 1931, p. 481.
35. Munro states with regard to these events, in commenting on the way in which the US intervened to maintain Díaz in power, that 'The intervention in Nicaragua in 1912 marks a turning point in American policy in the Caribbean. Before 1912, the Navy frequently undertook shows of strength to avoid fighting that could put foreigners in danger, or to discourage revolutionary activities . . . but there had been no case before 1912 in which American forces had fully entered into battle to suppress a revolution.' Munro, op. cit., p. 215.
36. Sequeira, op. cit., p. 11.

37. Ramón Romero, *Sandino y los Yanquis* (Mexico, Ediciones Patria y Libertad, 1961) p. 102.
38. Ernesto Martín, 'Una Carta al Hermano del Presidente Calles a Propósito del Escándalo de Nicaragua', *Revista Repertorio Americano*, vol. XIV, San José, 1927, p. 71.
39. Letter published in *Century Magazine* and in the US *Congressional Record* (13 January 1917, p. 1577) quoted in Selser, op. cit., p. 68, and in Juan del Camino, 'El Tratado Chamorro–Bryan es un Tratado Humillante y Fenicio', *Repertorio Americano*, vol. XXIV, San José, 1933, p. 22.
40. *Congressional Record. Proceedings and Debates of the 2nd. Session of the 67th Congress*, Washington, vol. LXLI, part 9a., pp. 8941–2; also Selser, op. cit., p. 73.
41. John Kennet Turner, 'Shall it be again?', quoted in Selser, op. cit., pp. 81–2.
42. Denny, op. cit., p. 245.
43. P.S., 'La Politique d'Intervention des Etas-Units au Nicaragua et au Méxique', *La Correspondance Internationale*, no. 16, 5 February 1927, p. 228. The author is only identified by initial. See also M. Tanin, 'L'offensive Impérialiste des Etats-Unis', *La Correspondance Internationale*, no.10, 22 January 1927, p. 132; George Harrison, 'Les Intrigues des Etats-Unis au Nicaragua', *La Correspondance Internationale*, 12 January 1925, p. 75; 'Izvestia', 'La Prestidigitation de la Diplomatie Américaine', *La Correspondance Internationale*, no. 16, 2 January 1927, p. 214.
44. In Rafael De Nogales, *The Looting of Nicaragua* (New York, R. M. McBride, 1928) p. 116 ff. Intervention by Senator Wheeler.
45. *La Prensa*, New York, 24 February 1927. Quoted in Romero, op. cit., p. 137.
46. Carleton Beals, *L'Amérique Latine: Monde en Révolution* (Paris, Payot, 1966) p. 72.
47. Nogales, op. cit., p. 116 ff..
48. Denny, op. cit., p. 247.
49. In his book *American Policy in Nicaragua*, commenting on his participation in these events, Stimson states, 'For a century (referring to all the Latin American countries) we have been scrupulous defenders of their independence, not only against Europe, but also sometimes against themselves. The latter is particularly true with regard to the Central American republics'. Henry L. Stimson, *American Policy in Nicaragua* (New York, Charles Scribner's Sons, 1927) p. 94.
50. Nogales, op. cit., p. 135.
51. Ibid, p. 285.
52. Ibid, p. 241.

2 The Indigenous Origins of the Sandinista Movement

1. Sandino recounted that when he was in Mexico, in 1925, and when his resolve to leave for Nicaragua was still in a state of development, he felt

most profoundly wounded when he was called 'a seller of his country, a shameless wretch, a traitor', because he was not fighting for his country. He added that at first he replied that as he was not a political man he did not feel he deserved such epithets, but that afterwards he reflected on the matter and understood that people who said such things were right, since, as a Nicaraguan, he had at the least a right to protest, and so decided to join Moncada's revolt. From then on, he said, he dedicated himself to searching for the hundred men who loved Nicaragua as much as he did, and who would fight to restore its complete sovereignty, placed in danger by yankee imperialism. See Sergio Ramírez Mercado (ed.), *El Pensamiento Vivo de Sandino* (San José, EDUCA, 1974) pp. 63–4.

2. Ejército Defensor de la Soberanía de Nicaragua.
3. It is important to point out that it was in the war against Sandino that the United States first put into practice the use of aircraft as support for infantry in counter-insurgent operations, and experimented with bombing by airborne patrols. The technical superiority of the US forces over a few hundred poorly armed men was not sufficient to defeat the *Sandinista* army, whose courage and heroism have been recognized even by American military experts. Sandino said that his arsenal was in the United States, as the only modern armaments they possessed were those which they managed to capture from the Marines. See Thomas Vernon Meggee, 'Contra las Guerrillas de Sandino en Nicaragua', *Revista Conservadora del Pensamiento Centroamericano*, vol. 24, no. 119, 1970, pp. 42–51. Also Ramírez Mercado, op. cit., pp. 12, 126 and 135.
4. Carleton Beals, 'With Sandino in Nicaragua', *The Nation*, no. CXXVI, 22 February–11 April 1928. Also quoted in Ramírez Mercado, op. cit., p. 132.
5. Ramón Belausteguigoitia, *Con Sandino en Nicaragua* (Madrid, Espasa Calpe, 1934) p. 111.
6. Neill Macaulay, *Sandino* (San José, Editorial Universitaria Centroamericana, 1970) p. 298.
7. Romero, op. cit., p. 163.
8. Macaulay, op. cit., p. 251.
9. Ibid, p. 142.
10. Ibid, p. 250.
11. Ramírez Mercado, op. cit., pp. 150–1.
12. Confederación Regional Obrera Mexicana.
13. Salomón de la Selva, 'Al pueblo de Nicaragua', *Repertorio Americano*, vol. XIV, San José, 1927, p. 65.
14. It is of interest to note here what the Communist Gustavo Machado wrote in this regard, from Sandino's camp: 'Political disorientation is more apparent among the intellectuals and among the "Patriots". They defend national sovereignty in the name of our race and the Hispano-American spirit, and are totally ignorant of the true economic situation of the country and the nature of the source of its oppresion. Against imperialism they still use romantic arguments, and political Girondinism continues to inspire the purest spirits. The producer class has scarcely

begun its reorganization, its struggle against imperialism places it "outside the law", and it only sees any guarantee of its security in the support of one of the two political parties, both of them composed of class enemies' (Gustavo Machado, 'La situación en Nicaragua', *Repertorio Americano*, vol. XVI, no. 26, San José, 28 April 1928, p. 269). Although Machado does not specifically mention Sandino, it is not too speculative to suggest that it was his recent contact with the General that provided the material for these conclusions.

15. Ramírez Mercado, op. cit., p. 95.
16. Anastasio Somoza, *El Verdadero Sandino o el Calvario de Las Segovias* (Managua, Tipografía Robelo, 1936) p. 56.
17. Selser, op. cit., p. 288 ff. It is interesting to note that in this Manifesto Sandino already uses the term *Indohispano*, which was frequently used in *Aprista* writings, though in the form 'Indoamerican' (*Indoamericano*).
18. Selser, op. cit., vol. I, p. 288 ff.
19. Italicized in the Spanish text (*translator's note*).
20. Quoted in Selser, op. cit., vol. II, pp. 47 and 58; and in Somoza, op. cit., p. 119 ff. My italics.
21. Somoza, op. cit., p. 294 ff.
22. Italicized in the Spanish text.
23. Selser, op. cit., vol. II, pp. 161–2.
24. Coquetear.
25. Somoza, op. cit., p. 312.
26. Selser, op. cit., p. 261.
27. Italicized in the Spanish text.
28. Ibid.
29. Xavier Campos Ponce, *Los Yanquis y Sandino* (Mexico D.F., Ediciones XCP, 1962) pp. 126, 278 ff.
30. Somoza, op. cit., p. 372 ff.
31. Ibid.
32. Ibid, p. 372 ff.
33. Selser, op. cit., vol. II, p. 197. My italics.
34. In the *Boletín de la Unión Panamericana* of February 1933, p. 73, it was reported that 'He (Sacasa) presented his credentials to the government of the United States on 15th April 1929, and remained in Washington until a few months before the elections of 6th November of last year, his agreeable personality and exceptional talent winning him many friends in social, governmental and diplomatic circles.'
35. Selser, op. cit., vol. II, p. 199.
36. Romero, op. cit., p. 210 ff.
37. Raymond Leslie Buel, 'The Central Americas', pp. 8–9.
38. Selser, op. cit., vol. II, p. 308.
39. Ibid, p. 297.
40. Ibid, p. 286.
41. Romero, op. cit., pp. 225–6.
42. On Sandino's esotericism, see Ramírez Mercado, op. cit., pp. 205, 206, 209, 210 and 288; Somoza, op. cit., pp. 177, 178, 203 and 210; Gustavo Alemán Bolaños, *Sandino el Libertador* (Mexico–Guatemala, Ediciones del Caribe, 1951) p. 119; and Selser, op. cit., vol. II, p. 122.

43. Alianza Popular Revolucionaria Americana, also referred to as 'Movimiento Aprista'.

44. Romain Rolland, 'A Coté de l'Amérique Latine', *Repertorio Americano*, vol. XIV, no. 9, San José, 1927, p. 133.

45. Letters from Sandino to Froylán Turcios of 8 and 20 September 1927, in Selser, op. cit., vol. II, pp. 293–4; letter from Sandino to Turcios of 24 September 1927, published in *Repertorio Americano*, vol. XVI, San José, 1927, p. 340.

46. Alemán Bolaños, op. cit., p. 38.

47. This appears in a clearly schematic form in Haya de la Torre, Víctor Raúl, '¿Qué es el APRA?', *Repertorio Americano*, vol. XIV, San José, 1927, p. 131; see also Magda Portal, 'Mensaje a las Mujeres de América Latina', *Repertorio Americano*, vol. XVI, San José, 1928, p. 62. It is useful here to recall the Fifth Congress of the Communist International, in which Haya de la Torre himself had taken part as an observer. For the International the United Front was conceived of fundamentally as a worker–peasant alliance for the achievement of a worker and peasant government. It was therefore no more than a new name for the proletarian dictatorship, a simple agitational formula. This, added to the Comintern's declared objective of the Bolshevikization of the different communist Parties, meant that there were substantial differences between the Communist understanding of the phrase and the apparently similar concept used by the APRA, in which the bourgeoisie and the petit bourgeoisie were expected to play a decisive role. In Zinoviev's interpretation the struggle would tend to move directly towards proletarian dictatorship and therefore entailed the political elimination of these classes and their emphatic separation from the Party, which thus had to remain free of centrists, semi-centrists, counter-revolutionaries, social democrats, and so on. See *La Correspondance Internationale*, no. 48, 4th year, 24 July 1924, p. 516.

48. Víctor Raúl Haya de la Torre, 'Carta a José María Zeledón', *Repertorio Americano*, vol. XVI, San José, 1928, p. 63.

49. Frente Unido de Trabajadores Manuales e Intelectuales de América.

50. Víctor Raúl Haya de la Torre, 'Carta a Froylán Turcios', *Repertorio Americano*, vol. XVI, San José, 1928, p. 343.

51. Ibid, pp. 231–2.

52. Esteban Pavletich, 'Carta a Joaquín García Monge', *Repertorio Americano*, vol. XVI, San José, 1928, p. 213.

53. Víctor Raúl Haya de la Torre, 'Del Cuzco Salió el Nuevo Verbo, y del Cuzco Saldrá la Nueva Acción', *Repertorio Americano*, vol. XVII, San José, 1928, p. 6.

54. Pavletich, op. cit., p. 219.

55. Víctor Raúl Haya de la Torre, 'Carta Abierta a Juan Ramón Avilés', *Repertorio Americano*, vol. XVIII, San José, 1929, p. 152.

56. Acción Comunal de Panamá, 'Algunas Palabras con Haya de la Torre', *Repertorio Americano*, vol. XVIII, San José, 1929, pp. 37–8.

57. See Macaulay, op. cit., p. 113, who accepts this information as true.

58. See Haya de la Torre's declarations made to *La Tribuna* of San José in December 1928.

59. See Gregorio Selser, *El Pequeño Ejército Loco* (Buenos Aires, Editorial Triángulo, 1958) pp. 311–12.
60. Selser, *Sandino, General de Hombres Libres*, vol. II, p. 28.
61. In *La Correspondencia Sudamericana*, 2a época, no. 7, Buenos Aires, 19 January 1929, pp. 18–19.
62. Ramírez Mercado, op. cit., pp. 295–6.
63. Alemán Bolaños, op. cit., p. 38.
64. Ramírez Mercado, op. cit., p. 180.
65. Ibid, p. 312.
66. Alberto Masferrer, 'La Misión de América', *Repertorio Americano*, vol. XVIII, San José, 1928, p. 1.
67. Macaulay, op. cit., p. 146.

3 Nicaragua, a Profitable Episode for the International: From Sandino the Hero to Sandino the Traitor

1. *La Correspondance Internationale*, no. 17, 5 February 1927, p. 228.
2. 'A bas l'impérialisme rapas et assassin des Etats-Unis', *La Correspondance Internationale*, no. 19, 9 February 1927, pp. 250–1.
3. See *La Correspondance Internationale*, no. 45, 28 April 1925, p. 355.
4. See 'L'Affaire de Tacna-Arica et l'Impérialisme Américain', *La Correspondance Internationale*, no. 32, 13 March 1926, p. 288.
5. Federación de Trabajadores Agrícolas de México.
6. See Augusto Benítez, 'Mella Centelleante Tránsito de un Dirigente Comunista', *Bohemia*, no. 28, Havana, Cuba, 18 July 1975, p. 93.
7. Carlos Deambrosis-Martins, 'La Expulsión de Haya de la Torre de Guatemala', *Repertorio Americano*, vol. XVII, San José, 1928, p. 230.
8. ISO, 'La Signification du Congrés de Bruxelles', *La Correspondance Internationale*, no. 27, 26 February 1927, p. 367. The article is signed with initials only.
9. Ibid, pp. 367–8.
10. US Government, 'Investigation of Un-American Propaganda Activities in the US', *The Communist Party of the US as an Agent of Foreign Power*, Washington, DC, 1947, p. 34.
11. Willy Münzenberg, 'La 2éme Conférence de Bruxelles de la Ligue Anti-Impérialiste', *La Correspondance Internationale*, no. 127, 21 December 1927, p. 1951.
12. Willy Münzenberg, 'A la Veille de la 2éme Conférence de la Ligue Anti-Impérialiste', *La Correspondance Internationale*, no. 122, 7 December 1927, p. 1822.
13. Ibid, p. 1823.
14. Willy Münzenberg, 'La 2éme Conférence de Bruxelles de la Ligue Anti-Impérialiste', op. cit., p. 1952.
15. *La Correspondance Internationale*, no. 73, 3 August 1928, p. 859.
16. In English in the original and the Spanish text (*translator's note*).
17. *La Correspondance Internationale*, no. 94, 30 August 1928, special issue XXIV. Macaulay states erroneously that the VI Congress and the Frankfurt Congress of the League were held simultaneously, when in fact they took place a year apart (see Macaulay, op. cit., p. 146).

18. See *La Correspondance Internationale*, no. 130, 30 October 1928, Special Issue XLIV, p. 1430.

19. '*Aprismo* has arisen as a petit-bourgeois current; it reflects the discontent of the petit-bourgeoisie of Peru with the regime of the dictator Leguía. The slogan of the APRA was in the beginning, the struggle against the feudalists and imperialism. The leaders of the APRA deny the leading role of the proletariat in the anti-imperialist agrarian revolution, according this role to the petit-bourgeois intellectuals. In the measure that the broad masses become radicalized, and the infuence of the Communist Parties increases, the *Apristas* go over to the side of the counter-revolution. The APRA enjoys great influence among the petit-bourgeois and the landowners less bound up with American imperialism. Thanks to the demagogy that it employs, it similarly also enjoys some influence among a section of the working class. The struggle against *Aprismo* is one of the essential tasks of the revolutionary labour movement in Peru', M.Ch., 'La Tactique de l'unité aux pays de l'Amérique Latine', *L'Internationale Syndicale Rouge*, no. 8, 30 April 1932, p. 410. The article is signed with initials only.

20. *La Correspondance Internationale*, no. 130, 30 October 1928, special issue XLIV, p. 1420.

21. *La Correspondance Internationale*, no. 106, 20 September 1928, special issue XXXI, p. 1133.

22. Ibid, p. 1142.

23. The campaign in support of Sandino in New York was also led in part by a revolutionary organization founded in 1926, the 'Spanish-Speaking Workers' Centre' (*Centro Obrero de Habla Española*). 'The centre was made up of workers of communist, anarchist and syndicalist tendencies from different Spanish-speaking countries.' It carried out aggressive street demonstrations under the slogans 'Hands Off Nicaragua', 'Down with Yankee Imperialism' and 'Long Live General Sandino'. See Torres, Lázaro, 'La ARNEC, una Combativa Organización Anti-imperialista', *Bohemia*, no. 23, Havana, Cuba, 6 June 1975, p. 91.

24. Macaulay, op. cit., p. 144.

25. See *La Correspondance Internationale*, no. 97, 2 September 1928, special issue XXVII, p. 1039.

26. See *La Correspondance Internationale*, no. 83, 16 August 1928, pp. 867–8.

27. Willy Münzenberg, 'Session de Berlin de la Ligue Anti-impérialiste', *La Correspondance Internationale*, no. 91, 25 August 1928, p. 973.

28. Julio Antonio Mella, 'Carta a Emilo Roy de Leuchsenring', in Gladys Blanco Cabrera, 'Emilio Roy de Leuchsenring, Verdadero Maestro de Nuestra Historia', *Bohemia*, no. 34, Havana, Cuba, 22 August 1975, p. 68.

29. Ibid, p. 73.

30. Get Out of Nicaragua – Fuera de Nicargua.

31. Ibid. See also Salvador De la Plaza, 'La lutte du Nicaragua, lutte de l'Amérique Latine pour son indépendance', *La Correspondance Internationale*, no. 9, 28 January 1928, p. 119.

32. Hands off Nicaragua Committee – Comité Manos Fuera de Nicaragua.

33. R. Lubrand, 'La l'ère Conférence de la Jeunesse Anti-impérialiste', *La Correspondance Internationalte*, no. 72, 12 August 1929.

34. See 'Un village d'enfants du S.O.I. aux Méxique', *La Correspondance Internationale*, no. 11, 6 February 1929, p. 114.

35. Hands Off Nicaragua Committee – Comité Manos Fuera de Nicaragua.

36. Willy Münzenberg, 'Session de Berlin de la Ligue Anti-impérialiste', p. 974.

37. Gustavo Machado, 'Carta a los Compañeros de la Unión Obrera Venezolana', *Repertorio Americano*, vol. XVII, San José, July 1928, p. 19.

38. Willy Münzenberg, 'De Bruxelles á Paris', *La Correspondance Internationale*, no. 51, 19 June 1929, p. 745. Henri Barbusse, to whom Münzenberg referred here, was in fact one of the organizers of the Frankfurt congress. It is of interest to transcribe here the message sent to Sandino by Barbuse which the latter published in his newspaper *Monde*: 'I bring to you in homage with my greetings those of the proletariat and revolutionary intellectuals of France and Europe, who previously have in many circumstances authorized me to speak in their name, in order to say to you that our attention is enthusiastically set upon the heroic figure of Sandino and his admirable forces. We salute in you a liberator, the magnificent soldier of a cause that, going beyond questions of races and nationalities, is the cause of the oppressed, of the exploited, of the peoples against the magnates. We salute in you all the ardent youth of Hispanic America that is stirring and rising up in the face of the executioners of the North, the Beasts of Gold, and all the multitude of workers and Indians who are in agitation along the length of the continent, impatient to begin the march to drive back the imperialist and capitalist machinery that has come from abroad, and in its place create a new world on the lands that are theirs. In the vanguard of the struggle and the continent, you, the General of Free Men, are playing a historic role that will be indelible, through your shining example and your splendid self-sacrifice. We are with you from the bottom of our hearts.' (Henri Barbusse, 'Saludo a Sandino', reprinted in *Repertorio Americano*, vol. VII, no. 17, San José, 1928, p. 267.)

39. Willy Münzenberg, 'Le Congrés de Francfort de la Ligue Anti-impérialiste', *La Correspondance Internationale*, no. 68, August 1929, p. 936.

40. Macaulay, op. cit., p. 146.

41. See *Repertorio Americano*, vol. XIV, San José, 1927, p. 344.

42. 'Manifeste du IIe. Congrés Mondial de la Ligue Anti-impérialiste', *La Correspondance Internationale*, no. 68, August 1929, p. 937.

43. Ibid, pp. 936–7.

44. Macaulay, op. cit., p. 147.

45. See Willy Münzenberg, 'Le Renforcement Prolétarien de la Ligue Anti-impérialiste', *La Correspondance Internationale*, no. 7, 23 January 1929, p. 75.

46. 'Phénoménes Sains dans la Ligue contre l'Impérialisme', *La Correspondance Internationale*, no. 102, 3 December 1930, p. 1346.

47. See Olga Cabrera, *Guiteras, La Epoca, el Hombre* (Havana, Editorial Política, 1974) p. 14.
48. See Augusto Arias, 'Carlos Aponte, Coronel de Sandino', *Repertorio Americano*, vol. XXXII, San José, 1936, p. 277.
49. Italicized (also capitalization) as in the Spanish text.
50. Arias, 'Carlos Aponte', p. 92.
51. Ibid, p. 91.
52. Ibid, p. 91.
53. Ibid, p. 92.
54. Ibid, pp. 92–3.
55. See David Luna, 'Algunas Facetas Sociales en la Vida de Agustín Farabundo Martí', *Revista Salvadoreña de Ciencias Sociales*, no. 1, January–March 1965, p. 97; also Thomas P. Anderson, *Matanza* (Lincoln, University of Nebraska Press, 1971) p. 35.
56. It is very probable that Martí may in fact have made the initial contact via Turcios, since in a letter sent from Las Segovias to a fellow Salvadorean, Santiago David García, he asked, 'There being many Salvadoreans in El Salvador who wish to come to join the liberation forces, I would ask for you to let them know that they can make the journey by taking out a passport in La Unión . . . They should obtain a passport for anywhere in Honduras and on arrival in Tegucigalpa should try to speak with don Froylán Turcios through an intermediary. Don Froylán will tell them the path to follow to reach our camps'. Reproduced in Jorge Arias Gómez, *Farabundo Martí* (San José, Editorial Universitaria Centroamericana, 1972) p. 51.
57. Comité Frente Unido Manos Fuera de Nicaragua.
58. Gustavo Machado, 'La Situación en Honduras', p. 269.
59. Augusto César Sandino, 'Carta a Gustavo Machado y Morales', *Repertorio Americano*, vol. XVII, San José, 1928, p. 19.
60. Macaulay, op. cit., p. 145.
61. Reproduced in Arias Gómez, op. cit., p. 51.
62. Ibid, p. 50.
63. See Carlos Fonseca Amador, 'The Macaulay Affair', *Prensa Política*, San José, Documentos, 3–15 March 1973.
64. Alemán Bolaños, op. cit., p. 75.
65. Ibid, p. 80.
66. Ibid, p. 82. The phrase used (cortos de alcance) would normally be understood as 'of limited intelligence', but could also be interpreted as 'of limited vision, ambition or understanding' (*translator's note*).
67. Ibid, p. 85.
68. Anderson, op. cit., p. 38.
69. Hernán Laborde, 'La Situation Politique au Méxique', *La Correspondance Internationale*, no. 72, 30 August 1930, pp. 951–2.
70. Ramírez Mercado, op. cit., pp. 198–200 (letter to Dr Pedro José Zepeda).
71. From *Izvestia*, reproduced in *La Correspondance Internationale*, no. 10, 1 February 1930, p. 97
72. *La Correspondance Internationale*, no. 1, 4 January 1930, p. 5. This obviously referred to the Mexican State of Yucatán.

73. Gregorio Selser, *Sandino, General de Hombres Libres*, vol. XXI, p. 94.
74. Coquetear.
75. Ramírez Mercado, op. cit., p. 201.
76. See Manuel Márquez Fuentes and Octavio Rodríguez Araujo, *El Partido Comunista Mexicano* (Mexico D.F., Ediciones El Caballito, 1973) p. 141.
77. Ibid, p. 201.
78. Ramírez Mercado, op. cit., p. 198.
79. Confederación Sindical Hispanoamericana.
80. Selser, *Sandino*, vol. II, p. 95.
81. Confederación Sindical Latinoamericana. (Sandino preferred to use the term 'Hispanic American'.)
82. See *La Correspondance Internationale*, no. 35, 23 April 1930, p. 426.
83. Ibid. My italics.
84. Márquez Fuentes and Rodríguez Araujo, op. cit., p. 128.
85. *New York Times*, 3 May 1930, p. 6.
86. Italicized in the Spanish text.
87. Somoza, op. cit., pp. 215–6.
88. Selser, *Sandino*, vol. II, p. 138.
89. Italicized in the Spanish text.
90. Luna, op. cit., pp. 105–6. My italics.
91. Anderson, op. cit., p. 38.
92. Italicized in the Spanish text.
93. Italicized in the Spanish text.
94. Italicized in the Spanish text.
95. Belausteguigoitia, op. cit., p. 185. My italics.
96. Italicized in the Spanish text.
97. Reproduced in Enrique Sorel, *Repertorio Americano*, vol. XXVIII, San José, 1934, p. 176.
98. Italicized in the Spanish text.
99. Sorel, *Repertorio*, p. 306.
100. Ibid, p. 214.
101. Somoza, op. cit., p. 354.
102. Alemán Bolaños, op. cit., p. 160.
103. J. Gómez, 'La Trahison de Sandino', *La Correspondance Internationale* , no. 23, 25 March 1933, p. 347.
104. Ibid, p. 347.
105. Ibid, pp. 347–8.
106. The quotes around 'General' are present in the original, put there obviously with the intention of ridiculing Sandino, now converted into a common traitor.
107. Gómez, op. cit., pp. 347–8.
108. Ibid, pp. 348–9. In Sandino's papers from the final period before his death what one does see is more the anguish of the General, who could not fully bring himself to believe that his allies were abandoning him. He repeatedly denounced the liquidation of his men and refused finally to disarm as long as the National Guard was not constitutionally regulated. Moreover, it is useful to note here that some *Sandinista* Generals continued the struggle after the death of Sandino, such as

Santos López, who returned to the Río Coco in 1962 to fight against the Somoza regime, as had Ramón Raudales, also one of Sandino's leading aides, in 1958. (See Fonseca Amador, op. cit., p. 3, and Romero, op. cit., p. 258.)

109. Gómez, op. cit., p. 348.
110. See Macaulay, op. cit., p. 300.
111. Gómez, op. cit., p. 348.
112. Luis Montes, 'Bananas, The Fruit Empire of Wall Street', *International Pamphlets*, no. 35, New York, Union Labor, 1933.
113. See Macaulay, op. cit., p. 245.
114. Sección Costarricense de la Liga Anti-imperialista, 'La Situación Política de Nicaragua y las Condiciones de Sandino para Deponer las Armas', *Trabajo*, Organ of the Communist Party of Costa Rica, San José, 14 January 1933, p. 2.
115. Italicized in the Spanish text.
116. 'Sandino en Managua', *Trabajo*, San José, 4 February 1933, p. 2. Unsigned article.

4 Historical and Political Origins of the Salvadorean Social Revolution of 1932

1. In Guatemala, on the other hand, the communist movement did not exist at this time. Repression against leftist ideas was so strong that General Ubico had prohibited the use of the word 'worker' as being communist. He ordered that the name of 'Jesus the Worker' should be changed to 'Jesus the Employee'.
2. The Communist movement was also non existent in Honduras. There were incipient labour organizations and a certain degree of radical activity, but a communist movement as such did not exist.
3. The US Department of Commerce, 'Salvador as a Market for Food-stuffs', *Trade Information Bulletin No. 692* (Washington, DC, US Government Printing Office, 1930).
4. Thomas F. Lee, *Latin-American Problems, Their Relations to our Investors Billions* (Brenver, Warren and Putman, New York, 1932) p. 148.
5. A. Altschult and W. W. Renwich, 'Del Problema de los Cereales en la República de El Salvador', *Boletín Oficial* (San Salvador, Ministerio de Economía, 1945) p. 55.
6. Lee, Thomas F., op. cit., p. 267.
7. See Thomas P. Anderson, *Matanza* (University of Nebraska Press, 1971) pp. 216 ff.; Alastair White, *El Salvador, Nation of the Modern World* (London 38; Tonbridge, Ernest Benn Ltd, 1973) p. 101.
8. For a description of the *tiendas de raya* in México, their place on the haciendas and their connection with the 1910 Revolution in that country, see Miguel Silva Herzog, *Breve Historia de la Revolución Mexicana* (México, Fondo de Cultura Económica, 1960) vol. 1, pp. 28 ff.
9. William Khrem, *Democracia y Tiranía en el Caribe* (Buenos Aires, Editorial Palestra, 1959) p. 42.
10. While the workers had to pay for the water they used, the houses of the estate owners even had large swimming pools, which for El Salvador in

1930 signified a fantastic expense. See Lilly Obsorne, 'El Salvador', *Bulletin of the Pan American Union*, March 1933, pp. 181–96.

11. US Department of Commerce, op. cit., p. 11.
12. See David Browning, *El Salvador: Landscape and Society* (Oxford, Clarendon Press, 1971) pp. 177–8.
13. Ibid, p. 178.
14. Ibid, p. 207.
15. Ibid, p. 217.
16. See Anderson, op. cit., pp. 16–17; Barón Castro, *La Población de El Salvador* (Madrid, Instituto de Cultura Hispánica, 1942) pp. 407–8; Ricardo Gallardo, 'Las Constituciones de El Salvador', in *Historia de la Integración Racial Territorial e Institucional del Pueblo Salvadoreño* (Madrid, Ediciones Cultura Hispánica, 1961) vol. 1, p. 566 ff.
17. See Jorge Arias Gómez, *Farabundo Martí* (San José, Costa Rica, Editorial Centroamericana, 1973) p. 36.
18. David Luna, 'Un Heroico y Trágico Suceso de Nuestra Historia', in *El Proceso Político Centroamericano* (San Salvador, Editorial Universitaria, 1964) p. 55.
19. See Arias Gómez, op. cit., p. 61.
20. It is of interest to point out that the workers of Costa Rica were not represented in the COCA.
21. See Roque Dalton, *Miguel Mármol: Los sucesos de 1932 in El Salvador* (San José, Costa Rica, Editorial Universitaria Centroamericana, 1972) p. 99. This book is valuable because it contains the memoirs of a man who was one of the principal leaders of the Communist Party of El Salvador from its foundation; see also Arias Gómez, op. cit., pp. 29–30.
22. In this Congress a particularly important part was played by the Nicaraguan Salomón de la Selva, and by the Venezuelan Ricardo Martínez (as a delegate for the Unión Obrera Venezolana, based in New York, of which Gustavo Machado was also a member). Martínez would later be a member of the Venezuelan Communist Party, and was sent to El Salvador by the Communist International to assist in the organization of the workers' movement. As an exile, he was also a member of the Mexican Communist Party. Although Martínez took part in the Congress of the Pan-American Federation and even the Salvadorean Communists thought that he was a recent convert, we believe that, together with Machado, he had already been connected with the International for several years. In August 1927 he took part in an insurrection in Bolivia, and he often merited the attention of *La Correspondance Internationale* (see *La Correspondance Internationale*, no. 91, 3 September 1927; no. 7, 25 January 1928, p. 99; no. 101, 5 October 1927, p. 1422). He was also involved with the Communist Party of Costa Rica, as he was one of their few contacts in New York.
23. See Arias Gómez, op. cit., p. 30.
24. See A. Lozovsky, 'Le Congrés de Syndicats de l'Amérique Latine', *La Correspondance Internationale*, no. 48, 9 June 1929, p. 698.
25. 'X Session of the Executive Committee', *La Correspondance Internationale*, no. 101, 8 October 1929, p. 1387.
26. See Dalton, op. cit., p. 150.

27. In this same speech, Ramírez also challenged Lozovsky for having said that the Mexican Communist Party (MCP) was sabotaging the progress of the RILU, saying that if he could speak Spanish he would be aware of the work being undertaken by the MCP in support of the creation of a new central labour organization, X Session of the Executive Commitee, p. 1387.

28. The idea of the Popular University originated in the same spirit as the University Reform of Córdoba of 1918. Haya de la Torre gave it its full political dimension through the APRA. 'I have always understood University Reform as being entirely the opposite of the refinement of a system so that it should better create a professional caste, that is to say, one that was stronger and more clearly defined. My idea of the Reform is just the opposite . . . To convert the student into a simple intellectual worker, with the class consciousness of a "simple intellectual worker", to democratize and, it may be said, to proletarianize the universities as much as possible; to make the members of the professions into a revolutionary element and not an instrument of reaction, a person that is consciously and resolutely at the service of the majority of society, that is, of the exploited classes; to move towards the social university and educate the student in direct and constant contact with the working classes. These are, in my opinion, the truly revolutionary aims of the Reform. And in Peru we have done no other than this. First, we ventilated the old and worm-eaten University of San Marcos, in Lima . . . Then we went further, and alongside the University that had been rejuvenated, but no more than rejuvenated by the Revolution, we created another that was young, strong, and perhaps its child . . . Our González Prada Popular University, where we fuse together our efforts and our revolutionary creed and the anguished rebellion of the workers. This will one day be the vast Social University of Peru, that will sing the funeral rites of the other kind. For the moment, it is a field of battle, a laboratory of experimentation, a bond of fraternity, a target for the terrorism of tyranny and a banner of agitation and hope for the people of Peru.' (Víctor Raúl Haya de la Torre, 'La Reforma Universitaria y la realidad social', pamphlet in the Personal Archive of Abel Dobles, Chacón, vol. 1. See also his 'Manifesto, Por las Universidades Populares González Prada del Perú'.) The influence of the APRA also accounts for the creation of universities of this kind in other countries of Central America, including Costa Rica, through intellectuals such as García Monge, Omar Dengo, etc. It is also important to point out that Esteban Pavletich, the leader of the APRA who had fought with Sandino, gave a number of talks in the University of the FRTS at the beginning of 1930. In July of that year he was discovered by the Salvadorean police under the false name of Esteban Trujillo (see Anderson, op. cit., pp. 28–9).

29. According to Miguel Mármol, it was among the participants in the Popular University that Agustín Farabundo Martí was democratically chosen to go, together with other Salvadorean workers, to join Sandino's guerrillas. We accept the possibility that Martí may have

submitted the matter to the consideration of the members of the Popular University, but we believe that his decision to take part in the events in Nicaragua had been set ever since the agents of the Anti-Imperialist League had proposed it to him, and that his designation in El Salvador was a formality.

30. Dana Munro, *The Five Republics of Central America* (New York, Oxford University Press, 1918) p. 110.
31. See Arias Gómez, op. cit., p. 36.
32. See Anderson, op. cit., p. 40.
33. See Dalton, op. cit., p. 144.
34. See Anderson, op. cit., pp. 24 and 84.

5 Farabundo Martí and the Communist International: Hunger in the Fields

1. See Dalton, op. cit., p. 155.
2. See ibid, p. 155.
3. See ibid, p. 155.
4. International Sindical Roja, *Tesis y Resoluciones del V Congreso* (Moscow, Pequeña Biblioteca de la Internacional Roja, September 1930) p. 5.
5. A. Lozovsky, 'El V Congreso de la I.S.R.', *La Internacional Sindical Roja*, no. 115–16, September–October 1930, p. 443 ff.
6. A. Lozovsky, 'El V Congreso de la I.S.R. Crisis Mundial, lucha económica y tareas del movimiento sindical revolucionario', *La Correspondencia Internacional*, no. 74, September 30, p. 1011.
7. A. Lozovsky, 'La apertura del Congreso de la I.S.R.', *La Correspondencia Internacional*, no. 69, 20 August 1930, p. 887..
8. International Sindical Roja, *Tesis y Resoluciones*, pp. 85–6.
9. El Debate del Congreso, *La Correspondencia Internacional*, no. 72, 30 August 1930, p. 1019.
10. Ibid, p. 86.
11. See Arias Gómez, op. cit., p. 83.
12. See Dalton, op. cit., p. 210.
13. International Sindical Roja, *Tesis y Resoluciones*, p. 16.
14. See Dalton, op. cit., pp. 216–17.
15. Ibid, p. 236.
16. In Anderson, op. cit., pp. 83–4.
17. See Dalton, op. cit., p. 157.
18. Willy Müzemberg, 'Cinco años del socorro Rojo Internacional', *La Correspondencia Internacional*, no. 100, 8 September 1926, p. 1118.
19. In *La Correspondencia Internacional*, no. 64, 10 September 1924, special no. XXI, p. 685.
20. In *La Correspondencia Internacional*, no. 56, 12 August 1924, p. 602.
21. In *La Correspondencia Internacional*, no. 45, 28 April 1924, p. 349.
22. 'Resolución sobre el Socorro Rojo Internacional', *La Correspondencia Internacional*, no. 64, 24 June 1925, p. 530.
23. Internacional Comunista, *Tesis y Resoluciones del VI Congreso de las I.C.* (Oficina de Ediciones, París, n.d.) p. 102.

24. Internacional Comunista, *Sindicatos Rojos y Socorro Rojo Internacional* (Oficina de Ediciones, París, 1931) p. 20.
25. Ibid, p. 78.
26. This was the same cadre who had made contact with the Costa Rican revolutionaries in the 1920s.
27. See Dalton, op. cit., p. 174.
28. In Anderson, op. cit., p. 68. This Gómez was one of the delegates from the US Communist Party to the VI Congress of the Comintern, as stated in the Minutes of the Congress, *La Correspondencia Internacional*, no. 124, 18 October 1928, p. 1346.
29. See Arias Gómez, op. cit., p. 64.
30. Ibid, pp. 65–6.
31. See Dalton, op. cit., p. 244.
32. See David Luna, *Análisis de una Dictadura Fascista Latinoamericana* (San Salvador, Editorial Universitaria, 1961) p. 110.
33. See Anderson, op. cit., p. 27.
34. Letter from the Caribbean Secretariat of International Red Aid to the General Secretary of the Section of International Red Aid in Guatemala, dated 22 September 1930. In Arias Gómez, op. cit., p. 68.
35. Supplement to no. 45 of *Opinión Estudiantil*, San Salvador, March 1931, published in facsimile in Arias Gómez, op. cit., p. 63.
36. Agustín Farabundo Martí, 'La Represión Fascista contra los Obreros y Campesinos de El Salvador', in David Luna, *Algunas Facetas Sociales en la Vida de Farabundo Martí*, pp. 101 ff.
37. With regard to Masferrer, see Alberto Masferrer, 'La Misión de América', *Repertorio Americano*, tom. XXV, no. 4, 1932, p. 55, where he presents his projected 'Constitution for a United Vitalist Central America', the ninth point of which contemplates 'containing the degeneration of the race by means of biological, eugenic and hygienic measures', and which states that the land should not be private property, that there should be absolutely no foreign intervention in the region, and that culture should be extended to the Indians. See Anderson, op. cit., pp. 46 ff.; Italo López Vallecillos, *El Periodismo en El Salvador*, pp. 361 ff.; Arias Gómez, op. cit., p. 86.
38. See Dalton, op. cit., p. 86.
39. See Arias Gómez, op. cit., 107.
40. Ibid, p. 247; David Luna, *Un Heroico y Trágico Suceso de Nuestra Historia*, p. 107.
41. See Dalton, op. cit., pp. 250–1. A further confirmation that the real organic links continued to be through International Red Aid.
42. Dalton, p. 250.
43. Ibid, p. 158.
44. Hernández Martínez is better known in the history of El Salvador by his second surname, for which reason we use here both the form shown and that of H. Martínez without distinction.
45. Dalton, p. 251.
46. See Anderson, op. cit., p. 88.
47. See Dalton, op. cit., p. 256.
48. Ibid, pp. 264–5.

6 The Rebellion of the Flower-Eaters: El Salvador, 1932

1. See Dalton, op. cit., p. 269 ff.
2. Although the date commonly accepted for the arrest of the three communist leaders is 20 January, since the news appeared in newspapers on the 21st, the Chief of Police at that time, Osmín Aguirre, declared to Thomas Anderson that the arrests were actually carried out on the 18th (see Anderson, op. cit., p. 93).
3. *Diario de Costa Rica*, 22 January 1932, p. 1.
4. See Dalton, op. cit., p. 275.
5. This document was given to the Costa Rican Vicente Sáenz in the Presidential Palace of El Salvador, together with other manifestos. Of all of them, the only one that from its content and style appears to us probably to be authentic is that quoted here. There is another that is a mixture of communist terminology and threats of death and firing squads for all and sundry, evidently prepared in order to justify the repression. Vicente Sáenz, *Rompiendo Cadenas* (México D.F., Editorial América Nueva, 1962) 4th edn, pp. 243 ff. Mármol complains that 'it was in documents like this one that afterwards sister parties of the International based themselves in order to say that ours was not a Party, but a machete gang thus giving credit to the reactionaries' (see Dalton, op. cit., p. 339).
6. The broadly based nature of the Salvadorean movement, its very organizational structure, made possible the leaking of a good deal of confidential information, which passed directly into the hands of the Government, which knew of a major part of the plans of the rebels (see Dalton, op. cit., p. 362).
7. Statement signed by Alberto Marín, Archivos Nacionales de Costa Rica, Box 365, File no. 001.
8. Letter from the Governor of Sonsonate, Ernesto Bara, to Presidente H. Martínez, dated 25 January 1932, Archivos Nacionales de Costa Rica, Box no. 365, File no. 001.
9. See Anderson, op. cit., p. 117.
10. It is important to point out here that in 1872 a major Indian uprising had broken out in Izalco, which, while it did not reach the magnitude of that of Anastasio Aquino, was of great significance in the definition of the hostility between peasants and landowners, as it arose out of the struggle for the land, the break up of the communal and common lands having already began (see Anderson, op. cit., p. 18). The revolt of Anastasio Aquino had also included Izalco, as well as the communities of Sonsonate, Ahuachapán, Chalatenango, Zacatecoluca and San Miguel (see Ricardo Gallardo, op. cit., p. 567).
11. See Dalton, op. cit., p. 3466; Anderson, op. cit., pp. 19 ff.
12. See Dalton, op. cit., p. 70.
13. Ibid, op. cit., p. 345.
14. Anderson, whose attitude is not precisely favourable to the insurgents, considers that this number is even perhaps greater than the real figure, but accepts it as a possibility.
15. The difficulties in calculating this figure are obvious, but all the different writers on the subject accept ten thousand as the minimum figure and

thirty thousand as the maximum. Italo López Vallecillos, *El Periodismo en El Salvador* (San Salvador, Editorial Universitaria, 1964) p. 106, accepts fourteen thousand as the correct number. David Luna, *Un Heroico y Trágico Suceso*, op. cit., p. 63, mentions twenty thousand as the most probable figure. Miguel Mármol (Dalton, op. cit., p. 355) gives the figure of 30 000 dead, which is that which has been accepted by the international communist movement.

16. Vicente Sáenz, *Rompiendo Cadenas*, op. cit., 4th Edition, pp. 341-242.
17. In fact a disembarkation was carried out on 24 January, but it has been kept in the strictest secrecy. An official of the British Foreign Service wrote, in July 1932, that 'thanks be to God' news of the disembarkation had never been published. The landing took place on the 24th but, when news was received that the Salvadorean government was not prepared to permit it, the British sailors and their equipment returned to the Skeena. This is described in the secret report of Commander Brodeur to the Navy Secretary in Ottawa of 7 April 1932, a copy of which is in the British Foreign Service archives (see Alastair White, op. cit., p. 113).
18. *Diario de Costa Rica*, 28 January 1932, p. 1.
19. See William Khrem, op. cit., p. 67; Anderson, op. cit., p. 136.
20. This led to protests in San José and Alajuela when they performed in Costa Rica. The Communist Party issued a call for their performances to be interrupted at the moment when this song was played. The leaders of the Party, Carlos Luis Fallas, Guillermo Fernández, Manuel Moscoa and Jaime Cerdas were imprisoned because of this (interview with Jaime Cerdas Mora, 29 November 1972).
21. See Dalton, op. cit., p. 324.
22. The repression carried out against the indigenous peasant population was so violent that aside from ceasing to speak the Pipil language (at least when they went to ask for work in the plantations) the Indians also adopted the dress of the 'whites' and sought to asimilate themselves as much as possible in the white population (see Alastair White, op. cit., p. 114).
23. Marcucci, *La Correspondencia Internacional*, no. 48, 8 June 1932, p. 933.
24. L. Deval, 'Las Luchas de Clase en América Central', *La Internacional Sindical Roja*, no. 10, 31 May 1932, p. 531. Miguel Mármol has stated, in contrast, that the means used by the CPES to give the labourers and sharecroppers an understanding of the concept of the bourgeois-democratic revolution was through the organization of effective strikes in the rural areas, over such basic issues as the demand for larger maize tortillas, or larger quantities of beans and coffee for the labourers, or for the abolition of company stores, for increased wages and better treatment for the workers, for repairs to the straw shacks lived in by the sharecroppers to be paid for by the landowners, and so on, which gave great momentum to the movement (see Dalton, op. cit., p. 161).
25. *El Comunista*, no. 11, March 1932, p. 2.
26. L. Deval, op. cit., p. 531.
27. L. Deval, 'Los Acontecimientos Revolucionarios en Chile', *La Internacional Sindical Roja*, no. 16, 31 August 1932, p. 793.
28. Ibid, p. 792.

29. On the soviets in Cuba see 'Declaración del SRI Cubano', *La Correspondencia Internacional*, no. 91–92, 11 November 1933, pp. 1331–2; 'El desarrollo de la Revolución en Cuba y el imperialismo americano', *La Correspondencia Internacional*, no. 87–88, 28 October 1933, p. 1064; G. Sinai, 'En Cuba se constituyen los soviets', *La Correspondencia Internacional*, no. 98–99, p. 1207; 'Communist Party of the USA, declaration on the events in Cuba', *La Correspondencia Internacional*, no. 72–73, September 1933, p. 895.
30. 'Manifiesto', *La Correspondencia Internacional*, no. 70–71, 2 September 1933, p. 860.

7 Costa Rica: An Original Democracy in Central America

1. Samuel Stone, 'Las convulsiones del istmo centroamericano: raíces de un conflicto entre élites', in *Estudios del Centro de Investigación y Adiestramiento Político Administrativo (CIAPA)*, San José, Litografía e Imprenta Lil S.A., 1979, no. 1.
2. See Ricardo Gallardo, *Las Constituciones de El Salvador*, vols. I–II (Madrid, Ediciones de Cultura Hispánica, 1961) and *Las Constituciones de la República Federal de Centro América* (Madrid, Instituto de Estudios Políticos, 1958); Luis Mariñas Otero, *Las Constituciones de Guatemala* (Madrid, Instituto de Estudios Políticos, 1958); Jorge Mario García Laguardia, *Orígenes de la Democracia Constitucional en Centro América* (San José, Editorial Universitaria de Centro América, 1971); Hernán G. Peralta, *El derecho constitucional en la independencia de Costa Rica* (San José, Trejos Hermanos, 1965) and *El Pacto de Concordia* (San José, Librería e Imprenta Lehman, 1965).
3. Samuel Stone, 'El surgimiento de los que mandan: Tierra, Capital y Trabajo en la forja de las sociedades centroamericanas', in *Estudios del Centro de Investigación y Adiestramiento Político Administrativo (CIAPA)*, San José, Litografía e Imprenta Lil S.A., 1980, no. 5. In the present text we follow the principal theses of Stone on this point, with which we are in complete agreement.
4. See Carlos Meléndez, 'Formas en la tenencia de la tierra en Costa Rica en la época colonial', *Revista de Historia*, año 1, no. 2, San José, 1975, pp. 104 ff., and *Costa Rica: Tierra y Poblamiento en la Colonia* (San José, Editorial Costa Rica, 1977); Elizabeth Fonseca, *Costa Rica Colonial, la Tierra y el Hombre* (San José, Editorial Universitaria Centroamericana, 1983); Carolyn Hall, *El café y el desarrollo histórico-geográfico de Costa Rica* (San José, Editorial Costa Rica, 1976).
5. Italicized in the Spanish text.
6. See Armando Rodríguez Ruíz, *La administración González Flores* (San José, Editorial Universidad de Costa Rica, 1968); Eduardo Oconitrillo García, *Los Tinoco (1917–1919)* (San José, Editorial Costa Rica, 1980); Cleto González Víquez, *El Sufragio en Costa Rica ante la Historia y la Legislación* (San José, Editorial Costa Rica, 1978); Hugo Murillo Jiménez, *Tinoco y Los Estados Unidos. Génesis y caída de un régimen* (San José, Editorial EUNED, 1981).

7. See Carlos Enrique Carranza Villalobos, *El Partido Unión Católica y su importancia en la vida política de Costa Rica*, unpublished graduate thesis, Universidad de Costa Rica, 1982.

8. See Samuel Stone, *La Dinastía de los Conquistadores* (San José, Editorial Universitaria de Centro América, 1975).

9. Tomás Soley Güell, *Compendio de Historia Económica y Hacendaria de Costa Rica* (San José, Editorial Soley Valverde, 1940) p. 128.

10. Tomás Soley Güell, *Historia Económica y Hacendaria de Costa Rica*, vol. II (San José, Editorial Universitaria, 1949) p. 10.

11. See Edelberto Torres, op. cit., p. 69; Rodolfo Cerdas, *La Crisis de la Democracia Liberal en Costa Rica* (San José, EDUCA, 1972) p. 31, and, same author, 'Del Estado Intervencionista al Estado Empresario', *Anuario de Estudios Centroamericanos*, no. 5 (San José, Editorial de la Universidad de Costa Rica, 1979).

12. Marco A. Fallas, *La Factoría de Tabacos de Costa Rica* (San José, Editorial Costa Rica, 1972); Rodolfo Cerdas, *La Formación del Estado en Costa Rica*, 2nd edn (San José, Editorial Universidad de Costa Rica, 1978); Víctor Acuña, 'Historia Económica del Tabaco, Epoca Colonial', unpublished doctoral thesis, Escuela de Historia y Geografía, Universidad de Costa Rica, 1974.

13. Rodrigo Facio, *La Moneda y la Banca Central en Costa Rica* (Mexico City, Fondo de Cultura Económica, 1947) p. 148.

14. See Soley Güell, *Historia Económica y Hacendaria*, vol. II, pp. 27–8.

15. See Dirección General de Estadística, *Anuario Estadístico año 1920* (San José, Imprenta Nacional, 1922) vol. XXIV, pp. 93 ff., and 208.

16. See *Informe de la Dirección General de Estadística Año 1925* (San José, Imprenta Nacional, 1926) pp. 7 and 20.

17. *Censo de Población de Costa Rica* (San José, Ministerio de Economía y Hacienda, Dirección general de Estadística y Censo, n.d.) pp. 52 ff.

18. Víctor Sanabria, *Genealogías de Cartago, hasta 1850* (San José, 1957) vol. I, p. 20. Sanabria, the Catholic Archbishop in the first half of this century, undertook an exhaustive study, in six volumes, of the families living in the central area of the country, where the most important concentration of population is to be found. 'The amount of chemically pure white blood that exists in the Republic is not great,' he concluded, 'there has been a genuine fusion of races.' Similarly, an analysis of all the family trees that have been recorded brings one to the conclusion, in his opinion, that there is not one of the 'principal' families that does not have a percentage of mixed blood, so that his study explains the uniform racial type that is found in most of the country.

19. Vladimir De la Cruz, *Las Luchas Sociales en Costa Rica* (1870–1930) (San José, Editorial Universidad de Costa Rica, 1983); Carlos Luis Fallas Monge, *El Movimiento Obrero en Costa Rica* (1830–1902) (San José, Editorial EUNED, 1983).

20. Sociedad Mutualista de Artesanos de Panadería.

21. Sociedad de Socorros Mutuos.

22. Federación de Artesanos, panaderos, construcción y carpinteros (capitalization as in Spanish text).

23. La Sociedad Mutualista de Tipógrafos.

24. Confederación General de Trabajadores.
25. See Stone, *La Dinastía de los Conquistadores*, p. 285.
26. Sociedad de Ebanistas y Carpinteros.
27. Mecánicos Unidos.
28. Club Obrero 28 de Noviembre.
29. Unión General de Cocheros.
30. See De la Cruz, op. cit., p. 121.
31. Marina Volio, *Jorge Volio y el Partido Reformista* (San José, Editorial Costa Rica, 1973).
32. Federación Obrera Costarricense.
33. COCA – Confederación Obrera Centroamericana.
34. Centro Socialista.
35. De la Cruz, op. cit., pp. 119, 121 and 130. There is a contradiction in the text of De la Cruz, as on p. 129 he links the dissolution of the Confederation to the foundation of the Socialist Party (1913) while on p. 121 he connects the same event to the foundation of the Reformist Party.
36. Liga Cívica.
37. Statutes of the *Liga Cívica*, published as a leaflet by the Imprenta La Tribuna, San José, no date. From the personal collection of the author. In this document one already sees the name of the worker Fausto Peraza, who will later be found in communist organizations.
38. Abel Dobles, unpublished memoirs, without pagination. They received *Internationale Syndicale Rouge*, which they were sent from Paris by Talhaimer; they had contact, by correspondence, with the French CGT, by means of Gustave Herclet; and in October 1929 sent a protest at the death of Guadalupe Rodríguez in Mexico to the Labour Defense Organization in the United States, which was published in the latter's magazine. In addition, the Bulletin of the RILU, *El Martillo*, of the Venezuela Communist Party, *Cultura Obrera*, published by the US Communist Party in Spanish, and many other publications can be found among the papers of Abel Dobles.
39. Invitation to a lecture by Jorge A. Vivó on political economy. Typewritten, in the personal collection of the author. The talk was held in a building of the Banco de Cooperación Nacional, and workers were specially invited to attend. Previously, other workers' leaders identified with socialism had also been noted as having passed through the country, such as Rodolfo Wedel Quirós, in 1925, and Francisco de Heredia, in 1927, both of them from Colombia. However, they do not seem to have been carrying out any specific missions on behalf of the International, nor is there any indication that they had any organizational links with it, as was the case with Vivó.
40. *La Tribuna*, San José, 19, 20 and 21 November 1926. It is of interest to point out that both Carlos Luis Sáenz and Gonzalo Montero Berry would later be prominent figures in the Communist Party of Costa Rica.
41. Typewritten copy of the manifesto dated San José, December 1927, in the personal collection of the author.
42. Partido Popular.
43. Dobles, memoirs; and *La Tribuna*, 23 May 1933.

44. Personal papers of Abel Dobles, vol. 3. The constitution of the Costa Rican section of the APRA, which had existed as a group since the previous year, was also made official in 1929. In their Declaration of Principles (San José, Imprenta La Tribuna, 1929) they expressed their adherence to the classic five points of *aprismo*, and stated that they would struggle with all their strength against imperialism. Some of the Section's members proceeded from the Civic League. They played an important part in the campaigns that took place during those years against the position of foreign companies in Costa Rica. ARCO – Asociación de Resistencia Cultural Obrera.

45. The latter committed suicide a few years later, out of 'revolutionary impatience', in the words of the communist writer Carmen Lyra, as 'the longings for justice of this dearly-loved young man could only be felt in their full intensity, to such a degree, that they became lost in infinity'. Carmen Lyra, 'Ricardo Coto Conde', *Trabajo*, 23 September 1931.

46. Agrupación de Reorganización Sindical.

47. Personal papers of Abel Dobles, vol. 3.

48. Día Continental de los Desocupados.

49. Dobles, vol. 2.

50. Unión General de Trabajadores.

51. Sociedad de Obreros y Ebanistas.

52. From documents from the personal papers of Gonzalo Montero Berry, in the possession of the author. Fausto Peraza had been invited to take part in a meeting organized by the League against Imperialism in Mexico, but had been unable to attend. Later he did go to the conference in Montevideo, but never returned to his country. In explaining his intervention in the incident with the police, over the law on tenancies proposed by the parliamentary deputy Albertazzi, Peraza declared, together with Montero Berry, that the organization they represented had to be built 'on the basis of the class struggle, because we consider that while the State machine is in the hands of capital', everything it did would favour the latter. *ABC*, 28 May 1930, p. 3.

53. *La Tribuna*, 29 May 1930.

54. Announcement of the meeting, San José, Imprenta Tormo, 7 November 1930. In the personal collection of the author.

55. See *La Tribuna*, 5 August 1930; *Internationale Syndicale Rouge*, Paris, Bureau d'Editions, no. 115–16, September–October 1930, no. 117–18, 1931; '8e session du Conseil Central de l'Internationale Syndicale Rouge, janvier, février, 1931'. No action in this direction on the part of the UGT is even mentioned, either in the corrrespondence received or in the organizational matters pending resolution.

56. Soley Güell, *Compendio de Historia Económica*, p. 163.

57. Ibid, p. 172. See also *Memoria de la secretaría de Hacienda y Comercio*, año 1923, San José, Imprenta Naconal, 1924.

58. Soley Güell, *Compendio de Historia Económica*, p. 173.

59. Arrests and clashes between the police and different sections of society were constantly reported during this period. See the incident involving teachers reported by *El Censor* on 8 May 1932. See also Dirección

General de Estadística y Censos, *Censo de Personas sin Trabajo*, San José, 1932.

8 The Foundation of the Communist Party and its Links with the International

1. *Diario de Costa Rica*, San José, 13 February 1931.
2. See Auditoría General de Obras Públicas, Caminos y Puentes, *Informe General del costo de obras ejecutadas en la administración del Lic. Ricardo Jiménez Oreamuno 1932–36*, T. Jesús Jiménez, Auditor, San José, Imprenta Juan Arias, no date.
3. Document in the personal papers of Gonzalo Montero Berry. Nothing definite on that could be proven existed, other than that there was a desire among the authorities to portray as such, as agents of the International, a number of Jews who had recently taken up residence in the country.
4. See Primer Libro de Actas del Partido Comunista de Costa Rica (Minute Book) p. 1. In the personal collection of the author.
5. Sindicato de Ebanistas.
6. *Trabajo*, official organ of the Communist Party, San José, 5 September 1931.
7. Primer Libro de Actas del PCCR, p. 6.
8. Biblioteca Lenin.
9. Document in the personal papers of Gonzalo Montero Berry.
10. See Arturo Fournier Facio, *La United Fruit Company y las huelgas bananeras*, unpublished graduate thesis, Universidad de Costa Rica, 1975, pp. 121 ff.; Adolfo Herrera García, Enrique V. Mora, and Francisco Gamboa, *Apuntes para la historia del Partido Comunista de Costa Rica* (San José, Imprenta Elena, n.d.) pp. 10 ff. Manuel Mora has said, at a workers' meeting in Siquirres, Province of Limón, on 28 August 1977, that, 'at that time the union (*sindicato*) and the Party blended into each other ... the Party and the union, I repeat, were practically a single body in this area', *Libertad*, San José, 15–21 June 1984, p. 7.
11. Interview with Emilio Valverde. Ricardo Martínez would later be one of the leading supporters of Browderism in Venezuela. 'The faction that controlled the leadership of the Party and which was led by Juan Bautista Fuenmayor and Ricardo Martínez,' wrote Salvador de la Plaza, in a report written in Caracas in April 1952, 'had found in Browder's revisionist deviation from Marxism in the United States a useful tool with which to justify "ideologically" their vulgar opportunism.' See Salvador De la Plaza and Jacques Duclos, *Antecedentes del Revisionismo en Venezuela* (Caracas, Fondo Editorial Salvador de la Plaza, 1973) p. 100. Other Browderists mentioned were Blas Roca and Gustavo Machado.
12. Interview with Jaime Cerdas Mora.
13. *Trabajo*, official organ of the Communist Party of Costa Rica, no. 1, San José, 14 July 1931, and *Trabajo*, 22 August 1931.
14. *Trabajo*, 10 October 1931.
15. *Trabajo*, 18 February 1933.

16. *Trabajo*, 25 November and 17 December 1933. They justified the incidents that they, when elected, went on to provoke in the Congress in a frankly anti-parliamentary manner, declaring, 'In this way the innumerable elements among the popular masses who still have faith in the effectiveness of bourgeois democracy will be convinced that one can now no longer struggle freely against capitalism within its structures. That the bourgeoisie is not prepared to let the workers use the so-called bourgeois freedoms to fight against it.' *Trabajo*, 16 June 1934.

17. *Trabajo*, July 1931 to April 1932. It figured as part of the masthead of the newspaper.

18. Published in leaflet form, San José, Imprenta Borrasé, no date. In the personal collection of the author.

19. Bloque de Obreros y Campesinos.

20. Leaflet, San José, Imprenta Falcó Hermanos, 3 November 1932. In the personal collection of the author.

21. *Trabajo*, 21 January 1933.

22. *Trabajo*, 28 January 1933.

23. Ibid. This was also still accompanied by actions of different kinds that were repressed by the police. See *El Censor*, 8 May 1932. On 19 June 1932 the Party leaders Luis Carballo, Jaime Cerdas and Manuel Mora were sentenced to terms of imprisonment.

24. Confederación Centroamericana de Estudiantes (CIADE).

25. 'El Segundo Congreso de Estudiantes y la actuación en sus deliberaciones de la fracción comunista', *Trabajo*, 21 May 1933, p. 2. Rómulo Betancourt said, in a letter dated San José, 4 August 1934, that 'I was personally able to confirm, in the CIADE affair, that nothing concrete, in the sense of a reform of the internal statutes of this kind of petit-bourgeois groupings, can be achieved through the debates.' See Estados Unidos de Venezuela, Servicio Secreto de Investigación, 'Las actividades comunistas en Venezuela' Caracas, 1936. Facsimile edition under the title *Libro Rojo del General López Contreras*, 1936 (Caracas, Ediciones Centauro, 1979) p. 190. Hereafter cited as *Libro Rojo*.

26. 'El segundo Congreso', *Trabajo*, 21 May 1933, p. 3. Reliable accounts exist that attribute the writing of this report to Betancourt, then a militant of the Communist Party of Costa Rica and a member of its leadership. In a letter written from Las Juntas de Abangares on 27 January 1932 Betancourt wrote, 'You know that I have been active here as a leader of the Communist Party. I write editorials in the newspaper, I am a member of the Executive Committee, I direct the Popular University. I have given several talks and made innumerable speeches.' *Libro Rojo*, p. 141.

27. Trabajo, 21 May 1933, p. 3. The quotes placed around the word 'hero' in order to refer mockingly to Sandino were, naturally, complemented by the title he was assigned in this article. By this time Sandino was for the entire Communist movement nothing other than 'the Traitor of Las Segovias'.

28. This and other groups such as the League against Imperialism would later send messages of protest to the Costa Rican government in solidarity with Jaime Cerdas Mora, who was wounded and imprisoned during the banana workers' strike of 1934, and following the measures

taken against Manuel Mora. See *Trabajo*, 30 September 1934. They also protested against the United Fruit Company directly in New York.

29. *Trabajo*, 21 May 1933, p. 3.
30. Ibid.
31. The greater part of the population of the Province of Limón is made up of blacks who were brought to the country for the building of the railway to the Atlantic coast in the last century. The majority were originally from Jamaica, though some migrants also came from the Bluefields region of Nicaragua. After the completion of the railway they chiefly took up cocoa growing, and their level of real involvement in unions and social movements was limited, though there are reports of a certain degree of participation in 1920, according to De la Cruz, in his work already quoted (p. 115), and of small-scale participation in the 1934 strike in the Estrella valley, as recalled by the Communist leader Jaime Cerdas Mora. Limón had for a long time been a centre of intense social agitation. In 1919 there were strikes on the railway in demand of better working hours, increases in wages, and so on, and there had even been some disputes in the last century, as we shall see.
32. The leaflet advertising the meeting went: 'Unemployed workers. A demonstration in the streets of the city by all those of us who lack work is now a necessity. If we remain passive and disunited, we will never get jobs. Today, Monday, in front of Porfirio Brenes, at half past two in the afternoon, a march will begin by those without work. Go there with your working tools. Holding them high, we will demand employment. No worker with any awareness should fail to be there. Unemployed Committee. San José, 22 May 1933.' The meeting place was none other than the Communist Party hall in the Pasaje Rescia, and the Chairman of the Committee was Carlos Luis Fallas, a leading militant of the Party and later a well-known writer. A copy of the leaflet is in the personal collection of the author, and it was also reprinted in *La Tribuna*, San José, 23. May 1933.
33. *La Tribuna*, 23 May 1933.
34. Ibid.
35. See *La Hora*, San José, 5 June 1933.
36. The Party newspaper felt obliged to explain the situation in an editorial, looking for support above all to the theses deployed by Lenin in his *Left-wing Communism. An Infantile Disorder*, which they quoted at length. 'The doctrine of Marxism is the most revolutionary in history. Its fundamental affirmation is that only through a radical transformation, by means of violence, of the present modes of existence can one arrive at a society without classes. However, the acceptance of this principle does not exclude, nor could it have excluded, the use of non-violent methods, that is, parliamentary, journalistic, propagandist, etc., methods of anti-capitalist action.' A reply was given to criticism that the mass meeting to choose the candidates, held in the *Teatro Adela*, had been entirely prepared in advance, and it was explained that Mora's non-acceptance of his nomination had been sanctioned by his suspension in his functions as General Secretary for a month, during which time he would be replaced by Jaime Cerdas Mora. The editorial

concluded among other things by saying that 'it is a matter of urgent importance to clarify that this nomination does not signify any kind of abandonment of principle, either by the Party or the candidate. No Communist principle or practice forbade it. The III International has never made any distinction in its sections between manual and intellectual workers.' *Trabajo*, 17 December 1933.

37. *Trabajo*, 23 April 1933.
38. See 'Plataforma Municipal del Bloque de Obreros y Campesinos, Sección de Alajuela', San José, Imprenta La Tribuna, 1935.
39. *Trabajo*, 8 April 1934.
40. Ibid, 5 May 1935. Previously, in *Trabajo* of 21 January 1933, they had declared, 'We Communists follow a line that is straight and direct and pursue a definite object: to conquer all political power for the workers and destroy the bourgeoisie as an exploiting class.'
41. Confederación General de Trabajadores.
42. *La Voz Sindical*, organ of the Confederación General de Trabajadores, year 1, no. 1, July 1934. In the personal collection of the author. Any possible financial aid received from abroad, which was at all events very limited, appears to have been directed fundamentally towards financing this kind of publication.
43. A letter signed by the Secretary for Correspondance of the Central Committee, R. Barrantes, of 6 August 1934 and addressed to the editor of *La Voz Sindical*, Montero Berry, states the following: 'In view of the varied conjectures that have been made regarding the publication of *La Voz Sindical*, in which, among other things, it has been stated that it is an organ of the Communist Party, and which have become known to the Central Committe of the Party, in which the matter was discussed extensively, and the lack of a line to be followed with regard to the material for publication was the object of censure; this Committee agreed in its last session to call on you in your position as editor of *La Voz Sindical* and member of the Union Organization Committee (Comité de Organización Sindical) and at the same time call on the Communist members of the Press Committee of that periodical, to attend a joint meeting that can be held in the course of any of the normal sessions of the Central Committee of the Party, but as what is to be discussed is of the greatest interest for the newspaper it should take place before the publication of the next edition.' In the personal collection of the author. The complete control of the Party over the union newspaper is evident.
44. *Trabajo*, 21 January 1933.
45. *Trabajo*, 7 April 1932.
46. *Trabajo*, 13 March 1932.
47. *Trabajo*, 14 April 1932.
48. See 'Con documento fehaciente se comprueba de los pactos realizados entre Octavio Beeche y el comunismo', *La Tribuna*, 2 February 1936; also Manue Mora, 'Manuel destruye las últimas calumnias del cortesismo', *La Tribuna*, 5 February 1936.
49. *El Partido Vanguardia Popular. Apuntes para su historia.* Typewritten pamphlet in the library of the Institute of Marxism–Leninism in

Moscow. Without precluding a further discussion of this issue later, it is useful to recall here what Rómulo Betancourt said as early as his letter of 15 August 1932 sent to Valmore Rodríguez from San José, where he wrote, 'I could tell you other things, a lot more, regarding the ineptitude and incapacity of the leadership of the III (International). I have filed away a picturesque collection of stupidities by that bureaucrats' central office, because it will serve us very well in the future to demonstrate that a Party that is guided by these abstract and pedantic directives is irredeemably condemned to failure.' *Libro Rojo*, p. 182.

50. Manuel Caballero, 'La Internacional Comunista y América Latina. La Sección Venezolana', *Cuadernos de Presente y Pasado*, Mexico City, 1978, p. 33.

51. Conferencia Sindical Latinoamericana.

52. Caballero, op cit. Caballero bases these claims on 'El Movimiento revolucionario latinoamericano. Versiones de la Primera Conferencia Comunista', published in the magazine *La Correspondencia Sudamericana*, Buenos Aires, June 1929, pp. 356–66; and on the newspaper *El Martillo*, central organ of the Communist Party of Venezuela (Venezuelan Section of the Communist International) clandestine, April 1939, p. 4. He uses the latter to justify his claim that the Bureau ceased to exist in 1938. In view of the inexactitudes contained in this account, it is important to mention here the comments made on this subject, regarding both the Caribbean Bureau and Ricardo Martínez, in Rodolfo Cerdas Cruz, *Stratégie et Tactique de L'Internationale Communiste en Amérique Latine*, Doctoral Thesis, Université de Paris V, 1973.

53. See Eudocio Ravines, *La Gran estafa. La penetración del Kremlin en Iberoamérica* (Mexico City, Libros y Revistas S.A., 1952).

54. Among them Arnoldo Ferreto, Secretary for Organization of the Party, and Enrique Mora, a member of the Party youth organization.

55. Confederación de Trabajadores de América Latina (CTAL).

56. Interview with Jaime Cerdas Mora, and De la Cruz, op. cit., p. 177.

57. Guzmán died in extreme poverty on 27 April 1959. See *Adelante*, San José, 3 May 1959, p. 1. In addition, there were also other contradictory versions on the subject of Guzmán's journey and subsequent events in circulation within the Party itself, which were later denied by Guzmán.

58. *Manifiesto del Partido Comunista a los trabajadores del país en el 1 de Mayo de 1934*, San José, Imprenta La Tribuna, 1934, leaflet in the personal collection of the author.

59. See *L'Internationale Communiste*, special number 17–18, September 1935, pp. 1484–7; also *La Correspondance Internationale*, no. 75–76, 31 August 1935, p. 1152.

60. Manuel Mora, *Tres Discursos en Defensa de la Democracia* (San José, Imprenta La Tribuna, 1936) p. 23.

61. For this reason the argument seems to me without foundation that is put forward by some authors (for example, Manuel Rojas Bolaños, *Lucha Social y Guerra Civil en Costa Rica*, San José, Editorial El Porvenir, 1980, pp. 69–70) who attribute to the influence of the Communist International the policy of alliances followed by the CPCR after the VII Congress of the Comintern and the subsequent dissolution of the

Party and transformation of it into the Popular Vanguard (Vanguardia Popular). This policy already existed; the strategy of Dimitrov, drawn from French experience, only served to confirm it and facilitate its growth, as it broke down all manner of self-imposed theoretical restrictions for the Costa Rican leaders. Moreover, even in the interpretation of such slogans as the Popular Front the CPCR went much further than was permitted to the local sections of the International. See also on this subject the interesting graduate thesis of Marielos Aguilar, *Carlos Luis Fallas. Su época y sus luchas* (San José, Editorial Porvenir, 1983, pp. 96–101). Manuel Mora himself has rewritten the history of the Party, without neverthelss entirely departing from the truth, saying that, 'in the very period of our foundation, 1929–1931, we drew up and published what we called a "minimum programme", that is, the plan of action and struggle that in our understanding corresponded to the economic and social contradictions of the country at that time. This was an advanced democratic programme . . . We were not, in those circumstances, asking for a communist society, nor even a socialist society. We were asking for a democratic society superior to the one in which we were living, but without presenting this plan to our people as the final goal of our struggle . . . The fact that we were communists did not mean that we were madmen or charlatans, like those who pretend they can leap through stages that are determined by the very level of development of our society in Costa Rica . . . We stated categorically that we would be the most determined defenders of the existing democratic system, but that we would fight to broaden and transform it until it was converted into a regime of socialist democracy, by which we meant that we would not be satisfied with purely constitutional institutions without a social and economic content. *We said – and this we have maintained throughout our entire history – that given the characteristics of our country, whether historical or social and political, we believed it possible for our revolutionary process not to develop by means of armed struggle.*' [Italicized in the Spanish text.] *Libertad*, 8–14 June 1984. This was a point of view that was inadmissible throughout the existence of the International, before, during and after the policy of the Popular Front.

62. See Stone, 'El surgimiento de los que mandan'.
63. In September 1936 the CPCR made public the following declaration by the Central Committee: '1. – We are not enemies of the democratic regime. On the contrary, we will sustain and defend it to the extent of our possibilities *and will make every effort to give it ever greater strength by giving it an economic content.* [Italicized in the Spanish text.] 2. – We are resolutely opposed to the transplantation to our country of formulas that do not accord with our economic, social and political structure. We declare that the problems of our country should be resolved in the light of a comprehensive and serious study of our national characteristics. 3. – We do not, as a popular organization, have either a religious or an anti-religious creed. 4. – We are not enemies of the great and noble national traditions. 5. – We are not enemies of the small property owner, but of that property which is formed precisely through the elimination of small

property, of that property which is formed through the elimination of small proprietors by means of robbery in its various forms. With respect to this large-scale property, no more do we think that its suppression is required at the present time. But we do believe that it can be restricted and regulated for the benefit of the people. 6. – We are not enemies of the family, rather, on the contrary, we believe the family should be provided with economic resources that could give it real human meaning.. 7. – We are determined enemies of crime and terror as a social system. We believe solely in the action of the masses, well prepared and organized, as an effective means of combat.' See Manuel Mora, *Por la afirmación de nuestra Democracia, por el progreso y bienestar de nuestra nación* (San José, 1939) pp. 10–11.

9 A Euro-Communism in the Central America of the 1930s

1. *Tico-Comunismo*: Tico is a common familiar or slang term in Central America for a Costa Rican or, as an adjective, for anything Costa Rican (*translator's note*).
2. See 'Los pequeños propietarios y el Partido Comunista', *Trabajo*, 5 September 1931.
3. See *Trabajo*, 22 May 1935.
4. See Stone, *La Dinastía de los Conquistadores*, pp. 109 ff.
5. See Manuel Mora, 'Discurso en el Teatro Latino sobre el Seguro de Riesgos Profesionales', *La Tribuna*, 2 August 1945, p. 3.
6. For example, see Manuel Mora, 'Si le niegan al pueblo sus derechos, un día u otro habrá una revolución', *Diario de Costa Rica*, 29 May 1942, p. 1. See also *Diario de Costa Rica*, 15 January 1942, p. 1.
7. See Manuel Mora, 'Sobre la base de un plan sencillo y eficaz de producción debe buscarse la unidad nacional', *La Tribuna*, 21 November 1944, p. 1.
8. Manuel Mora, *Por la afirmación de nuestra Democracia*, p. 11
9. With regard to the companies that were categorized as imperialistic, Mora went so far as to say, in 1943, that 'It has never been our intention to tear apart or to declare war on the United Fruit Company', *La Tribuna*, 19 August 1943.
10. See Manuel Mora, 'Colaboraremos sin vacilaciones con cualquier movimiento que con bases serias sea capaz de conducirnos a la nacionalización de nuestras riquezas eléctricas', *La Tribuna*, 12 August 1945; also *Diario de Costa Rica*, 20 May 1932. The Party newspaper *Trabajo* bore the subtitle 'At the service of Democracy'.
11. See, for example, Manuel Mora,.'En representación del Partido Comunista emplaza a todos los partidos políticos de Costa Rica para una armonía nacional en materia política', *Diario de Costa Rica*, 20 May 1942, p. 1
12. Mora, *Tres Discursos en Defensa de la Democracia*, pp. 10–11.
13. Mora, *Por la afirmación de nuestra Democracia*, p. 7. See also Manuel Mora, 'Queremos asegurar plenamente, dentro de un costarriqueñismo auténtico, nuestra posición de avanzada política de las fuerzas trabajadoras nacionales', *La Tribuna*, 16 June 1943; 'El Código de Trabajo que

se trata de dictar es hecho a la tica', *La Tribuna*, 17 August 1943; *Tres Discursos en Defensa de la Democracia*, pp. 10–11.

14. Hence, in referring to the displacement of Manuel Mora from the General Secretaryship of the Party as a consequence of the change in tactics of the Soviet Party brought on by the Central American crisis of the 1980s, Oscar Arias, General Secretary of the National Liberation Party (Partido Liberación Nacional), affiliated to the Socialist International, could declare that, 'It is to him (Mora) that we owe the fact that Costa Rican Communism has had an "indigenous", very *tico*, stamp', as he considered that the predominant element in Mora, rather than an orthodox Communist ideology, was his unquestionable nationalism (*La Nación*, 7 December 1983). A representative of a more anti-Communist position, J. A. Sánchez Alonso of the Free Costa Rica Movement (Movimiento Costa Rica Libre), regarded as far-rightist, stated that as he saw it 'the objective conditions of national realities have had their effect in Manuel Mora, and the "Orteguian" schema of human conduct as being subject to circumstance – that which surrounds us – did not pose any problems for the veteran Communist leader. Having contributed with his leadership to creating these conditions, he could not be very much inclined to the setting in motion of subjective conditions artificially created in order to torpedo them ... Whoever seeks to alter this status quo, will enter into a path that is generally unproductive, however strong the pressures may be becoming for the initiation of a climate that could precede a violent change.' *La Nación*, 9 December 1983. (Both concluded by expressing the hope that the new leadership would follow the same 'national' line of action as Mora. In doing so they disregarded the fact that this orientation had, objectively speaking, already been abandoned by the Costa Rican Communists many years previously.)

15. Mora, *Por la afirmación de nuestra Democracia*, p. 8.
16. See Manuel Mora, '16 reformas al Código Electoral planteó Vanguardia Popular', *La Tribuna*, 28 October 1944, p. 1; 'Hay que adicionar La Constitución con un capítulo de garantías electorales', *La Tribuna*, 5 November 1944, p. 1.
17. Thus Mora said in Congress, in 1936, 'In other words, what we wish to do is correct the failings to which we have pointed in the economic basis of the current regime. We are absolutely sure that, once these faults have been corrected, the other aspects of social life will improve almost by themselves.' *Tres Discursos en Defensa de la Democracia*, p. 28.
18. Formally speaking, both *clase trabajadora* and *clase obrera* mean the same thing and can equally be translated into English as 'working class'. However, *clase trabajadora* is much the older term and can be more easily understood to mean loosely 'all those who work; all those essentially dependent on their own labour to survive'. While the distinction is by no means precise, *clase obrera*, on the other hand – a more recent, more 'modern' introduction – is closely associated with political, and particularly Marxist or leftist, usage, and would more readily be taken to refer specifically to an industrial, manual working class (*translator's note*).

19. 'One cannot call what exists in the Soviet Union a Dictatorship. but the scientific organization of the economic life of societ,' Mora said in Congress in 1936. *Tres Discursos en Defensa de la Democracia*, p. 22.

20. See Manuel Mora, 'Carta a don Lico Jiménez sobre el conflicto de cafetaleros y trabajadores', *La Prensa Libre*, 18 July 1944, p. 1.

21. See *Por la afirmación de nuestra Democracia*, p. 8; also *La Tribuna*, 16 June 1943, p. 1. *A la tica* refers, again, to the word *tico* for Costa Rican.

22. Manuel Mora, 'La tesis de la lucha de clases tiene que ser reemplazada por la tesis de la colaboración de clases', *La Tribuna*, 23 February 1945, p. 4.

23. See *La Tribuna*, 23 February 1945 and 8 April 1945. The discussion on the Browderist deviation could be followed in the magazine *Revista Fundamentos*, published by the Cuban Communist Party, and the influence of which, aided by Blas Roca, reached as far as Venezuela. See De la Plaza and Duclos, op. cit., pp. 17 and 100.

24. Partido Guatemalteco del Trabajo.

25. See Manuel Mora, 'La colaboración de clases implica la ejecución de un plan económico poderoso en escala nacional', *La Tribuna*, 8 April 1945, p. 13; also *La Tribuna*, 17 August 1943, p. 1. Mora later said that Monsignor Sanabria had asked him 'if we would change our name and introduce modifications of some kind into our programme, without affecting its essential content. We accepted, and, instead of the Communist Party, now continue to call ourselves the Popular Vanguard Party', *Libertad*, 8–14 June 1984, p. 7.

26. Manuel Mora, 'Nuestro gobierno ya reconoció tácitamente al de la Unión Soviética', *La Tribuna*, 6 July 1943, p. 1.

27. Manuel Mora, 'Oumansky fue asesinado por el falangismo continental', *Ultima Hora*, 26 January 1945, p. 1.

28. See article by Mora in *Libertad*, official review of the Popular Vanguard Party, 23–29 June 1978. My italics.

Conclusion

1. This was so in the case of the use of aircraft as support for infantry in counter-insurgency operations, and of bombing by air patrols against moving guerrilla columns, both tactics that were experimented with in Nicaragua and later employed in China. See Meggee, op. cit.

2. The term *macheteros* came, of course, from the long work knife used by all peasants and field-hands in the region. Politically it had strongly pejorative connotations.

3. *Libro Rojo*, pp. 141–2.

4. Ibid, pp. 195ff.

5. Ibid, p. 151.

6. Rodríguez, op. cit., p. 121.

Bibliography

Acción Comunal de Panamá, 'Algunas palabras con Haya de la Torre', *Repertorio Americano*, vol. XVIII (San José, 1929).

Acuña, Víctor, 'Historia Económica del Tabaco, Epoca Colonial', unpublished doctoral thesis, Escuela de Historia y Geografía (San José, Universidad de Costa Rica, 1974).

Aguilar, Marielos, *Carlos Luis Fallas. Su época y sus luchas* (San José, Editorial Porvenir, 1983).

Alemán Bolaños, Gustavo, *Sandino, El Libertador* (México–Guatemala, Ediciones del Caribe, 1957).

Alonso, José A., 'Elites gobernantes y familismo en Nicaragua', *Revista de Estudios Centroamericanos*, vol. 20, no. 296.

Anderson, Thomas P., *Matanza* (Lincoln, University of Nebraska Press, 1971).

André, Pierre, *Compte rendu des débats d'aprés les journeaux des Moscou* (Paris, Bibliothéque du Parti Socialiste de l'Humanité, 1920).

Arias, Augusto, 'Carlos Aponte, Coronel de Sandino', *Repertorio Americano*, vol. XXXII (San José, 1936).

Arias Gómez, Jorge, *Farabundo Martí* (San José, Editorial Universitaria Centroamericana, 1972).

Attschult, A. and Renwich, W.W., 'Del problema de los Cereales en la República de El Salvador', *Boletín Oficial* (San Salvador, Ministerio de Economía, 1945).

Auditoría General de Obras Públicas, Caminos y Puentes, *Informe General del Costo de Obras Ejecutadas en la Administración del Lic. Ricardo Jiménez Oreamuno 1932–1936* (San José, Imprenta Juan Arias, n.d.).

Bara, Ernesto, *Letter to President H. Martínez*, 25 January 1932, Archivos Nacionales de Costa Rica, Box 365, File no. 001.

Barbusse, Henri, 'Saludo a Sandino', *Repertorio Americano*, vol. VII, no. 17 (San José, 1928).

Barón Castro, Rodolfo, *La Población de El Salvador* (Madrid, Instituto de Cultura Hispánica, 1942).

Beals, Carleton, *L'Amérique Latine: Monde en Révolution* (Paris, Payot, 1966).

Belausteguigoitia, Ramón, *Con Sandino en Nicaragua* (Madrid, Espasa Calpe, 1934).

Belli, Pedro, 'Prolegómenos para una Historia Económica de Nicaragua de 1905 a 1966', *Revista del Pensamiento Centroamericano*, vol. XXX, no. 146 (Managua, January–March 1975).

Benítez, Augusto, 'Mella, Centelleante Tránsito de un Dirigente Comunista', *Bohemia*, no. 28 (Havana, 18 July 1975).

Blanco Cabrera, Gladys, 'Emilio Roy de Leuchsenrig, verdadero maestro de nuestra historia', *Bohemia*, no. 34 (Havana, 22 August 1975).

Bloque de Obreros y Campesinos, Sección de Alajuela, *Plataforma Municipal* (San José, Imprenta La Tribuna, 1935).

214

Boersner, Demetrio, *The Bolsheviks and the National Colonial Question (1917–1928)*, thesis 106, University of Geneva (Geneva, Institut Universitaire des Hautes Etudes Universitaux, 1957).

Browning, David, *El Salvador, Landscape and Society* (Oxford, Clarendon Press, 1971).

Buell, Raymond Leslie, *The Central Americas*, Foreign Policy Association, Pamphlet no. 69 (New York, December 1930).

—— 'The United States and Central American Stability', *Foreign Policy Reports*, vol. VII, no. 9 (Washington, DC, 8 July 1931).

Bukharin, N. 'La situation internationale et les tâches de l' I.C.', *La Correspondance Internationale*, no. spécial XI, no. 12, 1 August 1928.

Caballero, Manuel, 'La Internacional Comunista y América Latina. La Sección Venezolana', *Cuadernos de.Presente y Pasado* (Mexico City, 1978).

Cabrera, Olga, *Guiteras, la época, el hombre* (Havana, Editorial Política, 1974).

Campos Ponce, Xavier, *Los Yanquis y Sandino* (México D.F., Ediciones XCP, 1962).

Carranza Villalobos, Carlos Enrique, 'El Partido Unión Católica y su importancia en la vida política de Costa Rica', unpublished graduate thesis (San José, Universidad de Costa Rica, 1982).

Cerdas, Rodolfo, *La Crisis de la democracia liberal en Costa Rica* (San José, EDUCA, 1972).

—— 'Del Estado Intervencionista al Estado Empresario', *Anuario de Estudios Centroamericanos*, no. 5 (San José, Editorial de la Universidad de Costa Rica, 1979).

—— 'Stratégie et tactique de l'Internationale Communiste en Amérique Latine', doctoral thesis (Université de Paris, 1973).

Claudín, Fernando, *La Crisis del Movimiento Comunista. De la Komintern a la Kominform* (París, Ruedo Ibérico, 1970).

Collotti, Erica and Robertazzi, Chiara, *La Internacional Comunista y los Problemas Coloniales 1919–1935* (Paris–Geneva, Droz, 1973).

Communist International, *Minutes* (Petrograd 17 June, Moscow 23 July; Petrograd, 7 August 1920).

Communist Party of Costa Rica, *Primer Libro de Actas* (*Minute Book*) (San José, 1931).

—— *El Partido Vanguardia Popular. Apuntes para su historia*, typewritten pamphlet (San José, n.d.).

—— 'Los pequeños propietarios y el Partido Comunista', *Trabajo*, 5 September 1931.

—— *Manifiesto del Partido Comunista a los trabajadores del país en el 1º de mayo de 1934* (San José, Imprenta La Tribuna, 1934).

Communist Party of the USA, 'Declaration on the Events in Cuba', *La Correspondencia Internacional*, no. 72–73, September 1933.

Dalton, Roque, *Miguel Mármol: Los sucesos de 1932 en El Salvador* (San José, EDUCA, 1972).

Deambrosis-Martins, Carlos, 'La expulsión de Haya de la Torre de Guatemala', *Repertorio Americano*, vol. XVII (San José, 1928).

Degras, Jane (ed.), *The Communist International 1919–1943. Documents*, vol. I (London, Frank Cass, 1971).

De la Cruz, Vladimir, *Las luchas sociales en Costa Rica (1870–1930)* (San José, Editorial de la Universidad de Costa Rica, 1983).

De la Plaza, Salvador, 'La lutte du Nicaragua, lutte de l'Amérique Latine pour son indépendance', *La Correspondance Internationale*, no. 72, 12 August 1929.

De la Plaza, Salvador and Duclos, Jacques, *Antecedentes del revisionismo en Venezuela* (Caracas, Fondo Editorial Salvador de la Plaza, 1973).

De la Selva, Salomón, 'Al pueblo de Nicaragua', *Repertorio Americano*, vol. XIV (San José, 1927).

De Nogales, Rafael, *The Looting of Nicaragua* (New York, R. M. McBride, 1928).

Del Camino, Juan, 'El Tratado Chamorro-Bryan es un tratado humillante y fenicio', *Repertorio Americano*, vol. XXIV (San José, 1933).

Denny, Harold Norman, *Dollars for Bullets (The Story of American Rule in Nicaragua)* (New York, The Dial Press, 1929).

Deval, L., 'Las luchas de clases en América Central', *La Internacional Sindical Roja*, no. 10, 31 May 1932.

—— 'Los Antecedentes Revolucionarios en Chile', *La Internacional Sindical Roja*, no. 16, 31 August 1932.

Dirección General de Estadística de Costa Rica, *Anuario Estadístico año 1920*, vol. XXIV (San José, Imprenta Nacional, 1922).

—— Informe año 1925 (San José, Imprenta Nacional, 1926).

Dirección General de Estadística y Censos de Costa Rica, *Censo de personas sin trabajo* (San José, 1932).

—— Censo de Población de Costa Rica (San José, Ministerio de Economía y Hacienda, n.d.).

Dobles, Abel, *Memorias*, unpublished (San José, n.d.).

Facio, Rodrigo, *La Moneda y la Banca Central en Costa Rica* (Mexico City, Fondo de Cultura Económica, 1947).

Fallas, Marco A., *La Factoría de Tabacos de Costa Rica* (San José, Editorial Costa Rica, 1972).

Fallas Monge, Carlos Luis, *El Movimiento Obrero en Costa Rica (1830–1902)* (San José, EUNED, 1983).

Fonseca Amador, Carlos, 'The Macaulay Affair', *Prensa Política*, Documentos, San José, 3–15 March 1973.

Fournier Facio, Arturo, 'La United Fruit Co. y las huelgas bananeras', unpublished graduate thesis (San José, Universidad de Costa Rica, 1975).

Gallardo, Ricardo, 'Las Constituciones de El Salvador', *Historia de la Integración Racial, Territorial e Institucional del Pueblo Salvadoreño* (Madrid, Ediciones Cultura Hispánica, 1961).

—— *Las Constituciones de El Salvador*, vols. I–II (Madrid, Ediciones de Cultura Hispánica, 1961).

—— *Las Constituciones de la República Federal de Centro América* (Madrid, Instituto de Estudios Políticos, 1958).

García Laguardia, Jorge Mario, *Orígenes de la Democracia Constitucional en Centro América* (San José, Editorial Universitaria de Centro América, 1971).

Gómez, J. 'La Trahison de Sandino', *La Correspondance Internationale*, no. 23, 20 March 1933.

—— 'Les événements révolutionnaires á Cuba et les tâches du PC', *La Correspondance Internationale*, no. 75–76, 11 September 1933.

González Víquez, Cleto, *El sufragio en Costa Rica ante la historia y la legislación* (San José, Editorial Costa Rica, 1928).

Hall, Carolyn, *El café y el desarrollo histórico geográfico de Costa Rica* (San José, Editorial Costa Rica, 1976).

Harrison, George, 'Les intrigues des Etats-Unis au Nicaragua', *La Correspondance Internationale*, 12 January 1925.

Haya de la Torre, Víctor Raúl, 'Carta abierta a Juan Ramón Avilés', *Repertorio Americano*, vol. XVIII (San José, 1929).

—— 'Carta a Froilán Turcios', *Repertorio Americano*, vol. XVI (San José, 1928).

—— 'Carta a José María Zeledón'' *Repertorio Americano*, vol. XVI (San José, 1928).

—— 'Del Cuzco Salió el Nuevo Verbo, y del Cuzco Saldrá la Nueva Historia', *Repertorio Americano*, vol. XVII (San José, 1928).

—— *La Reforma Universitaria y la Realidad.Social*, pamphlet, n.d.

—— '¿Qué es el APRA?', *Repertorio Americano*, vol. XIV, San José, 1927.

Herrera García, Adolfo, Mora V. Enrique y Gamboa, Francisco, *Apuntes para la Historia del Partido Comunista de Costa Rica* (San José, Imprenta Elena, n.d.).

Humbert-Droz, Jules, *De Lénine a Staline* (Neuchatel, Editions de la Baconniére, 1971).

Internacional Comunista, *La Internacional Comunista. Ensayo Histórico Suscinto* (Moscow, Editorial Progreso, n.d.).

—— *Sindicatos Rojos y Socorro Rojo Internacional* (Paris, Oficina de Ediciones, 1931).

—— *Tesis y Resoluciones del VI Congreso de la IC* (Paris, Oficina de Ediciones, n.d.).

Internacional Sindical Roja, *Tesis y Resoluciones del V Congreso* (Moscow, Pequeña Biblioteca de la Internacional Roja, September 1930).

ISO, 'La Signification du Congrés de Bruxelles', *La Correspondance Internationale*, no. 27, 26 February 1927.

Izvestia, 'La prestidigitation de la diplomatie Américaine', *La Correspondance Internationale*, no. 16, 2 January 1927.

Khrem, William, *Democracia y Tiranía en el Caribe* (Buenos Aires, Editorial Palestra, 1959).

Laborde, Hernán, 'La situation politique au Méxique', *La Correspondance Internationale*, no. 72, 30 August 1930.

Latin American Center, University of California, *Statistical Abstracts of Latin America 1966* (Los Angeles, University of California, 1967).

Lee, Thomas, *Latin American Problems, Their Relation to Our Investors' Billions* (New York, Brower, Warren and Putnam, 1932).

Lenin, V.I., *Collected Works* (Moscow, Progress, 1966).

—— *The Beginning of the Revolution in Russia* (Moscow, Progress, 1956).

—— *Selected Works* (Moscow, Progress, 1968).

Liga Cívica, *Statutes* (San José, Imprenta la Tribuna, n.d.).

López Vallecillos, Italo, *El Periodismo en El Salvador* (San Salvador, Editorial Universitaria, 1964).

Lozovski, A., 'El V Congreso de la I.S.R.', *La Internacional Sindical Roja*, no. 115–116, September–October 1930.

—— 'El V Congreso de la I.S.R. Crisis mundial, lucha económica y tareas del movimiento sindical revolucionario', *La Correspondencia Internacional*, no. 14, September 1930.

—— 'La apertura del Congreso de la I.S.R.', *La Correspondencia Internacional*, no. 69, 20 August 1930.

—— 'Le Congrés de Syndicats de l'Amérique Latine', *La Correspondance Internationale*, no. 48, 9 June 1929.

Lubrand, R., 'La 1ère Conférence de la Jeunesse Anti-impérialiste', *La Correspondance Internationale*, no. 72, 12 August 1929.

Luna, David, *Análisis de una Dictadura Fascista Latinoamericana* (San Salvador, Editorial Universitaria, 1961).

—— 'Algunas facetas sociales en la vida de Agustín Farabundo Martí', *Revista Salvadoreña de Ciencias Sociales*, no. 1, January–March 1965.

'Ricardo Coto Conde', *Trabajo*, 23 September 1931.

Macaulay, Neill, *Sandino* (San José, Editorial Universitaria Centroamericana, 1970)

Machado, Gustavo, 'Carta a los compañeros de la Unión Obrera Venezolana', *Repertorio Americano*, vol. XVII (San José, July 1928).

—— 'La situación en Nicaragua', *Repertorio Americano*, vol. XVI, no. 26 (San José, 28 April 1928).

Mannings, William R. (ed.), *Correspondencia de las Naciones Latinoamericanas* (Buenos Aires, Editorial La Facultad, 1931).

Marín, Alberto, *Statement* (Archivos Nacionales de Costa Rica, Box 365, File no. 001).

Mariñas, Otero, Luis, *Las Constituciones de Guatemala* (Madrid, Instituto de Estudios Políticos, 1958).

Márquez Fuentes, Manuel and Rodríguez Araujo, Octavio, *El Partido Comunista Mexicano* (México D.F., Ediciones El Caballito, 1973).

Martín, Ernesto, 'Una carta al Hermano del Presidente Calles a Propósito del Escándalo de Nicaragua', *Repertorio Americano*, vol. XIV (San José, 1927).

Marx, Karl, *Capital* (London, Penguin, 1976).

Marx, Karl and Engels, Friedrich, *On Colonialism* (New York, International Publishers, 1972).

—— *Selected Works* (Moscow, Progress, 1968).

Masferrer, Alberto, 'La Misión de América', *Repertorio Americano*, vol. XVII (San José, 1928).

Meggee, Thomas Vernon, 'Contra las guerrillas de Sandino en Nicaragua', *Revista Conservadora del Pensamiento Centroamericano*, vol. 24, no. 119, 1970.

Meléndez, Carlos, 'Formas en la tenencia de la tierra en Costa Rica en la época colonial', *Revista de Historia*, año 1, no. 2 (San José, 1975).

—— *Costa Rica, Tierra y Poblamiento en la Colonia* (San José, Editorial Universitaria Centroamericana, 1983).

Montes, Luis, *Bananas, The Fruit Empire of Wall Street*, International Pamphlets, no. 35 (New York, Union Labour, 1933).

Mora, Manuel, 'Carta a don Lico Jiménez sobre el conflicto de cafetaleros y trabajadores', *La Prensa Libre*, 18 July 1944.

—— 'Colaboraremos sin vacilaciones con cualquier movimiento que con bases serias sea capaz de conducirnos a la nacionalización de nuestras riquezas eléctricas', *La Tribuna*, 12 August 1945.

—— '16 Reformas al Código Electoral planteó Vanguardia Popular', *La Tribuna*, 25 October 1944.

—— 'Discurso en el Teatro Latino sobre el Seguro de Riesgos profesionales', *La Tribuna*, 2 August 1945.

—— 'El Código de Trabajo que se trata de dictar es hecho a la tica', *La Tribuna*, 17 August 1943.

—— 'Manuel Mora, en representación del PC emplaza a todos los partidos políticos de Costa Rica para una armonía nacional en materia política', *Diario de Costa Rica*, 20 May 1942.

—— 'Hay que adecuar la Constitución con un capítulo de garantías electorales', *La Tribuna*, 15 November 1944.

—— 'La colaboración implica la ejecución de un plan económico poderoso en escala nacional', *La Tribuna*, 8 April 1945.

—— 'La tesis de la lucha de clases tiene que ser reemplazada por la tesis de colaboración de clases', *La Tribuna*, 23 February 1945.

—— ''Nuestro gobierno reconoció tácitamente al de la Unión Soviética', *La Tribuna*, 6 July 1943.

—— 'Oumansky fue asesinado por el falangismo continental', *Ultima Hora*, 26 January 1945.

—— *Por la afirmación de nuestra Democracia, por el progreso y bienestar de nuestra nación* (San José, 1939).

—— 'Queremos asegurar plenamente dentro de un costarriqueñismo auténtico, nuestra posición de avanzada política de las fuerzas trabajadoras nacionales', *La Tribuna*, 16 June 1943.

—— 'Si le niegan al pueblo sus derechos, un día u otro habrá una revolución', *Diario de Costa Rica*, 29 May 1942.

—— 'Sobre la base de un plan sencillo y eficaz de producción debe buscarse la unidad nacional', *La Tribuna*, 21 November 1944.

—— *Tres discursos en defensa de la democracia* (San José, Imprenta La Tribuna, 1936).

Munro, Dana, *The Five Republics of Central America* (New York, Oxford University Press, 1928).

—— *Intervention and Dollar Diplomacy in the Caribbean, 1900–1921* (Princeton, NJ, Princeton University Press, 1964).

Müzenberg, Willy, 'Cinco años del Socorro Rojo Internacional', *La Correspondencia Internacional*, no. 100, 8 September 1926.

—— 'Le Congrés de Francfort de la Ligue Anti-impérialiste', *La Correspondance Internationale*, no. 68, August 1929.

—— 'De Bruxelles á Paris', *La Correspondance Internationale*, no. 51, 19 June 1929.

—— 'A la veille de la 2éme Conference de la Ligue Anti-Impériáliste', *La Correspondance Internationale*, no. 122, 7 December 1927.

—— 'La 2éme Conference de Bruxelles de la Ligue Anti-Impérialiste', *La Correspondance Internationale*, no. 127, 21 December 1927.

—— 'Le reenforcement prolétarien de la Ligue Anti-Impérialiste', *La Correspondance Internationale*, no. 7, 23 January 1929.

—— 'Session de Berlin de la Ligue Anti-Impérialiste', *La Correspondance Internationale*, no. 91, 25 August 1928.

Murillo Jiménez, Hugo, *Tinoco y los Estados Unidos. Génesis y caída de un régimen* (San José, EUNED, 1981).

M.Ch. 'La tactique de l'unité aux pays de l'Amérique Latine', *L'Internationale Syndicale Rouge*, no. 8, 30 April 1932.

Oconitrillo García, Eduardo, *Los Tinoco (1917–1919)* (San José, Editorial Costa Rica, 1980).

Osborne, Lilly, 'El Salvador', *Bulletin of the Pan American Union*, March 1933.

Pavletich, Esteban, 'Carta a Joaquín García Monge', *Repertorio Americano*, vol. XVI (San José, 1928).

Penelon, J. F., 'Chile and Anglo-American Imperialism', *Communist International*, no. 23, 1926.

Peralta, Hernán G., *El Derecho Constitucional en la independencia de Costa Rica* (San José, Trejos Hermanos, 1965).

—— *El Pacto de Concordia* (San José, Librería e Imprenta Lehmann, 1965).

Pérez, I. 'Le Honduras sous le joug de l'impérialisme', *La Correspondance Internationale*, no. 100–101, 9 December 1933.

Portal, Magda, 'Mensaje a las mujeres de América Latina', *Repertorio Americano*, vol. XVI (San José, 1928).

P.S., 'La politique d'intervention des Etats-Unis au Nicaragua et au Méxique', *La Correspondance Internationale*, no. 16, 5 February 1927.

Ramírez Mercado, Sergio (ed.), *El Pensamiento Vivo de Sandino* (San José, EDUCA, 1974).

Ravines, Eudocio, *La gran estafa. La penetración del Kremlin en Iberoamérica* (Mexico City, Libros y revistas S.A., 1952).

Rodríguez Ruiz, Armando, *La Administración González Flores* (San José, Editorial de la Universidad de Costa Rica, 1968).

Rodríguez, Carlos Rafael, *Lenin y la cuestión colonial* (Chile, Editorial Prensa Latinoamericana S.A., 1973).

Rojas Bolaños, Manuel, *Lucha social y guerra civil en Costa Rica* (San José, Editorial El Porvenir, 1980).

Rolland, Romain, 'A coté de l'Amérique Latine', *Repertorio Americano*, vol. XIV, no. 9 (San José, 1927).

Romero, Ramón, *Sandino y los yanquis* (México, Ediciones Patria y Libertad, 1961).

Rosmer, Alfred, *Moscou sous Lenine*, vol. I (Paris, Maspero, 1970).

Roy, M. N., *Memoirs* (Dehara Dun, Bombay, New Delhi, Calcutta, Allied Publishers, 1964).

—— *Selected Works* (ed. Sibnarayn Ray) vol. I, 1917–1922 (New Delhi, Oxford University Press, 1987).

Sáenz Vicente, *Rompiendo cadenas*, 4th edn (Mexico D.F., Editorial América Nueva, 1962).

Sanabria, Víctor, *Genealogías de Cartago hasta 1850*, vol. I (San José, 1957).

Sandino, Augusto César, 'Carta a Gustavo Machado y Morales', *Repertorio Americano*, vol. XVII (San José, 1928).

Sección Costarricense de la Liga Anti-imperialista, 'La situación política de Nicaragua y las condiciones de Sandino para deponer las armas', *Trabajo* (Organ of the Communist Party of Costa Rica, San José, 14 January 1933).

Secretaría de Hacienda y Comercio, *Memoria del año 1923* (San José, Imprenta Nacional, 1924).

Selser, Gregorio, *El Pequeño Ejército Loco* (Buenos Aires, Editorial Triángulo, 1958).

—— *Sandino, General de Hombres Libres* (Buenos Aires, Editorial Triángulo, 1958).

Sequeira, Diego Manuel, *Emission et Amortissements d'Emprunts Extérieurs de la République de Nicaragua Pendant le Premier Quart du Siécle*, doctoral thesis (Paris, Librairie Générale de Droit et de Jurisprudence, 1931).

Servicio Secreto de Investigación, Estados Unidos de Venezuela, *Las actividades comunistas en Venezuela. Libro Rojo del General López Contreras, 1936*, facsimile edn (Caracas, Ediciones Centauro, 1979).

Silva Herzog, Miguel, *Breve Historia de la Revolución Mexicana* (México, Fondo de Cultura Económica, 1960).

Socorro Rojo, 'Declaración del SRI cubano', *La Correspondencia Internacional*, no. 91–92, 11 November 1933.

Soley Güell, Tomás, *Compendio de Historia Económica y Hacendaria de Costa Rica* (San José, Editorial Soley Valverde, 1940).

—— *Historia Económica y Hacendaria de Costa Rica*, vol. II (San José, Editorial Universitaria, 1949).

Somoza, Anastasio, *El verdadero Sandino o el Calvario de Las Segovias* (Managua, Tipografía Robelo, 1936).

Sorel, Enrique, 'Sandino El Libertador y Martí el Comunista', *Repertorio Americano*, vol. XXVIII (San José, 1934).

Stimson, Henry L., *American Policy in Nicaragua* (New York, Charles Scribner's Sons, 1927).

Stone, Samuel, 'El surgimiento de los que mandan: tierra, capital y trabajo en las sociedades centroamericanas', *Estudios del Centro de Investigación y Adiestramiento Político-Administrativo-CIAPA*, no. 5 (San José, Litografía e Imprenta Lil. S.A., 1980).

—— *La Dinastía de los Conquistadores* (Editorial Universitaria de Centro América, 1975).

—— 'Las convulsiones del istmo centroamericano: raíces de un conflicto entre élites', *Estudios del Centro de Investigación y Adiestramiento Político-Administrativo-CIAPA* (San José, Litografía e Imprenta Lil. S.A., 1979).

Tanin, M., 'L'offensive impérialiste des Etats Unis', *La Correspondance Internationale*, no. 10, 22 January 1927.

Torres, Edelberto, *Interpretación del Desarrollo Social Centroamericano* (San José, EDUCA, 1971).

US Congress, *Congressional Records, Proceedings and Debates of the 2nd Session of the 67th Congress*, vol. LXLI (Washington, DC).

US Department of Commerce, 'Salvador as a Market for Foodstuffs', *Trade Information Bulletin no. 692* (Washington, DC, US Government Printing Office, 1930).

US Government, 'Investigation of Un-American Propaganda Activities in the US', *The Communist Party of the US as an Agent of Foreign Power* (Washington, DC, 1947).

Varga, Eugéne, 'La situation économique mondiale au prémier trimestre 1926', *La Correspondance Internationale*, no. 48, 28 May 1926.

—— 'La situation économique mondiale', *La Correspondance Internationale*, no. 63, 10 June 1927.

Volio, Marina, *Jorge Volio y el Partido Reformista* (San José, Editorial Costa Rica, 1973).

White, Alastair, *El Salvador, Nation of a Modern World* (London and Tonbridge, Ernest Benn, 1973).

Wurm, Charles, 'The Intervention of the US in Nicaragua', *Communist International*, vol. 9, no. 4, January 1927.

Periodicals

ABC, 28 May 1930

Adelante (San José), 3 May 1959

Bohemia (Havana), no. 23, 6 June 1975

Boletín de la Unión Panamericana, February 1933

Communist International, no. 166–67, 1921
   no. 14, 1925
   no. 9, 1 March 1927

Diario de Costa Rica (San José)
   13 February 1931
   22 January 1932
   28 January 1932
   20 May 1932
   15 January 1942

El Censor, 8 May 1932

El Comunista, no.11, March 1932

Internationale Syndicale Rouge (Paris, Bureau d'Editions)
   no. 101, June 1929
   no. 115–116, September/October 1930
   no. 117–118, January /February 1931

La Correspondance Internationale (Paris)
   no. 47, 4th year, 24 July 1924
   no. 45, 28 April 1925
   no. 32, 13 March 1926
   no. 138, 20 December 1926
   no. 140, 23 December 1926
   no. 142, 28 December 1926
   no. 9, 19 January 1927
   no. 17, 5 February 1927
   no. 19, 9 February 1927
   no. 90, 31 August 1927
   no. 53, 7 June 1928
   no. 73, 3 August 1928
   no. 94, 30 August 1928
   no. 83, 16 August 1928
   no. 97, 2 September 1928, special issue XXVII
   no. 106, 20 September 1928, special issue XXI
   no 106, 20 September 1928, special issue XXXI
   no. 118, 9 October 1928, special issue XXXVIII

no. 122, 15 October 1928, special issue XL
no. 125, 19 October 1928, special issue XL
no. 122, 15 October 1928, special issue XL
no. 130, 30 October 1928, special issue XLIV
no. 139, 20 November 1928, special issue XLVII
no. 11, 6 February 1929
no. 37, 4 May 1929
no. 68, August 1929
no. 89, 18 September 1929
no. 1, 4 January 1930
no. 11, 5 February 1930
no. 10, 1 February 1930
no. 35, 23 April 1930
no. 102, 3 December 1930
no. 70–71, 2 Sepember 1933
no. 98–99, 15 December 1933
no. 44–45, 1 June 1935
no. 75–76, 31 August 1935
no. 95–96, 19 October 1935
La Correspondencia Internacional
no. 124, 18 October 1928
no. 64, 24 June 1925
no. 64, 10 September 1924
no.56, 2 August 1924
no. 45, 28 April 1924
no. 72, 30 Augu 1930
no. 70–71, 2 September 1933
no. 87–88, 28 October 1933
no. 98–99, December 1933
no. 7, 25 January 1928
no. 101, 5 October 1927
no. 91, 3 September 1927
no. 7, 25 January 1928
no. 101, 8 October 1929
no. 48, 8 June 1932
La Correspondencia Sudamericana (Buenos Aires), 2nd época, no. 7, 19 January 1929
La Hora, 5 June 1933 (San José)
La Nación (San José)
7 December 1983
9 December 1983
La Tribuna (San José)
19 November 1926
20 November 1926
21 November 1926
December 1928
5 August 1930
23 May 1933
2 February 1936

5 February 1936
16 June 1943
17 August 1943
19 August 1943
8 April 1945
La Voz Sindical (San José), year 1, no. 1, July 1934
Libertad (San José)
  23–29 June 1978
  8–14 June 1984
  15–21 June 1984
L'Internationale Communiste (Paris)
  no. 22, 20 November 1934
  no. 17–18, September 1935, special edition
New York Times, 3 May 1930
Repertorio Americano (San José)
  vol. XIV, 1927
  vol. XVI, 1927
Trabajo (San José)
  14 July 1931
  22 August 1931
  5 September 1931
  16 October 1931
  4 February 1932
  13 March 1932
  7 April 1932
  14 April 1932
  21 January 1933
  25 January 1933
  28 January 1933
  18 February 1933
  23 April 1933
  21 May 1933
  25 November 1933
  17 December 1933
  8 April 1934
  16 June 1934
  30 September 1934

Index